D1272771

SELF-RESPECT AND INDEPENDENCE OF MIND

JAPAN LIBRARY

SELF-RESPECT AND INDEPENDENCE OF MIND

THE CHALLENGE OF FUKUZAWA YUKICHI

KITAOKA SHINICHI

TRANSLATED BY
JAMES M. VARDAMAN

Japan Publishing Industry Foundation for Culture

KITAOKA, Shinichi. Translated by James M. Vardaman.
Self-Respect and Independence of Mind: The Challenge of Fukuzawa Yukichi

Published by Japan Publishing Industry Foundation for Culture (JPIC),
3-12-3 Kanda-Jinbocho, Chiyoda-ku, Tokyo 101-0051, Japan

Published in 2017. Printed in Japan.

Originally published in the Japanese language under the title of *Dokuritsu jison: Fukuzawa Yukichi no chôsen* by KODANSHA LTD. in hardcover in 2002 and by CHUOKORON-SHINSHA, INC. in paperback form in 2011.
Nonexclusive English language rights arranged with CHUOKORON-SHINSHA, INC.

Jacket and cover design by NIIZUMA Hisanori
Front and cover photo of Fukuzawa Yukichi: Courtesy of the Fukuzawa Memorial Center for Modern Japanese Studies, Keio University

ISBN 978-4-916055-62-0
http://www.jpic.or.jp/japanlibrary/

Translator's Note

Names in this volume follow the Japanese order with family name preceding the given name. Japanese authors whose works appear in English translation or who prefer the Western order with family names last, however, follow the original citation.

This volume follows the Hepburn system of Romanization. Macrons have been omitted.

Where possible, Chinese and Korean names are used for relevant texts, personal names and place names. Alternate names are given in parentheses or brackets.

Dates in the original text are given with era names (for example, Meiji 1). To prevent confusion, all dates have been converted to the Western system, although in some select cases the era form of the date follows the Western date. Further, months and days have been converted to the Western calendar system.

Preface to the English Edition

A half-century ago, the majority of Japanese historians viewed the Meiji Restoration as an imperfect revolution. The reason for their conclusion was that compared with the French and Russian revolutions, there was no conclusive breaking up of the existing political system and even after the restoration, it was the samurai who retained real power. Today those who make such claims are in the minority. Around the world, those who praise the Russian Revolution are rare and those who hold that the French Revolution was a fortuitous event continue to decline in number. Economist Kenneth Boulding, on the basis of his sojourn in Japan asserted that in terms of sustained, cumulative development achieved at such minimal expense, the two most conspicuous cases in world history are the American Revolution and the Meiji Restoration.[1] It is reasonable to say that this is now the mainstream view worldwide.

Meriting particular attention is the Meiji Restoration of 1868. The driving force behind this movement was the lower-ranking samurai class from Satsuma, Choshu and other domains. While samurai were all members of a single class, there was a major distinction in status between the lower-rank and upper-rank samurai. Although it was not difficult for a member of one of the classes below the samurai to rise to the status of samurai, it was highly exceptional for a lower-ranking samurai to rise to the higher ranks of the same class. The lower-ranking samurai who grasped power through the restoration, upon deciding that the existence of the feudal domains, including Satsuma and Choshu upon which their very own status was based, was an impediment to the modernization of Japan, abolished the domains (*han*) which had existed for several hundred years, gathered all of the feudal lords (*daimyo*) in Edo (now Tokyo), and placed the whole country under a centralized government. That was a mere three years after the restoration. In addition, they recognized that their own existence as members of a distinct samurai class was also an obstacle, and eight years after the restoration, they abolished the traditional system of four classes and eliminated status distinctions. Such an enormous reform in Japan, which has such a long history, was even more striking than the American Revolution.

The leading figures on the side of those who grasped power to carry out the Meiji Restoration included Okubo Toshimichi, Saigo Takamori, and Kido Takayoshi, followed in the next generation by Ito Hirobumi and Yamagata Aritomo. The central figure on the intellectual side is Fukuzawa Yukichi.

Born in 1835 in Oita Prefecture to a lower-ranking samurai family, Fukuzawa, out of dissatisfaction with the discrimination he observed within his own domain, left for Nagasaki in 1854 with the intention of beginning to study Dutch Learning. It was the year after Commodore Matthew Perry reached Japan's shores. In 1855 Fukuzawa relocated to Osaka where he began serious studies of Dutch. Within Japan's self-seclusion policy, so-called Dutch Learning was the only window left open for learning about the West. After becoming one of the leading scholars of Dutch Learning in Japan, Fukuzawa then went to Edo and began to teach. With the issuance of the United States-Japan Treaty of Amity and Commerce and other maritime trade treaties, several ports were opened to foreign commerce. One of these was Yokohama, and in 1859, Fukuzawa visited the port area and received a shock strong enough to knock him off his feet. The Dutch he had so assiduously studied was of no help at all. The language that dominated Yokohama was English.

Fukuzawa immediately shifted his efforts toward studying English and by a stroke of luck was able to visit the United States in 1860, to travel around Europe for almost a year in 1862, and travel to the United States a second time in 1867. During the Bakumatsu period, it was extremely rare for anyone to visit the West on so many separate occasions.

Fukuzawa grasped Western civilization not just in terms of the number of warships a country had or the miles of railroad track it had laid but also in terms of the social system that made such things possible. He further understood the modern spirit upon which they were founded. Fukuzawa was not simply a person who introduced diverse aspects of Western civilization but a thinker with a thorough, deep understanding of the foundations of the West. Fukuzawa astutely observed that "a nation's independence stands upon the independence of the self," which meant that for Japan, fearful of the Western advance, what was necessary to attain independence was neither warships nor wealth but rather the cultivation of individuals who were fundamentally endowed with an independent spirit.

Very few thinkers in Japan are as much discussed as Fukuzawa. Some who take him as their subject rely heavily on his autobiography. While it is one of the world's more fascinating works of that genre, it contains mistaken memories endemic to autobiographies, some self-justification and some falsehood. Some people see Fukuzawa as the precursor of post-Meiji overseas expansionism, but documentary evidence for their case has recently been called into question. In my view, Fukuzawa is rather the origin of the discourse on behalf of Japan becoming a trading nation. Other critics try to understand Fukuzawa's thought systematically, but it is doubtful whether one can adequately assess his way of thinking without placing him in the context of his times, because he continued to write in order to rouse the people of an actual country.

This being the case, in the context of the development of Japanese politics, there are surprisingly few volumes even in Japanese that take up what Fukuzawa wrote as well as what he did. I have written this volume with hopes of partially filling that gap. Fukuzawa was a world-class intellectual. The basis for this claim is that he attempted to find a solution to the problem of how a non-Western nation, faced with the advance of the Western nations, could maintain their independence, modernize, and take a place among the advanced countries. This is still a major issue for many non-Western nations.

Fukuzawa's *Autobiography*, *An Encouragement of Learning* and *An Outline of a Theory of Civilization* have been translated into English and there are excellent studies on his thought.[2] However, there are no books that are easily accessible to the general reader. It would be an unexpected joy for this author if this volume were to at least partially remedy that situation.

Kitaoka Shinichi
February 2017

Contents

Foreword

No Japanese intellectual is more written about or commented on than Fukuzawa Yukichi. Thanks to the long-term efforts of many people connected to Keio Gijuku (Keio University), which Fukuzawa founded, more historical documents about Fukuzawa have been gathered than about any of his contemporaries. Thus, the facts of his life may be dissected in the finest detail. However, is the merit that Fukuzawa offers truly appreciated?

Not only was Fukuzawa a representative Japanese intellectual of his age, but he was a world-class thinker. *The Autobiography of Fukuzawa Yukichi (Fukuo Jiden)* is a masterpiece among the autobiographies of the genre, including those of figures such as Benjamin Franklin, and those who have not yet read it are missing something.

Some may doubt the veracity of such high praise. If such is the case, one reason may be the style of his writing. Fukuzawa often wrote in exceptionally plain prose. In "Preface to The Collected Works of Fukuzawa Yukichi" (*Fukuzawa Zenshu Shogen*) we find his motto for writing: to make things so clear that if you read it aloud and a servant girl fresh from the country happens to hear it from the other side of the *shoji*, she will easily understand it. Due to such simplicity, however, Fukuzawa's writing does not appear very profound at first glance.

Further, in Fukuzawa's works, the most up-to-date learning of his time is not on display like clusters of brilliant stars. The Western works that he was able to make use of were limited in number. Of course, his breadth of reading was limited compared to contemporary Western scholars. It was also rather limited when compared to the reading undertaken by those Japanese scholars who were some ten years younger than Fukuzawa. If the number of books read and the range of academic methodologies employed are necessary requirements for being an intellectual, then perhaps one could claim that Fukuzawa did not meet that standard.

Despite these doubts, what qualifies Fukuzawa as a first-rank intellectual is the breadth of the subject matter that he confronted head-on, and the depth of the answers he presented. In *An Encouragement of Learning (Gakumon no Susume)* and *An Outline of a Theory of Civilization (Bunmeiron no Gairyaku)*, Fukuzawa grasped the distinctive features of Japanese civilization in comparison with the West, and by precisely indicating those intricacies distinct to Japanese politics, he tackled head-on what would be necessary for Japan's development. Such issues were not just for Japan to face alone. When considered broadly in terms of what differentiates the Western from the non-Western world, and whether it is possible for the latter to modernize, this subject has significance for world history as a whole. Considering these factors, it is difficult to find intellectuals of his day who showed potential solutions that were superior to those of Fukuzawa, even if one considers figures outside of Japan.

The role Fukuzawa played in the radical reforms of the Meiji period was truly enormous. Although it is difficult to compare intellectuals and politicians, the role that Fukuzawa played from the Bakumatsu period through the Sino-Japanese War stands well in comparison with the three great leaders of the Meiji Restoration—Okubo Toshimichi, Saigo Takamori and Kido Takayoshi.

Character sketches were one of the popular pastimes of the Meiji period. While Japanese society was undergoing systematic changes during that era, more often than not it was individual talent that was the impetus for such change. Furthermore, new figures were coming on the scene one after another, and delineation of character became almost a distinct literary genre. The most prominent of these writers was Toyabe Shuntei, who was known for his broad knowledge, balanced judgment and lucid prose. Toyabe once took up Fukuzawa as a topic and wrote the following:

It seems to me that his past history is truly and deeply intertwined with

> the spirit of the Meiji era. He is not related to this spirit by actions but rather by words. His contributions may not dazzle the eyes with the brilliance of the three great leaders of the Restoration, but in terms of influencing the thinking of the period and assisting social progress, the three great leaders pale by comparison. Needless to say, even Ito Hirobumi and Itagaki Taisuke cannot match him. (*Fukuzawa Yukichi-o, Taiyo,* 1898)

In other words, in terms of who influenced changes in intellectual thought regarding progress in society, Toyabe asserted that the role played by Fukuzawa exceeded that of the three leaders generally considered the main forces behind the transformation of society and Ito Hirobumi and Itagaki Taisuke as well.

To reiterate, Fukuzawa encountered a period of world-wide historical change and acted without hesitation. *The Autobiography,* in which he left behind the rare, free, open-minded spirit that permeated his life, is one of the world's outstanding biographical works precisely because it was such a period of change. If one takes a broad view of the Meiji Restoration and seeks to find a figure most representative of the era, without a doubt Fukuzawa Yukichi is that person.

Japan's national power has stagnated since the early 1960s. Many people, including the author, believe that it was because Japan was unable to cope with the new international realities that followed the end of the Cold War, such as regional conflicts, rise of new powers, international terrorism, and the IT revolution. They argue that Japan has to transform its political and economic system, calling this the third opening of the nation, following the first at the time of the Meiji Restoration and the second during the post-1945 reforms. Consequently, as Japan today finds itself feeling trapped in a sense of despair, it is to the Meiji era that we should turn, and more than to anyone else, the person we should turn to is Fukuzawa Yukichi.

With the general reader in mind, this volume brings together the results of research into the accomplishments of Fukuzawa as part of an overall appraisal of the man himself.

Surprisingly, such books are few in number.

Among the volumes that take up Fukuzawa's writings, for example, there are several whose primary focus is *The Autobiography*. To be sure, it is a great work, but, as is natural with memoirs, there are mistaken memories and some significant inaccuracies. In addition, twelve of the fifteen chapters portray his youth and there is comparatively little about his prime years. That is to say, an introduction to *The Autobiography* is not even an introduction to his entire life story.

In presenting an overall view of Fukuzawa, one naturally has to introduce the content of *An Encouragement of Learning* and *An Outline of a Theory of Civilization,* but among the biographical works, there is, on the whole, comparatively little coverage of his ideas within these works.

On the other hand, there are many works that discuss Fukuzawa's thinking, focusing on the two aforementioned works. In discussing a thinker, the standard approach is to place the main works in the center of one's purview. Yet with this method, there is a risk that the result will be abstract and overly-complicated. A more difficult issue is the relationship of *An Encouragement of Learning* and *An Outline of a Theory of Civilization* with Fukuzawa's later works. Studies on Fukuzawa generally offer high praise for these two works but are harshly critical of his later works, seeing them as pro-government or too hard line.

Contrasting *An Encouragement of Learning* and *An Outline of a Theory of Civilization,* which Fukuzawa wrote during his thirties to describe how Japan was then, with the writings that laid out practical policies and which Fukuzawa published once he had attained considerable influence (these generally appeared in *Jiji Shimpo*, founded in 1882) is bound to turn up some differences. Moreover, the issues that needed solving changed along with the development of the Meiji State. From this perspective, I believe it is quite necesssary to grasp Fukuzawa's thinking in a unified manner within the context of the development of Meiji Japan and Fukuzawa's personal growth.

This volume is a biographical work centered on Fukuzawa's thinking. But by the term "thinking," we shall not deal with a system of abstract logic but instead deal with thinking of a more pragmatic nature. It is this author's hope to convey to the reader what Fukuzawa wanted for Japan by looking at his vision and methodology as well as at his rhetoric.

Here I would like to make a personal comment. I taught at Rikkyo University beginning in 1976 and since 1997 at the University of Tokyo. During these years, roughly twice every three years, I have used *The Autobiography of Fukuzawa Yukichi* and *An Encouragement of Learning* or alternately *The Autobiography* and *An Outline of a Theory of Civilization* in my classes. I am neither a specialist in the history of Japanese political thought nor a specialist on Fukuzawa Yukichi, but I have considerable experience in reading Fukuzawa's main works.

The reason for dealing with his works with such frequency is that they are perfectly suited for understanding the upheavals of the Meiji period and they brilliantly depict the distinctive features of Japanese political affairs. In addition, I simply wanted students to learn about Fukuzawa's life itself.

The title of this volume, *Self-Respect and Independence of Mind (Dokuritsu Jison)*, is a phrase Fukuzawa was particularly fond of. It applies to his life itself. When Fukuzawa left the domain where his family lived in order to begin studying Dutch, he was not at all confident that he would be successful. To the contrary, one could even call his actions somewhat reckless. However, Fukuzawa was not motivated by self-interest or his own gains or losses. Such concerns were considered to demean one's self. Fukuzawa was not guided by such ambitions, but he listened instead to his own inner voice and did what he really wanted to do, what he felt was truly the right thing to do. He chose to walk an independent path, while maintaining his own integrity, currying favor with, depending on, and fearing no one.

Needless to say, people blessed with Fukuzawa's talent are rare. However, one does not have to be like Fukuzawa to live—or at least to attempt to live—a life of integrity. It is this independence of mind and sense of self-respect that is most essential in turbulent times. Without such spirit, Japan will not be able to extricate itself from its long-lasting stagnation. It would bring the author great pleasure if this book enables those who are searching for some way out of the present turmoil to learn something of the essence of Fukuzawa Yukichi.

Kitaoka Shinichi
March 2002

Chapter 1

The Nakatsu Period

Former residence of Fukuzawa Yukichi. The Fukuzawa family resided here from about 1849.

Nakatsu Domain

The Autobiography of Fukuzawa Yukichi[3] opens with the following lines:

> My father, Fukuzawa Hyakusuke, was a samurai of the Nakatsu Okudaira domain in Buzen Province (present-day Oita Prefecture). My mother, called Ojun, was the eldest daughter of another samurai in the same domain named Hashimoto Hamaemon. My father's status was barely high enough for him to be granted a formal audience with the lord of the domain. He was a few ranks above the *ashigaru*, the common foot-soldiers, but he was in the lower echelon of samurai. Today his position would correspond to *hanninkan*, the lowest rank of government official, and he worked as the overseer of the treasury (*motojimeyaku*), which meant that for long periods of time he was assigned to duties at the Nakatsu domain warehouse and headquarters in Osaka.
>
> As a consequence, our entire household moved to Osaka and all of the children were born there: a son, three daughters, then myself, the youngest. I was born on January 10th, 1835, when my father was forty-one years old and my mother was twenty-nine. A year and a half later my father died. My mother was left with five children to raise, my brother was only nine and I was a mere infant. Unable to remain in Osaka, the only thing my mother could do was to take us all back to Nakatsu.

With minor additions, such as the mention of Oita Prefecture and the date according to the new calendrical year, the above passage stands basically as he published it. The original passage is worth reading aloud. Some Japanese readers may be unfamiliar with pre-war terms like *hanninkan* (middle and lower-rank members of the public official bureaucracy) and *soryo* (the oldest son of the family). With these exceptions, however, the reader cannot help but be amazed at how easy the passage reads and how comfortable its tempo is. It is based on notes taken from lectures, but it was written in 1898, well over a century ago.

Such readability can only result from both strong conviction and long experience. Unless one possesses an uncommon degree of self-confidence, one cannot write such flowing prose. Without the completely new sensibility underlying this writing, it would probably be impossible for modern readers to easily absorb its meaning. The opening passage of *The Autobiography* is, I believe, stirring and direct.

The beginning of *The Autobiography of Fukuzawa Yukichi* gives us various reasons to pause and contemplate. As Professor Iida Kanae has pointed out, Fukuzawa severely criticized the Nakatsu domain, and yet he was fortunate enough to have been born there. If he had been born for example in Tohoku (northern Honshu), his chances of coming into contact with Western civilization would have been slim. The fact that Nakatsu was close to Nagasaki was a considerable advantage. Further, if he had been born in a larger domain, the domain itself would in great likelihood have become embroiled in the politics of the Bakumatsu years, (i.e., the closing days of the Tokugawa regime); the talented young Fukuzawa might have become caught up in these events and become involved in politics rather than learning. As a result of that, he might well have died young.[4]

Going one step further, if Fukuzawa had been born into a family of higher status, he probably would not have been able to cast his domain aside so easily. If he had not been born into a samurai family, it would have been difficult for him to get involved in Dutch Studies (*Rangaku*). At the time of Commodore Matthew Perry's arrival, he was eighteen years old, a perfect age to be. In other words, these momentous events occurred just as he was entering his prime, just as he was ready to take a major step forward in life. Fukuzawa began his work in Dutch Studies in earnest at age twenty, switched to English Studies at age twenty-four and at age twenty-five boarded the *Kanrin Maru* bound for the United States. Had Fukuzawa been born earlier, he might well have established his position as a scholar of Dutch Studies and then would have found it difficult to switch over to English as the language of scholarship. In contrast, had he been born later, he would have missed being in the vanguard of the full-scale introduction of Western ideas, and some other person might well have come along and become the leading authority instead.

However, such hypotheticals are for historians to contemplate. When Fukuzawa embarked on his life's journey, he had no outlook or hopes for success. He simply did what he believed was correct, and he moved forward as he felt he should. Memoirs of so-called eminent figures usually begin with the great ambitions they possessed as a child or statements about what a child prodigy the person was, but Fukuzawa's autobiography is not that kind of thing. Let us instead retrace the course he followed.

Nakatsu domain was about fifty kilometers northwest of present-day Oita City. Although it was in what is now Oita Prefecture, it was on the border of Fukuoka Prefecture. Compared with the major feudal lords (*daimyo*) of Kyushu—the Shimazu (720,000 *koku*[5]) of Satsuma Kagoshima, the Hosokawa (540,000 *koku*) of Higo Kumamoto, the Kuroda (470,000 *koku*) of Chikuzen Fukuoka, and the Nabeshima (350,000 *koku*) of Hizen Saga—the Nakatsu domain (100,000 *koku*) was not large. Nakatsu Castle, which today stands along the Nakatsu River, projects a tranquil atmosphere and does not present the imposing image of a major domain. In terms of the domains established throughout the country, however, it was neither particularly large nor small. At the time, there were said to be some 300 domains, many of which were only 10,000 to 20,000 *koku*, whereas only 50 domains were over 100,000 *koku*.

Of particular interest was the position of Fukuzawa's family as a lower-echelon samurai family. In order to understand the impact of the environment in which Fukuzawa was raised and educated—and by extension, the fact that the Meiji Restoration was implemented by the same class of lower-echelon samurai—let us examine the relationship between the higher echelon and lower echelon of the samurai class in Nakatsu domain by means of the "Conditions in an Old Feudal Clan" (*Kyuhanjo*[6]), written by Fukuzawa in 1877.

The Difference Between the Upper and Lower Samurai

The Nakatsu domain had some 1,500 samurai retainers in total. In terms of status and official duties, they could be classified into one hundred or more categories, but overall they were sharply divided into an upper echelon and a lower echelon. The upper echelon ranged from major vassals to pages, together with certain special cases such as the Confucian scholars and physicians. The lower echelon consisted of *yuhitsu* (secretaries), *nakakosho* (usually grooms and stablemen), *tomokosho* (close attendants), and *koyakunin* (minor functionaries) as well as *ashigaru* (common foot-soldiers) and others who had been granted the privilege of wearing a sword. It was said that the ratio of upper to lower retainers was roughly one to three, which would have meant that there were fewer than 400 in the upper echelon and some 1,100 in the lower echelon.

A major barrier lay between the upper and lower echelons. The top of the lower echelon were the secretaries. During the 250-year Tokugawa shogunate, only three to five retainers crossed this barrier to rise to *koshogumi*, the lowest position within the upper echelon. Furthermore, marriages between members of the upper and lower echelons were rare.

In contrast, there was great mobility within each echelon. Within the upper, it was not unusual for a member of the lowest rank *(koshogumi)*, to be promoted to a kind of chamberlain *(yonin)*, and if the second or third son of a major vassal established a branch family, it was customary for him to be appointed as a close attendant *(kosho)*. Further, within the lower echelon, while there was a major disparity between the lowest rank of samurai *(ashigaru)* and secretaries *(yuhitsu)*, it was not unheard of for an *ashigaru* to be promoted to a *nakakosho*. Not only that, it was not unheard of for a peasant to become a samurai and then end up rising to the middle ranks of the lower echelon. In sum, in comparison with the virtual impossibility of rising from the lower to the upper echelon, it was not that difficult to rise from outside the samurai class altogether to the ranks of the lower-echelon samurai.

Let us examine several examples of practical differences between the upper and lower echelons. Even if it was raining, for example, an *ashigaru*, encountering a middle-rank samurai of the lower echelon who was higher in rank, was expected to remove his wooden clogs and prostrate himself at the side of the road. A lower-echelon samurai, upon encountering a higher-echelon samurai, was required to display a similar etiquette. Similarly, when a samurai of the lower echelon called at the home of an upper-echelon samurai, he was required to make his salutations from the anteroom before entering the main room. In contrast, when an upper-echelon samurai called on one from the lower echelon, he was free to walk straight into the reception room with sword in hand.

When addressing one another, the upper echelon used *kisama* as a form of address when speaking to lower-echelon samurai, and the lower echelon used *anata* when speaking to the upper echelon. The upper ranks said *kiyare* for "come," while the lower ranks used the more polite *oide nasai*. Within the lower echelon, the lower-ranking *ashigaru* called the upper echelon not by personal name but by *danna-sama*. If the superior was a major retainer, he would always be addressed as *danna-sama*, the term a servant would use in speaking to his master.

Raised wooden floors inside the front door of a household were permitted in the upper-echelon houses. The upper echelon traveled on horseback; the lower echelon walked. Further, in principle, learning was not part of the work of the lower echelon, so they were not permitted to travel to other provinces to pursue studies.

There was a major economic gap between the two echelons. There was also a major gap among members of the upper echelon, with major retainers receiving 1,000 to 2,000 *koku* or more, while the *koshogumi* (attendants) and physicians received stipends less than ten *buchi*, one *buchi* being a relatively fixed ration for one person. However, as a general rule, the largest group received—under the pretense of 100, 200 or 250 *koku*—an actual total of from 22-23 *koku* to 40-60 *koku*. Those who held an important post might receive a nominal 100 *koku* or more. At any rate, if they received between 20 and 30 *koku*, the ordinary household would be able to live and even provide a measure of education to their children.

In contrast, the stipends of the lower echelon ranged from 15 *koku* and rations *(buchi)* for three men, 13 *koku* and rations *(buchi)* for two men, to 10 *koku* and rations *(buchi)* for one man. Below this, there were some who were simply paid in cash. It is said that even the upper levels of the lower echelon only received a net of 7 to 8 *koku*. This might be sufficient for a husband and wife, but if there were children or elderly people to care for, basic subsistence would be difficult, so both men and women would have to take up some kind of handicraft or do spinning to get by. Fukuzawa wrote that "these jobs might in theory be mere side-jobs, but in reality the samurai came to regard them as their main occupation while regarding their official clan duties as work on the side. In effect, they were not samurai but simply workmen."

As a consequence, the lower echelon of the samurai class did not have the economic means to provide their children with high-level education. It was normal for their offspring to finish the Nine Chinese Classics, *Mengqiu* (*Mogyu*, a textbook aimed at children and beginners), and possibly one or two volumes of *Tso-chuan (Saden)*. Additionally, writing and arithmetic were seen as essential. For a lower-echelon family, to have some degree of leeway in their livelihood, it was necessary that children obtain a minor official post and for this reason academic accomplishments were seen as being absolutely essential.

There was also a major difference in manners and customs. Upper-echelon households had maids and servants, so they themselves did not go into the street to do shopping. Nor did they go to the public baths. When going out, the men wore formal *hakama*, pleated trousers, and wore two swords at their side. At night, they were accompanied by someone carrying a lantern to light the way. If they carried anything at all, it was kendo equipment or a fishing pole and they never carried anything in a *furoshiki* wrapping cloth.

In contrast, the lower-echelon households ordinarily did not employ servants. Aside from mid-day, in the evening, both men and women went out to do their own shopping. In the neighborhood, the men might cover their faces with a cloth *(tenugui)*, carry two swords, just one, or even go unarmed, and they often did not wear formal trousers *(hakama)*. When a banquet was held, it was these men who livened things up by entertaining. Fukuzawa tells us that the upper echelon had a sophisticated, profound air, yet they knew little of worldly affairs. Meanwhile, the lower echelon was somewhat crude and lacking in manners but was nevertheless high-spirited.

The Influence of Yukichi's Scholarly Father Hyakusuke

We now turn to Fukuzawa's family.

Fukuzawa's father Hyakusuke was first called to service in 1819 and he successfully held posts as a minor official in *motojimekata* affairs. Two years later he took over as head of his family. In October 1822, he was ordered to serve as *kaimaikata*, which meant residing in Osaka. The *moto-jimekata*, the overseer, was charged with managing the domain's accounts, while the *kaimaikata* was the official who managed the day-to-day operations of the clan storehouse *(kurayashiki)*. His duty was to collect rice and other products from the domain that were stored in the Osaka warehouses and have them converted into money. In actual fact, the position required that he negotiate loans from the wealthy Osaka merchants, using the domain's produce as collateral.

The nature of the work was filled with temptations, so it was a fundamental principle that the manager be rotated every two years. Because Hyakusuke was both competent and honest, however, he was repeatedly reappointed such that his term of office continued for thirteen years. During this period, he repeatedly requested a transfer, but each time the domain turned his request down and instead promoted him. As a result of this chain of events, he was promoted—within the lower echelon—from *koyakunin* (a minor official) to *tomokosho* and eventually to *oumaya*, which was later renamed *nakakosho*. This was the highest rank within the lower echelon. It is apparent from this just how trusted he was within the domain hierarchy. As mentioned earlier, promotion within the lower echelon was often by way of functions within the treasury warehouse.

Due to the fact that Hyakusuke was of a scholarly frame of mind, he did not care for such work. Fukuzawa comments that his father was the type of pure scholar who felt debased by simply looking at money. He must have felt this strongly because when he heard that Yukichi's brother, Sannosuke, was being taught multiplication tables at the training school at the storehouse headquarters, he made Sannosuke drop out. Despite the fact that the abacus was indispensible in Hyakusuke's gaining promotions, it might have had the reverse effect of making him dislike such things even more.

From childhood, Hyakusuke had loved learning. He had hoped to study at Kan Chazan at Bingo Fukuyama, but because his family was unable to afford it, he went to study with the domain Confucianist Nomoto Setsugan. Hyakusuke went on to study with Hoashi Banri in the Bungo Hiji domain, where it is said he came to be recognized as one of Hoashi's more talented students.

While in Osaka it was, naturally enough, possible to keep company with a large number of scholars and other experts. Among them, he showed little interest in Rai Sanyo in Kyoto and instead revered Ito Togai. Annotated works by Ito Togai were among the prized volumes in his private library. Among his close friends was a Confucian scholar named Noda Tekiho and he grew close to Nakamura Ritsuen, who studied in the schools of both Nomoto Sengan and Hoashi Banri. Noda, from the Tango Tanabe domain, was involved in domain administration, as was Hoashi. Nakamura was also involved in administrative affairs.

About the time Yukichi was born, Hyakusuke was delighted that he was finally able to obtain a 64-volume set of Chinese classics that he had long hoped to possess: *Joyujorei* (Ch: Shang-yu T'iao-Li). Because this acquisition coincided with his joy over the birth of another son, Hyakusuke took the second character *yu* from the title of the collection and named his son *Yu*kichi.

The collection *Joyujorei*, covering the Qing period 1735 to 1750 was divided into imperial rescripts, imperial ordinances and government ordinances arranged by year. It was not the sort of compilation that the ordinary Japanese scholar of Chinese classics would show an interest in. Given what he held in his library and the nature of his acquaintances, Hyakusuke was not the type of scholar who favored prose and poetry. His preferences ran toward legal systems, economics and what might be referred to as enlightened rule and the succor of the people.

It is said that Hyakusuke's private library contained some 1,500 volumes. Today, that does not sound so impressive; however, in his day it was an astounding figure, and for a samurai of the lower echelon, assembling such a collection must have required extraordinary sacrifice. When Hyakusuke suddenly died, his close friend Nakamura Ritsuen immediately rushed to conduct funeral rites for him and he composed a lengthy eulogy. One passage from it read, "You were so absorbed in books and the classics that you were liable to forget both thirst and hunger." Surely that was no exaggeration.

A Free and Rational Spirit

Yukichi was only one and a half when his father died in 1836. There was no other choice for the family than to return to Nakatsu. The house which they had left vacant for so long, with no one to look after it, was in a state of ruin.

Their household finances were in a bad way and because the family had grown completely acclimatized to the culture of Osaka, they did not get along well with those around them. Even language was an issue. While in Osaka one might say, "*so de omasu,*" in Nakatsu people said, "*so ja chiko.*" The family also wore their clothes and their hair in an Osaka style. By nature, Yukichi was both a lively boy and well-built, however, he had difficulty climbing trees and swimming like the local children. This was because he did not spend much time playing with friends of his own age.

The family modestly closed ranks around their courageous, affectionate mother and got on with their lives. Their late father often came up in conversations. When Yukichi heard that his father had talked about having Yukichi enter the Buddhist priesthood so that he could advance beyond the bounds of his social status, Yukichi believed that his father had suppressed his own sense of bitterness throughout his life. Yukichi began to feel that the feudal system of lineage was his parents' enemy.

His mother, however, seems to have possessed a freer spirit. She did not discriminate and even once picked the lice off a female beggar; she was kind to all types of people. She possessed a strong sense of obligation, and when forced to borrow money, she paid it back regardless of the difficulty. It seemed she was not a follower of any particular religion, but she was extremely devout all the same.

Yukichi was dexterous and easily repapered *shoji* screens, replaced the cover of *tatami* mats, repaired holes in the roof, mended wooden pails and fixed the straps of wooden *geta*. He worked hard at side-jobs like making *geta* and fitting out the sheath, cords and metal fittings of swords. In winter, when his hands chapped and cracked, he sewed the cracks closed with thread, and poured hot oil over them to fill them in. He was so tough that one winter he slept on the *tatami* without a *futon*. In a poem written in 1879, he reflected back on his youth and how he was skilled at mundane tasks, fondly recalling the days when his robust spirit took on any small task at hand.

Yukichi was a free-spirited youth filled with a sense of the rational. He was once scolded by his brother for stepping on a scrap of paper inscribed with the name of his feudal lord. Unable to grasp what was so enormous about stepping on a piece of paper, he tried stepping on an *ofuda*, a strip of paper with talismanic writing, from a Shinto shrine. Nothing happened. He then tried switching the stones of the object of worship at an Inari shrine to see if he would incur some form of divine punishment for doing so. Again, nothing happened.

Once his brother asked him what his goal in life was and he responded that he wanted to earn huge sums of money and use it in any way he pleased. His brother was appalled by this response. When Yukichi asked what his brother's goal was, Sannosuke replied, "filial piety and fidelity until death." His brother was a truly serious youth.

Yukichi was fourteen or fifteen when he first pursued academic studies. His was a delayed start. In almost no time, however, he began to distinguish himself. He was particularly good at *Tso-chuan (Saden)*. Typically, students gave this topic up after reading three or four of the fifteen volumes, but Yukichi read everything. Not only that, he read through them eleven times and even memorized some of the most interesting passages. Yukichi writes that he became a senior student *(zenza)* in Chinese literature as a result.

Please allow me a brief comment on *Tso-chuan*. Among Confucianists there were nine works considered to be scriptures: The Four Books *(Shisho)* and Five Classics *(Gokyo)*. The Four Books consist of *The Great Learning* (Ch: Daxue; J: Daigaku), *The Doctrine of the Mean* (Ch: Zhongyong; J: Chuyo), *The Analects* (Ch: Lunyu; J: Rongo), and *Mencius* (Ch: Mengzi; J: Moshi). The Five Classics (Ch: Wujing; J: Gokyo) consist of *The Book of Changes* (Ch: Yijing; J: Ekikyo), *The Book of Documents* (Ch: Shu jing; J: Shokyo), *The Book of Odes* (Ch: Shi jing; J: Shikyo), *The Book of Rites* (Ch: Li ji; J: Raiki) and *The Spring and Summer Annals* (Ch: Chun qiu; J: Shunju).

Of these, *The Spring and Autumn Annals* contain the chronical or annals of the kingdom of Lu (Ro) during the Spring and Autumn Period. This volume was particularly revered because it was thought to be the only one of the Five Classics written by Confucius himself. In actual fact, it is now thought that Confucius did not compose the whole work but rather compiled previously-existing works and added his own amendments to them.

However, *The Spring and Autumn Annals* are extremely succinct and many people have published annotated editions of them. Three of these are particularly well-known and perhaps the best is by Zuo-shi. This is the version known as *Tso-chuan* (*Saden*). Neither the author nor when it was compiled is known.

Despite this anonymity, *Tso-chuan* has an established reputation, such resting upon its vivid portrayal of the actions of rival local barons. As a work of Chinese history, *The Scribe's Records* (Ch: Shih-chi; J: Shiki) is famous, but concerning the Spring and Autumn Period, this latter work fundamentally follows *The Spring and Autumn Annals*. Some say that the dynamism of *Tso-chuan* is superior. As time passed, *The Annals* came to be seen as a third volume—together with *The Analects and Mencius*—that made up the fundamentals of a Japanese education in the classics.

To have read this through eleven times is no ordinary accomplishment. The fact attests to Fukuzawa's competence in Chinese and the clarity and rhythm of his later writing is undoubtedly related to his knowledge of Chinese literature. We can perhaps also see here the strong interest he developed in history and, in particular, the rise and fall of nation-states.

Departing Nakatsu

Fukuzawa disliked Nakatsu. Looking back on it from the modern perspective, Nakatsu was not that bad a place. It had a degree of tradition both with respect to learning and Dutch Studies. (Maeno Ryotaku, one of the translators of the *Kaitai Shinsho* [New Book of Anatomy] was originally a physician in the Nakatsu domain). Nakatsu also lacked the serious political strife that often occurred in the larger domains. Nonetheless, Yukichi felt it to be unbearably stifling. All things considered, he was unhappy with the discrepancies in social status. His father, Hyakusuke, had been forced to take on the unpleasant duty of being a *motojimekata*, subsequently rising to the top of the lower echelon of samurai before dying suddenly. Indeed, we have already seen how deep the divide was between the upper and lower echelons. For a youth who was capable of doubting the omnipresence of the lord of the domain and even the Inari deity, to have every aspect of daily life partitioned—from language usage to daily etiquette—into fine gradients that depended on one's status, was more than the young Fukuzawa could take. He looked for any excuse at all that would allow him to leave Nakatsu.

In July 1853, U.S. Commodore Matthew Perry sailed into Uraga Bay; in August Russian Vice-Admiral Yevfimy Putyatin arrived at Nagasaki. The impact of these events reverberated even in Nakatsu, and the necessity of artillery technology and Dutch Studies was clear. Even Yukichi's brother Sannosuke became interested in mathematics and gunnery and began to see the necessity of studying Dutch. However, there was no one in Nakatsu who could handle "writing sideways," that is, writing in a foreign language such as Dutch. At the very least, the tradition established by Maeno Ryotaku had not been handed down. Sannosuke told Yukichi about the existence of these "languages written sideways"—European languages written horizontally instead of vertically like Japanese was in those days—and through this information the latter first learned about the field of Dutch Studies. Yukichi became interested in reading such strange languages. He felt that if other people could do it, he could, too.

In due course, Sannosuke had to tend to some business in Nagasaki, and Yukichi accompanied him. He simply went along in order to escape from Nakatsu. In 1854 Yukichi turned nineteen. This was right around the time of Perry's second visit to Japan.

At the time, a young man named Okudaira Jugaku was studying in Nagasaki. A relative of the lord of the Nakatsu domain, his father was one of the chief counselors *(karo)*, and he himself became a counselor, subsequently taking the name Okudaira Iki. Sannosuke asked Okudaira to take Yukichi in as a sort of attendant. Okudaira was then temporarily living at a Buddhist temple called Koei-ji. It was a temple with a history that belonged to the Jodo Shin sect and it still exists today. Back then, the temple was related to the Okudaira household by marriage. Yukichi, as a consequence of becoming a dependent of Okudaira, also began to live and board at the temple.

Shortly thereafter, through Okudaira, Yukichi was introduced to Yamamoto Monojiro, an instructor of gunnery, who took him in as a boarder. Yamamoto was a follower of Takashima Shuhan and in 1857 was said to have cast two cannons which he presented to the bakufu. By the time Yukichi went to live with him, however, Yamamoto's eyesight had grown so poor that he could no longer read. Thus, Yukichi became the eyes of Yamamoto and also gave lessons to his son. Yukichi also eventually took on the chores of negotiating household debts, drawing water from the well, sweeping the house, taking care of the dogs and cats, and completing any kind of work that needed doing. By and by, Yamamoto even asked him to become his adopted son. All of a sudden, the boy who was skilled in mundane tasks became a person of some merit. Yukichi was willing to go all out in his chores, and despite the fact that he had an incomparable love of alcohol, he did not imbibe a single drop during his time in Nagasaki. Yukichi had liked liquor since childhood, and when his mother shaved the front part of his head, as was then the custom, she coaxed him to put up with the unpleasantness by promising a small drink after it was over.

Yamamoto had a large collection of books on gunnery which the bakufu had confiscated from Takashima Shuhan. Part of Yamamoto's income was derived from fees from lending out these books or by selling handwritten copies of them. Fukuzawa was put in charge of these various transactions and his name came to be known among the students of gunnery in Nagasaki.

Somewhat displeased by these developments, the young Okudaira came up with a plan. In the middle of March 1855, Yukichi received a letter from a cousin back in Nakatsu named Fujimoto saying that his mother was ill and that Yukichi should return home. Sannosuke was posted in Osaka at that time, his three sisters were all married, and his mother was living by herself in the Nakatsu house. Yukichi was stunned by the letter.

Another letter accompanying it, however, said that he should not be anxious about his mother's health. According to this second letter, Fujimoto had been summoned by Okudaira Jugaku's father, who said that

Yukichi's presence in Nagasaki was hampering his own son's studies, so Fujimoto should write to Yukichi, telling him his mother was ill and that he should immediately depart for Nakatsu. The gist of this second letter was that Yukichi should not worry but that he should come home promptly.

All the more because his efforts were just beginning to yield some results, Yukichi was absolutely furious with this turn of events. However, his better judgment told him that it was useless to argue. Pretending to be completely fooled by this ruse, he decided to leave Nagasaki. While explaining that his mother had taken ill, he took his leave of the Yamamoto family. Upon leaving Nagasaki, he dropped by a drinking place in Isahaya and for the first time in a year drank alcohol to his heart's content.

After leaving Nagasaki, however, Yukichi did not return to Nakatsu but instead intended to go straight to Edo. He had met a student of medicine named Okabe and asked Okabe to write a letter introducing him to Okabe's father in Edo. Yukichi hoped to be taken in as a dependent. He was broke, so he used various ruses to make his way eastward. Forging a letter to get free lodging and an advance of money, he then proceeded to make his way by boat from Shimonoseki to Akashi. There he disembarked and in the middle of the night headed on foot to Osaka, some thirty-eight miles distant. He reached his brother's residence at the Nakatsu domain storehouses and residence in Osaka's Dojima district.

Yukichi had been born in Osaka. He had no memories of the city himself but he encountered many people who remembered him from his infancy there. Among these people was his wet-nurse who was the wife of a wharf laborer; there was also a faithful servant of the family. As this man walked him around the area, Yukichi wrote, "I could not hold back the tears prompted by his memories of those days." Thinking back on the days in Nakatsu, when he was treated as an outsider and driven out of Nagasaki by crafty plotting, Yukichi commented, "It was a truly wonderful feeling, just as if I had returned to my real home."

When he explained to his brother why he had suddenly come to Osaka, Sannosuke more or less understood. But his brother would not condone his going on to Edo and instead persuaded Yukichi to stay in Osaka and enter the *Tekijuku*, a school run by Ogata Koan, in April 1855. There Yukichi met the man who would be his teacher to the end of his life.

Chapter 2

Ogata's *Tekijuku*

Copy of the *Doeff Halma*, a Dutch-Japanese dictionary used at Ogata Koan's *Tekijuku* academy.
(Courtesy of the Oita Prefecture Ancient Sages Historical Archives, Keio University Fukuzawa Memorial Center)

Studying with Ogata Koan

And so Yukichi became a student at Ogata Koan's *Tekijuku*, a school for Dutch Studies. This had a decisive impact on Yukichi's life. Had he not met Ogata, he would not have become the Yukichi now known to history.

Ogata Koan was born in Bitchu in 1810 and in 1838 at the age of 28, he opened a medical practice in Osaka and at the same time established a school for Dutch Studies. The school was originally named *Tekitekisaijuku*, but it was gradually shortened to *Tekijuku*. When Yukichi entered the school, Ogata was forty-five years old and had hit his stride. Ogata and Sugita Seikei in Edo were considered the two greatest authorities in Dutch Studies in the country.

At that time, the *Tekijuku* was the foremost school of Dutch Studies. At its peak, it enjoyed an enrollment of one hundred students, while during its entire existence, more than one thousand individuals passed through its gates. Among the school's many alumni, the following rose to particular prominence: Hashimoto Sanai (of the Fukui domain, went on to become a reformer of the Bakumatsu period); Murata Ryoan (later known as Murata Zoroku and subsequently called Omura Masujiro, a top expert on military affairs in the late years of Edo and early years of Meiji); Sano Eiju (later known as Sano Tsunetami, became Minister of Agriculture and Commerce, subsequently invested as a count within the peerage of Meiji Japan, founder of the Japanese Red Cross Society); Otori Keisuke (later a leader of the bakufu infantry forces, appointed Minister to the courts of China and Korea, subsequently invested as a baron within the peerage of Meiji Japan); Nagayo Sensai (later a head of the Bureau of Hygiene, Ministry of Home Affairs); Mitsukuri Shuhei (later a member of the *Meirokusha* [the Meiji Six Society], also a member of the Tokyo Academy); Hanabusa Yoshimoto (later appointed Minister to Czarist Russia, subsequently invested as a viscount within the peerage of Meiji Japan): Motono Morimichi (later a diplomat, went on to become the president of the *Yomiuri Shimbunsha*, a major Japanese newspaper); and Ikeda Kensai (later a physician, subsequently invested as a baron within the peerage of Meiji Japan).

Many of those who came to study at the school were from provinces lying to the west of Osaka. Each time the Lord of Chikuzen, Kuroda Mino, passed through the city, he invited Ogata to his residence, and Ogata succeeded in borrowing from the lord whatever Western book he had most recently acquired. In addition, Nabeshima Kanso of Saga, Yamauchi Yodo of Tosa, and Matsudaira Shungaku of Echizen all deeply trusted Ogata. Thus, they sent many of their medical students to study with him.

Ogata taught in Osaka for twenty-four years. However, in 1862, after the bakufu had repeatedly requested that he become the shogun's personal physician, Ogata finally consented and relocated himself to Edo. As a physician, his new position represented the highest honor. As an educator, however, Ogata had hoped to continue his school.

Yukichi started at the *Tekijuku* on April 25th, 1855, and commuted from the headquarters of the Nakatsu domain warehouses. A year later, in April 1856, while caring for a friend suffering from typhoid, he was infected himself. Ogata compassionately took care of Yukichi during his illness. Although he diagnosed Yukichi himself, Ogata called in another physician to compound the medicines used for treatment. Ogata explained that it was difficult to treat the illness, because he felt as close to the patient as he would to his own son.

Yukichi wrote, "It will be seen that the relation between teacher and student at the time was of the intimate, father-and-son kind. When Ogata-sensei felt it difficult to treat my illness, his was the same feeling that he would have felt toward his own son. This has changed nowadays with the increase of students and the teacher-student relation has turned into something of a public affair; and I fear even the little regard for each other will grow less as the new school system progresses. But when I was in Ogata's school, I could not but feel that I was a member of his family."[7] Having lost his father at a young age, Yukichi clearly saw Ogata as a second father.

His illness proved to be quite serious. Within a few days he lost consciousness and for a week he remained in a coma. However, because he was naturally robust and young, Yukichi recovered quickly and by May he was well enough to walk outside again.

Meanwhile, his brother Sannosuke was in poor health. His rheumatism worsened and he could no longer write with his right hand. Fortunately, Sannosuke's two-year term of office came to an end around that time, so Yukichi and his brother decided to return together to Nakatsu.

In Nakatsu, Yukichi recovered his health and in September he returned to Osaka. Renting a section of the headquarters' office of the Nakatsu domain, he then resumed his attendance at the *Tekijuku*. Shortly thereafter, on the first of October, his brother Sannosuke suddenly passed away. Yukichi immediately proceeded to Nakatsu and by the time he arrived, the family's relatives had gathered and decided that Yukichi would become the head of the household. Prior to this, he had already been adopted into the Nakamura family and had become Nakamura Yukichi, but now he was to become Fukuzawa Yukichi once again.

No matter what it took, he was still determined to continue his studies. However, he now bore heavy responsibilities as the head of the family and he could not easily leave Nakatsu. No one around him sympathized with his own hopes and desires. He was particularly anxious about the fact that returning to Osaka would mean leaving his mother behind alone. Yukichi went directly to her, described the progress he had made in studying Dutch, how he felt that there was no future for him in Nakatsu and how much he wanted to continue his studies in Osaka. She was a woman of considerable fortitude and she understood his hopes and gave him permission.

Despite this, it was not easy to leave Nakatsu. First of all, he would have to pay back an enormous inherited debt of 40 *ryo*. The family sold everything, from the library of rare books that his father had been so proud of to everyday trays and bowls. Everything was sold to pay off the entire debt. The only thing that they did not sell was the previously mentioned thirteen-volume *Ekikyo shitchu* set on Chinese ethics which Ito Togai had carefully annotated in his own hand. It was the one treasure that his father had particularly prized and so they kept it. His father had written a note saying that those thirteen volumes should be passed down from generation to generation in the Fukuzawa family. Seeing this inscription as being equivalent to a last will and testament, they had no heart to sell the set. Additionally, two porcelain bowls remained, the price at which they were offered being so ridiculously low that it seemed foolish to sell them. Everything else was sold off.

Next, it was necessary to obtain permission from the domain authorities. It had been easy when Fukuzawa was still a dependent of his brother, but now that he was head of the household, it was difficult. When he submitted his petition to be allowed to leave the domain to study Dutch, he was told that there was no precedent for doing so. Someone privately advised him that he might be more successful by applying to study gunnery, because there was a precedent for that. And that is exactly what he did. (Actually, he wrote this petition later, so there may be a mistaken memory at work here.)

Just as he was preparing to depart, Fukuzawa's mother took ill, so he spent what little money he had to obtain expensive medicine and she eventually recovered. On the day of his departure from Nakatsu, only his mother and sister saw Yukichi off and they prayed for his safe journey. No other relatives or friends bade him farewell. It was a lonely, unblessed departure, but perhaps it shows just how counter to the common practice in those days his decision was. It was extremely difficult for Yukichi to leave his mother. But without such determination, the Yukichi later known to history would not have existed.

Yukichi returned to Ogata's school in November 1856. He had no money to pay his tuition, but when he explained his circumstances to Ogata-sensei, Ogata agreed to take him on as a "free boarder." Because such behavior might be construed as preferential, Ogata accepted Yukichi as a boarder, the pretext being that Yukichi was to translate the volume on fortifications that he had earlier copied in Nakatsu.

The particulars of their arrangement were as follows. When Yukichi returned to Nakatsu, Okudaira Iki had also returned. This was the same Okudaira who had Yukichi driven out of Nagasaki. In any event, when Yukichi went to call on him, Okudaira had a copy of a book on constructing fortifications. "It was only 23 *ryo*, so it was inexpensive," Okudaira had commented. To Yukichi that was a staggeringly high price. Nonetheless, he was extremely interested in seeing it. The *Tekijuku* was poorly supplied with books other than works on medicine. Of course, he had no real expectation that he could borrow the book, but he came up with a plan, saying he just wanted to look at the drawings and the table of contents and asking if he could borrow the volume for four or five days. Astonishingly Okudaira loaned it to him. Yukichi immediately devoted himself to transcribing the entire volume. He asked a friend to double-check his transcription to be sure he had everything down correctly. Within thirty days, he had copied the entire book and returned it safely.

The translation of this volume was eventually copied and spread in all directions. It is said that the volume on constructing fortifications was based on Enomoto Takeaki's *Goryokaku*, a Western-style fort in Hakodate, Hokkaido.

The Read-and-discuss System

We turn now to life in Ogata's *Tekijuku*. Yukichi was there for three years and seven months, but in reality he studied there only for two years and nine months. Few autobiographies portray the author's youth with such open-mindedness as Fukuzawa's *The Autobiography.*

The read-and-discuss format was the heart of studying at the *Tekijuku.* New students began by studying two books on Dutch grammar: *Waranbunten zenpen* followed by *Waranbunten kohen seikuhen.* The original title of the former was *Grammatica* and the latter was titled *Syntaxis.* The older students would first read these works aloud—a practice called *kaidoku*—and then elucidate the passages. Once students obtained a basic knowledge of the fundamentals, they would move on to reading and discussing the works.

Courses at the school were divided into seven or eight grades, and six times monthly (twice every ten days or so), reading and discussion sessions were held. The senior students led the sessions and the participants drew lots and were assigned passages to translate and interpret. Each student would explain his portion of the reading, and then the other students would ask questions and debate. The winner of a debate would have a circle posted next to his name while the loser received a black dot next to his. If someone gave such a clear interpretation during a debate that no one challenged at all, he received a triangular mark in the record book. This triangle was worth three circles. The student who achieved the top rank for three months in succession would be advanced to the next grade. That was how the system worked.

So, first they copied out the text. The school only had ten books on physics and medicine. (As a result of this experience, Keio Gijuku acquired a large number of books after it was founded.) The students all drew lots to determine who would be allowed to copy the text next. One portion for each segment was from three to five pages of *hanshi* writing paper.

All the students were on good terms and learned from one another, but no one ever shared knowledge covered in the reading and discussion sessions. To do so would have been considered unsportsmanlike.

Therefore one had no choice but to depend on one's own ability and a dictionary. The school had only two dictionaries. One was the *Doeff Halma*, a Dutch-Japanese dictionary edited and translated by Hendrik Doeff, head of the Dutch Trading Representatives at Nagasaki. This work was based on an earlier Dutch-French dictionary. The second was the Weiland Dutch dictionary. It would only be used by the senior students, so ordinarily the rank-and-file of the assembled students depended solely on the Doeff volume. These dictionaries were located in the so-called Doeff Room and that was where students gathered to look words up. As the day for reading aloud in class approached, the room filled with students and no one got any sleep. Fukuzawa would later emphasize the importance of competition as a developmental mainspring within society, with the read-and-discuss system he encountered at the *Tekijuku* probably representing the formative experience behind his belief.

Whatever the difficulties, however, the students actually studied. As already noted, Fukuzawa had fallen ill in April 1856. He bound a mat with a rope to make a sort of stuffed pillow, but when he recovered slightly and wanted to use his "regular" pillow, he couldn't locate it even after exhaustively searching the warehouse. Eventually he realized he could get along without any pillow at all. Even when it grew dark in the late afternoon he would continue to read, and when he grew weary and sleepy, he would just put his head down on his desk or sleep with his head on the edge of the *tokonoma*, an alcove in the room, using it as a pillow. He did not bother to spread out his bedding.

Yukichi later became a boarder at the *Tekijuku*, but he continued to live in a similar fashion. In the evening when it was time to eat, if he had money he would drink saké. Then, after a short nap, he would wake up around ten o'clock and read until dawn. When he heard the sounds of the breakfast preparations commencing, he would again fall asleep. When breakfast was finally ready, he would take a morning bath, eat his breakfast and then resume his reading. This became his daily routine.

Yukichi was also completely indifferent to how he dressed. Osaka was warm, so winter presented no real obstacle, but the summer heat was hard to bear. Consequently, not only did he wear no outer clothing, but he did not wear a loincloth or underwear, either. He was stark naked. At mealtimes in the dining room, he would, just for appearance sake, put on a *haori*—a loose overgarment—to cover his complete nakedness, and because there was no place to sit, he would eat standing up.

He occasionally committed blunders. Once when he was sleeping upstairs, he heard a woman's voice from downstairs calling his name repeatedly. Having returned from a bout of drinking and then fallen asleep, he wondered what the maid wanted at such an ungodly hour. Jumping up and without stopping to put on his clothes, he ran down the stairs only to discover that it was not the maid but Mrs. Ogata. Naked as he was, it seemed inappropriate to either kneel in front of her or bow. He was at a loss as to what to do. Perhaps feeling sorry for his situation, Mrs. Ogata simply walked away without a word. The next morning he could not bring himself to apologize for his rudeness the night before, but he never forgot that incident. In *The Autobiography*, he writes that when he had reason to visit Osaka a few years later, he visited the Ogata house and remembered the incident with shame.

The students at the *Tekijuku* studied hard but they also had fun. With little money to spend, their amusement was pretty much limited to drinking and making a lot of racket. Yukichi was particularly fond of liquor. Whenever he had money, he would drink. If he had a little more money, he would go to a restaurant. Such occasions were rare and usually eating out meant going to a place that served chicken or an even cheaper place where beef was on the menu. It was never quite clear whether the beef had come from a cow that had died of illness or been slaughtered. The meat was often tough and had a powerful smell. All of the customers were either tattooed hoodlums *(gorotsuki)* or students from the *Tekijuku.*

The reason they were comfortable eating meat was that they were students of Dutch Studies and were completely at ease with both death and meat. In those days, that was unique, so one day when the proprietor of a local beef stew shop *(gyunabe-ya)* bought a pig but proved too softhearted to kill it himself, he asked the students to do it. He promised them the head of the pig if they would slaughter it for him. They suffocated the animal, decapitated it, and after mercilessly poking and studying the brain and the eyes of the beast, cooked up the pieces and ate them.

The hijinks the students got into were numerous. They made trouble at temple markets, forged letters from prostitutes, tricked a companion into eating potentially poisonous globefish by telling him it was sea bream, and pocketed cups and trays from restaurants.

They also conducted dangerous experiments. They succeeded in making hydrochloric acid, melting zinc in it and then plating iron with tin. When they tried to make sulphuric acid, they got into considerable trouble. When they attempted to make ammonium chloride, it gave off such a stench that people in the neighborhood complained. Subsequently, they hired a boat to continue their experiments in the middle of a river, so determined were they to succeed one way or another. *The Autobiography* is filled with examples of such youthful exuberance.

There were, however, few books at the school that could be studied. Thus, any new additions to the library were precious. After a while, there was simply nothing else to read, so the students even read the introductions to books and volumes on meaningless topics. On one occasion, Lord Kuroda passed through Osaka on his annual journey to Edo under the "alternate attendance system" *(sankin kotai)*, and Ogata Koan returned from paying respects to his lordship with a curious book he had borrowed from Kuroda. One chapter of this volume dealt with electricity. Several students decided to copy out at least that chapter while they had access to the book. Over a period of two nights and three days, they worked straight through with one student reading aloud, one taking down dictation and a third reading for corrections. When they had to return the book, they "handled it with such affection that it seemed as if they were parting from a parent," reports Fukuzawa.

The Spirit of the Students

From time to time the students requested that Ogata-sensei lecture to them. Yukichi recalls the impact of these lectures in the following passage.

> I remember how impressed I was by the minuteness of his observations, and at the same time by the boldness of his conclusions. How many times, on returning to our dormitory, we young men talked together about the lecture and expressed our admiration of Ogata-sensei's learning and ability, feeling ourselves petty and unlearned by comparison.[8]

Although Yukichi writes these lines in a rather casual tone, his respect for Ogata clearly shines through. The comment about the preciseness and boldness of his interpretations represent essential conditions for sterling translations. A fearless interpretation that lacks precise accuracy is no more than an empty boast, while scrupulous accuracy alone is devoid of meaning. What is essential for an excellent translation is a combination of preciseness and a rich imagination.

Needless to say, it was because Yukichi had outstanding ability that he was able to appreciate the capabilities of such a teacher. It must have been a blissful opportunity for an excellent student to study directly under an excellent teacher.

At the same time, Ogata's wife would later comment that when

Fukuzawa was attending the school, he differed greatly from the other students. Her husband said that he was sure the young man would one day make a name for himself and she agreed. She could not have imagined, however, just how prominent he would actually become.[9] Nothing could bring more pleasure to a teacher than to have excellent students.

In Yukichi's view, the *Tekijuku* run by Ogata Koan was the best school of Dutch Studies in the entire country. In Edo, whether within the bakufu or in the residences of the various daimyo, there was a great demand for Western learning. If one could read Western books to some degree, one could gain employment, and translation was well rewarded. In Osaka, meanwhile, Western learning was unrelated to earning a living. Yukichi comments that it was precisely this lack of practical application that accounted for the advance of learning there.

Yukichi describes the spirit of the school's students this way.

> In short, we students were conscious of the fact that we were the sold possessors of the key to knowledge of the great European civilization. However much we suffered from poverty, whatever poor clothes we wore, the extent of our knowledge and the resources of our minds were beyond the reach of any prince or nobleman of the whole nation. If our work was hard, we were proud of it, knowing that no one knew what we endured. 'In hardship we found pleasure, and the hardship was pleasure.'[10]

The students' happiness came from being absorbed in something that had no immediate, direct purpose. They had a good teacher, amiable companions and vigorous competition. As a result of living in such an environment for a total of two years and nine months, Yukichi's life changed.

In August 1856, the year after Yukichi entered the *Tekijuku*, Townsend Harris arrived in Japan. In December 1857, Harris was granted an audience at Edo Castle and the pressure was on to formally sign what is now known as the United States-Japan Treaty of Amity and Commerce. Once the decision to sign the treaty was made, Hotta Masayoshi, as head of the *roju*, senior councilors of the shogunate, was dispatched to Kyoto to submit the matter to the Emperor for his approval. But he was unsuccessful in obtaining imperial consent.

Greatly shocked by this development, in June 1858, the bakufu passed control of the *roju* to Ii Naosuke, conferring on him the special title of *tairo* (chancellor). Ii resolved to sign the treaty of his own volition and he began a furious suppression of the Hitotsubashi faction which opposed his actions. This disturbance turned into what came to be called the Ansei Purge. As a result, a major political upheaval began to unfold with Kyoto at its epicenter. There is no evidence that Yukichi had any strong interest in political affairs at this time. He was simply a member of the faction that had a vague desire to open the country.

Chapter 3

Going to America

Photograph taken with daughter of the photographer in a studio in San Francisco in 1860. (Courtesy of the Keio University Fukuzawa Memorial Center)

Leaving for Edo

While he was studying at Ogata's *Tekijuku*, Fukuzawa came to be known among various people even outside the school. In the autumn of 1858, he received a directive from the Nakatsu domain to proceed to Edo. The domain was looking for somebody to teach Dutch Studies there, and although he was not the only person who could fill such a position, because he belonged to the domain, it seemed natural to select him for the role.

Fukuzawa was not the sort of person who obeyed simply because he received an order from his domain. His decision to follow the order was probably due to the fact that he perceived it as a turning point. He had completed the curriculum at the *Tekijuku* and there were not many books in the school's collection. He must surely have been curious about what changes had taken place in Edo since the arrival of Perry in 1853. If he received a suitable remuneration from the Nakatsu domain, he would surely be able to see his mother. The *Tekijuku* may have been the best school in the land, but he was not going to Edo to study; he was going there to teach. More than that, however, he probably wanted to know what was happening in the political center of Japan.

After returning to Nakatsu once and seeing his mother, Fukuzawa then headed for Edo. He received expenses from the domain sufficient to allow him a traveling attendant. A fellow student at the *Tekijuku*, Okamoto Shukichi (who later changed his name to Furukawa Setsuzo or Masao), went with him. Along the way at Oumi, he was able to meet his father's close friend Nakamura Ritsuen. Ritsuen was absolutely delighted to see him and told Fukuzawa about how he had immediately headed to Nakatsu upon hearing about Hyakusuke's death and how he had carried little Yukichi, who was only one at the time, to the boat when the family left Osaka to return to Nakatsu. Fukuzawa stayed one night with the older man and later recalled the event writing, "I felt as if I had actually met my father."

Fukuzawa and Okamoto reached Edo in the middle of November. As they walked through the city, Fukuzawa, noting an apprentice painstakingly setting the teeth of a saw, was greatly impressed by the advance of civilization in Edo. As one might expect, he was highly conscious of the city's culture.

Fukuzawa immediately set up housekeeping in a row house in the secondary residence, *nakayashiki*, of the Nakatsu domain located in the Tsukiji Teppozu District. It was there that he opened his school of Dutch Studies, known as "Keio Gijuku," in November 1858.

While proud of the scholarship he undertook at the *Tekijuku*, learning in Edo weighed on Fukuzawa's mind. On one occasion he called on a former classmate at the *Tekijuku*, a physician named Shimamura, who was translating a book from Dutch and was struggling to untangle a difficult passage. True enough, it was rough going even for Fukuzawa, but within half an hour he had worked it out. In *The Autobiography*, he writes,

> The passage, as I recall, dealt with the relation between light and the human eye. When you lighted two candles and did something to one of the lights, something happened. I do not remember exactly, but it will be found in Shimamura's translation entitled *Seiri Hatsumo*.[11]

That he remembered this vividly some forty years later indicates how proud he was of his successful reading. When he heard from Shimamura that no one else he had asked had been able to elucidate the passage, Fukuzawa was filled with self-confidence.

Moreover, brimming with mischief, Fukuzawa sometimes took difficult passages that were easy to misinterpret to other Dutch scholars, pretending not to grasp the meaning. In many cases they mistranslated the pro-offered passages, which of course left Fukuzawa feeling smug regarding his own expertise.

Resolving to Learn English

In July 1859, roughly half a year after Fukuzawa arrived in Edo, the United States-Japan Treaty of Amity and Commerce came into effect and Japan commenced overseas trade. Yokohama, a port near Tokyo, was officially opened to overseas trade. Filled with a sense of curiosity, Fukuzawa promptly went to have a look at the port in July or August.

When he reached Yokohama, however, he was shocked. He could not communicate with the newly-arrived foreign merchants at all; no one understood what he said and he could not understand what they said. He was unable to even read signboards on buildings or labels on bottles for sale in the stores. Fukuzawa writes that the words were not written in Dutch but in some language he could not comprehend.

> ...I had been walking for twenty-four hours, a distance of some fifty miles, going and coming. But the fatigue of my legs was nothing compared with the bitter disappointment in my heart. I had been striving with all my powers for many years to learn the Dutch language. And now when I had reason to believe myself one of the best in the country, I found that I could not even read the signs of merchants who had come to trade with us from foreign lands.[12]

This is probably the most well-known passage in *The Autobiography*. For the optimistic Fukuzawa to suddenly feel that his youthful years had come to naught must have turned his entire world upside down. Yet it was typical of him to bounce right back. The language he heard and saw must have been either English or French, and since English seemed to be the dominant language among the merchants, what he had encountered must have been English.

But there was almost no one in Edo who could teach English to him.

After some asking around, he found an interpreter named Moriyama Takichiro. From Fukuchi Gen'ichiro, a bakufu interpreter and friend who also wanted to learn English, he heard that there were only two people in Edo to try: one was Moriyama, who could read English, and the other was Nakahama Manjiro, who knew how to speak English.

Fukuzawa first approached Moriyama, who granted his request. It meant making a five-mile trek to Moriyama's home each time, and as it turned out, Moriyama was an extremely busy person and could set aside time for teaching Fukuzawa only early in the morning or late at night. After making several trips to Moriyama's home only to be told that sudden business had come up or Moriyama had had to leave home to perform some duty, Fukuzawa gave up and decided to learn the language on his own. He managed to purchase a small Dutch-English conversation book in Yokohama, but he had no dictionary. He learned by chance that the bakufu school, the *Bansho Shirabesho* (the Institute for the Investigation of Barbarian Books), possessed some dictionaries, but to gain access to them, he would have to register as a student. He gained admission to the institute, but upon learning on his very first day that he could not take books out of the building, he gave up on that as well.

During this period, he asked some merchants dealing with foreigners in Yokohama to keep an eye out for a Dutch-English dictionary. In due course, one of them found a small Dutch-English, English-Dutch dictionary comprised of two volumes. However, it cost five *ryo*. Unable to pay such a sum himself, he petitioned the Nakatsu clan's authority in Edo to purchase it for his use. The petition was granted and he began studying on his own.

It was difficult to study without a companion. He first turned to Kanda Takahira (later a member of the Chamber of Elders, a member of the House of Peers, and subsequently invested as a baron within the peerage of Meiji Japan), but Kanda proved reluctant to join him. Fukuzawa then approached Murata Zoroku, who responded that significant works written in English would soon be translated into Dutch, so one could just wait to read the Dutch versions when they were published.

Murata was then thirty-six and in his prime. He had opened a private school named *Kyukyodo* and at the same time entered service in the *Kobusho* and the *Bansho Shirabesho*. Actually, he later began to study English as well, so Tomita Masafumi speculates that perhaps he disliked the way Fukuzawa approached him with the idea of studying together (Tomita, *Kosho Fukuzawa Yukichi, volume one*).

Next Fukuzawa tried Harada Keisaku, who enthusiastically agreed with his suggestion. They began studying and discovered that the hardest part of learning the language was pronunciation. They got help from English-speaking children and Japanese fishermen who had been shipwrecked, picked up by Western ships, and acquired a bit of English before being brought back to Japan. Other than this issue, the two students discovered, once they got started, that the grammar was almost the same as the first European language they had studied. Thus, they were able to make fairly rapid progress. Harada later changed his name to Harada Ichido, his son Toyokichi became successful as a geologist, and his grandson Kumao made a name for himself as the secretary of the *genro*, the elder statesman Saionji Kinmochi.

Voyage of the *Kanrin Maru*

At that time, the bakufu was preparing to send a mission to the United States. Its purpose was to exchange official documents of ratification of the United States-Japan Treaty of Amity and Commerce in Washington, D.C., and for that purpose America dispatched a warship to carry the envoy and vice-envoy. The bakufu, however, hoping to gain actual experience in ocean navigation, sent another ship, the famous *Kanrin Maru*.

The decisions regarding these matters took time, but in October it was decided that Shinmi Masaoki would serve as ambassador and Muragaki Norimasa would serve as his deputy. Kimura Yoshitake, Settsu-no-kami, was appointed to serve as the naval commissioner in December, and on January 15th, 1860, it was decided that the *Kanrin Maru* would accompany the other ship. The ship would weigh anchor off Shinagawa on February 4th, 1860.

Fukuzawa was quite eager to go to America. Searching for some vital connection that would allow him to join the diplomatic mission, he discovered that Katsuragawa Hoshu, a physician of Dutch medicine with whom he was acquainted, happened to know Kimura Yoshitake. Katsuragawa's wife was Kimura's sister. Katsuragawa introduced Fukuzawa to his brother-in-law and Kimura readily consented to take Fukuzawa along as a junior member of the mission. Fukuzawa writes that in those days almost no one was eager to take the risks of traveling abroad.

All things considered, if Fukuzawa had been the least bit late in visiting Yokohama the first time or in switching from studying Dutch to studying English, he would have missed his chance to travel to America. He was extremely fortunate, but good fortune comes only to those who are prepared for it.

Fukuzawa with evident pride writes that only a few years had passed since the Japanese had seen their first steamship but that they had succeeded in navigating the seas. It is well-known, however, that the *Kanrin Maru*'s crossing of the Pacific was only possible due to the dedicated efforts of the American captain John M. Brooke and others. In considerable detail, Brooke describes in his journal how the Japanese were unable to adjust to the seas, how timid they were and how little training they had. When the ship encountered strong winds and rain, the Japanese seemed to retreat to their cabins and had no idea how to cope with the situation. Brooke writes that the Japanese crept into their cabins when the winds rose, just like an ostrich trying to hide itself completely by burying its head in the sand. However, Brooke said repeatedly after the event that the voyage was the result of Japanese efforts. It seems that he possessed a gracefully modest character.

Aboard the *Kanrin Maru*, Kimura served as commodore and Katsu Kaishu served as captain. According to Fukuzawa, Katsu suffered severe seasickness and kept to his cabin. Additionally, Kimura and Katsu did not get along. Kimura had been supervisor of the Nagasaki Naval Training Academy but he was unable to actually navigate a ship, and Katsu was discontented by this fact. Refusing to cooperate with Kimura almost entirely, at one point in mid-ocean Katsu told him to lower a boat because he intended to go back to Japan. At all events, Katsu's actions during the voyage were peevish in the extreme and Fukuzawa must have had a low opinion of him. This probably foreshadows the "strained endurance," *yasegaman no setsu*, that he would refer to in his later years. In contrast, Fukuzawa had a very high opinion of Kimura.

Visiting San Francisco

Upon arriving in San Francisco, the mission received a warm welcome. The fact that a group of Japanese had come across the Pacific to be introduced to a new civilization in the United States led to a great stir among the American population. This sensation combined the natural kindness of the country with a consciousness of it having to act as a guardian of its Japanese guests. In being feted this way, the Japanese could not help but be delighted.

Everything was new to the eyes of the Japanese. Even commonplace things like horse-drawn carriages were interesting to the visitors. They were also surprised by liquor that was served with ice. Despite having previously seen carpet off-cuts used as materials for purses and tobacco pouches, it was astounding to see a valuable carpet laid over an entire room—and then see people walking on it in their street shoes. Fukuzawa was also amazed to see empty cans and discarded ironware lying scattered in garbage piles around the city. In those days in Edo, after a fire, people would scavenge through burnt-out areas simply to collect nails because iron was so valuable. As seen by these examples of carpets and ironware, the sheer quantity of materials made a deep impression on Fukuzawa. He was also astonished by the high price of goods.

On the other hand, he was not surprised in the realm of science. He was already aware from books he had read about the mechanism of telegraphic communication, how chemical substances were created and how they changed.

The unexpected discoveries included aspects of the social system in America. When he asked where the descendants of George Washington might be, no one seemed to know, and moreover, no one seemed particularly interested in knowing. Fukuzawa was favorably impressed that, in comparison with Minamoto Yoritomo or Tokugawa Ieyasu in Japan, there was so little attention paid to family lineage in the United States.

The most important purchase he made was a Webster's Dictionary (the revised *American Dictionary of the English Language*). His shipmate, Nakahama Manjiro, also purchased a copy of the same dictionary. Fukuzawa later claimed that theirs were the first copies of this dictionary to be imported into Japan.

The official mission left for Washington, D.C., while Fukuzawa and some of his companions sojourned in San Francisco. The entrourage arrived in the city on March 18th, stayed more than a month and departed on May 9th.

The ship called at Hawaii on May 24th and on the 27th it departed for Japan. After the ship left Hawaii, Fukuzawa showed his companions a photograph. It was one he had taken in San Francisco with a young woman, the 15-year-old daughter of the photographer. He had purposely waited until they left Hawaii to show it to them so that they would be unable to imitate him and have a similar photo taken themselves. Fukuzawa was proud of the fact that he had never visited such places as the pleasure quarters in Japan and he treated coldly those who did. But he made fun of his companions who couldn't imagine making a play for an American woman. Able to speak a little English, being of large stature, being young, taking initiative in everything, Fukuzawa was able to pull off having himself photographed with an American girl.

Fukuzawa returned to Japan on June 23rd. When he landed at Uraga, he asked someone who had come to meet the mission if anything important had happened during their absence. The man started to say something but Fukuzawa cut him off, saying, "Let me guess. Could it be something like a group of samurai from Mito storming into Chancellor Ii Naosuke's residence?" It seemed that he had guessed correctly about the Sakuradamon Incident, which had occurred two months earlier. The man was astounded, but it is said that Fukuzawa had heard about the assassination of Ii immediately upon landing and was just putting the man on.

To be sure, such an event had not been unpredictable. Following the opening of Japan's ports in 1859, there had been a conspicuous outflow of currency and prices had risen. All of this was the result of Chancellor Ii Naosuke's signing the United States-Japan Treaty of Amity and Commerce the previous year of his own volition. The criticism of Ii was particularly fierce among the Hitotsubashi faction which was suppressed by Ii, particularly in the Mito domain, during what is known as the Ansei Purge. This led to the Sakuradamon Incident and the fury of anti-foreign sentiment *(joi)*.

Upon Fukuzawa's return from America, the number of students attending his school gradually increased. Not yet having full confidence in his English ability, however, their "learning experience" was more a case of studying together. In September, he translated *Ka-Ei Tsugo* (a Chinese-English dictionary). The original was a book he had bought together with the Webster's Dictionary in San Francisco. It had English words and conversational phrases for daily life with pronunciation using Chinese characters and translations. Fukuzawa added Japanese pronunciations and meanings in *katakana* and published it as *Zotei Ka-Ei Tsugo* (the "Enlarged Chinese-English Dictionary"). For example, the English word "Venus" was followed by the *katakana* pronunciation *"benusu"* and the Chinese characters 金星 (read as *"kinsei"* in Japanese). In the same fashion, the English word "Planet" was followed by *"puranneto"* in *katakana* and the Chinese characters 行星.

In December 1860, Fukuzawa was employed by the bakufu to liaise with the foreign legations in Japan, through what we would call the Foreign Ministry today. His remuneration was 15 *ryo* and rations for 20 men (20 *ninbuchi*). The work involved translating diplomatic documents. No small portion of these documents came with a Dutch version attached. Translating these was excellent practice for Fukuzawa. Because he was working for the bakufu, there were many books available for reference purposes and he was allowed to take them home. During this period he was able to learn while he taught others.

Some of the diplomacy that Fukuzawa was involved in during this period involved very serious matters. One of the first documents he translated concerned the assassination of Henry Heusken, interpreter for the American legation, by samurai of the Satsuma domain at Azabu Nakanohashi on January 15th, 1861. This event led to heightened tensions, with the British, French and Dutch legations withdrawing from Edo to Yokohama. Furthermore, on July 5th, 1861, *ronin* (unemployed samurai) from the Mito domain attacked the British legation at Tozenji. This event followed the Tsushima Incident, in which a Russian warship anchored in a bay off Tsushima Island attempted to construct a base (March 13th, 1861).

Six months later, the Russians were driven off with cooperation from British warships.

During this period, the bakufu was attempting to develop an alliance between the Imperial Court and the shogunate. Through such an alliance, the bakufu hoped to strengthen its own authority. Negotiations were completed and the Princess Kazu (Kazunomiya) arrived in Edo in December 1861 as a bride for the shogun.

In all likelihood, it was toward the end of 1860 that Fukuzawa moved from his row house in the grounds of the secondary residence, *nakayashiki*, of the Nakatsu domain in the Tsukiji Teppozu District to a place he rented in the Shiba Shinsenza District. In the winter of 1861, he married Okin, the daughter of Toki Tarohachi, a Nakatsu samurai of the upper echelon. Fukuzawa was twenty-six and Okin was fifteen. As we have seen, a marriage across the gap of the upper and lower samurai echelons was a rare event. The Toki family received a stipend of 210 *koku* and *yakuryo* of 50 *koku*, which was a major difference from the Fukuzawa household stipend of 13 *koku* and a mere 2 *ninbuchi*.

Chapter 4
Learning about Europe

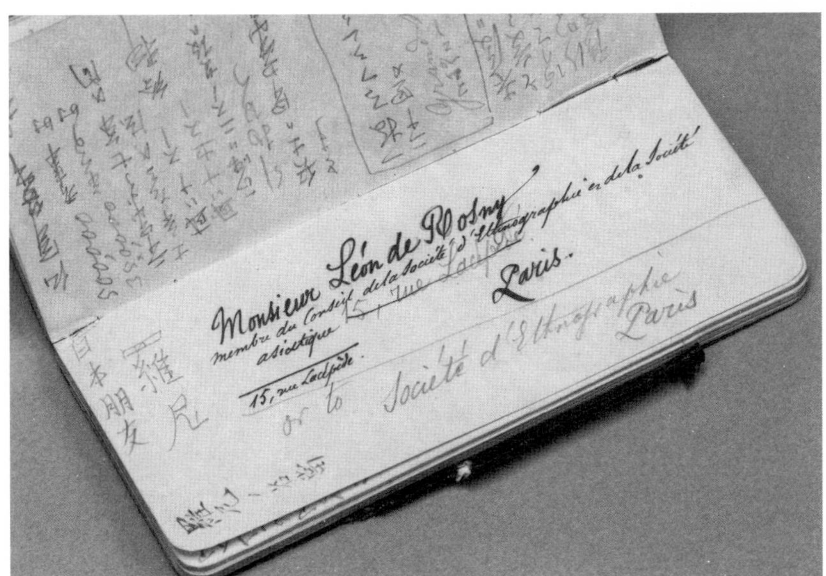

Pocket Diary of the West, in which Fukuzawa kept notes during his travels in Europe. The name "Rosny" can be seen here. (Courtesy of Keio University Fukuzawa Memorial Center)

Going to Europe

On January 22nd, 1862, Fukuzawa set sail from Shinagawa on board the British frigate HMS *Odin* as a member of the bakufu mission to Europe. The mission would return to Japan on January 29th, 1863. This excursion had far greater impact on Fukuzawa than his previous trip to the United States, and it helped form the fundamental underpinnings of his understanding of the West. Fukuzawa's first best-selling book, entitled *Conditions in the West (Seiyo Jijo)*, was based on observations made during this journey. The journal that Fukuzawa kept still exists, later being published as part of a 19-volume report of the mission entitled *Diary of the West (Seiko ki)*. Thus, through this source it is possible to trace Fukuzawa's words and deeds during his travels. Among modern works, we also have Haga Toru's fine book entitled, *Taikun no shisetsu* [Embassy of the Shogun], which employs a great store of primary sources in addition to the above. Using these resources, let us try and follow Fukuzawa's activities abroad.

What led to the mission being dispatched is as follows: under an agreement reached in 1858, the bakufu promised that within a certain period of time, it would open up to Western access the two cities of Edo and Osaka, along with the five ports of Kanagawa, Nagasaki, Hakodate, Niigata and Hyogo. Due to anti-foreign agitation against opening Edo, Osaka and the port at Hyogo, however, the bakufu hoped to somehow negotiate a postponement before the agreement was enacted. Additionally, because Niigata was seen as an unsuitable treaty port, the bakufu authorities wanted to negotiate a substitute. During this period as well, from the standpoint of unifying the Imperial Court and the shogunate, the bakufu was endeavoring to go along with the wishes of the Court, and because the Court embraced a strong exclusionist sentiment, the bakufu was searching for a way to make the aforementioned changes to the agreement.

Naturally, when the bakufu appealed to the five foreign signatories

(Great Britain, France, the United States, Holland and Russia) in order to implement the aforementioned changes, it failed to achieve its aims. The British and French envoys, however, suggested that Japan send a mission to Europe to negotiate directly, and the envoys proposed that their own governments would shoulder the expenses involved. In making such an offer, the motivation of London and Paris was to recapture the diplomatic initiative in dealings with Japan, and thus circumvent the strides made by the United States.

The bakufu accepted this Anglo-French offer and subsequently dispatched a special mission to Europe to request an extension for the opening of the contentious cities and ports. The mission was to be led by Takenouchi Shimotsuke-no-kami Yasunori as senior envoy, Matsudaira Iwami-no-kami Yasunao as vice-envoy, while Kyogoku Noto-no-kami Takaaki was to be the *ometsuke* (inspector). The traveling party would be comprised of 36 members (two additional members would be added later), with Fukuzawa being assigned as an official linguist, along with Mitsukuri Shuhei and Matsuki Koan (later known as Terashima Munemori). Both gentlemen were fellow scholars of Western learning with whom Fukuzawa was on good terms. Slightly senior to this trio was Fukuchi Gen'ichiro, yet another linguist. Together, the four of them were a true group of Western scholars. With six members from the earlier mission to the United States included, the mission that would go to Europe boasted an enormous amount of talent, although not perfect.

During the mission's initial planning phase, it is said that Fukuzawa was not listed among those on the trip. Instead, a decision on his inclusion only occurred on January 19th, shortly before the planned date of departure. Only eighteen months had passed since Fukuzawa had returned from the United States where he had served as a valet of Kimura Settsu-no-kami. Now, on the trip to Europe, he was to travel as a fully-fledged bakufu retainer. Thus, he was to receive an allowance of some 400 *ryo*. Moreover, in that all the expenses incurred were to be borne by the public purse, Fukuzawa had no particular need for the money. And because he was not extravagant by nature, this allowance left him with new-found wealth.

Five years earlier, Fukuzawa had found it necessary to sell off virtually all his family's possessions in order to cover a debt of 40 *ryo* left by his deceased father. Also, as remuneration for hand-copying the book on fortification construction which he had duped Okudaira Iki into loaning him, he had received 23 *ryo*. But recall that just two years before that, when commencing his English studies, he had found a small dictionary for sale. However, at a price of 5 *ryo*, Fukuzawa had been unable to afford to buy it himself. Thus, he had to ask his domain to purchase it on his behalf. Thinking back on episodes such as these, Fukuzawa must have been overwhelmed by his subsequent good fortune.

Of the 400 *ryo* he received as an allowance for his bakufu position, Fukuzawa forwarded 100 *ryo* to his mother. Three years had passed since he had left her to travel to Edo. Since returning from the United States, he had not seen her at all, and it pained him to think that he was once again headed abroad. He must have wanted to somehow repay his mother for the affection she had shown him and the hardships she had endured, and more than anything else, he must have wanted to let her know how high he had risen in the world.

Together with the 100 *ryo*, Fukuzawa also forwarded to his mother the photograph that he had had taken with the American girl in San Francisco. The picture became a sensation in Nakatsu and countless people visited his mother especially in order to see it. At the time, Aoki Shuzo (later a Japanese foreign minister) was studying there. He and his teacher also called upon Fukuzawa's mother to witness the 100 *ryo* and the "famous" photograph. It is said that Aoki was so impressed by this event that it influenced him to pursue Western learning. It is not difficult to imagine that such items would have had a powerful impact on the people of the Nakatsu domain.

The Decline of Ancient Civilizations

The delegation to Europe boarded the HMS *Odin*, a superb frigate attached to the British East Indies Squadron. She was equipped with paddle wheels on both sides, displaced some 2,000 tons, and was mounted with 16 large cannon. Furthermore, the *Odin's* complement of officers and men exceeded 300 sailors. In preparing for the passage, the *Odin* had been refitted in Hong Kong. Then upon reaching Edo, Japanese craftsmen were hired to paper the walls of cabins with Japanese motifs, lay down *tatami* matting and install sliding *shoji* screens throughout the ship. This was done to create rooms decorated in a Japanese taste. The intention of the British was to exceed the level of hospitality offered by the Americans during the earlier mission to the United States.

The mission sailed from Edo on January 22nd and reached Nagasaki on the 28th. During this leg of the journey, the seas were quite rough and the Japanese passengers experienced bouts of seasickness. They were amazed by how the British sailors performed their duties while being unfazed by the rough conditions.

While in Nagasaki, Fukuzawa called at the home of Yamamoto Monojiro, who had previously looked after him. He also met with twenty or so old friends including Nagayo Sensai. On receiving the hospitality of Yamamoto-sensei, Fukuzawa confessed that he had managed to abstain from drinking during his previous sojourn in Nagasaki although the experience had been almost unbearable. In reality, he continued, he was actually a heavy drinker, and Yamamoto and his wife were subsequently astounded at how much Fukuzawa could drink.

Departing Nagasaki on January 30th, 1862, the mission to Europe reached Hong Kong on February 4th. Needless to say, as a result of the Treaty of Nanking concluded in 1842, Hong Kong had been ceded to Great Britain. Subsequently, the island of Hong Kong had undergone a remarkable transformation, it previously being considered a barren wilderness only inhabited by pirates. The colony that the British had established was then competing with Canton (Guangzhou) to be the center of regional trade. Furthermore, as a result of the Peking Treaty of 1860 following the Arrow War, Great Britain also took over Kowloon, north of Hong Kong Island.

Fukuzawa had a memorable experience when visiting Hong Kong. One day, a group of Chinese peddlers boarded the *Odin* and they eagerly tried to sell shoes to those on board. Out of boredom, Fukuzawa tried to haggle with one of the party when, an Englishman standing nearby, perhaps believing that the peddler was doing something dishonest, suddenly grabbed the shoes, told Fukuzawa to hand him two dollars, which he then threw at the Chinese man, and without uttering another word heartily drove the peddler from the ship with his walking stick. Shocked by the incident, Fukuzawa was abruptly reminded of the power exercised by Great Britain and the absolute helplessness of the Chinese, and at the same time, he imagined how satisfying it would be to exercise such power. In later years, Fukuzawa repeatedly mentioned this episode, so it must have made a considerable impression on him.

The Japanese mission stayed in Hong Kong for a week. At the time, the United States was embroiled in the Civil War. Great Britain was supportive of the Southern cause so, from time to time, problems arose when British and Northern warships encountered one another. Fully conscious of the hostilities, the *Odin* carefully observed the movement of any American ships it encountered during the passage.

As soon as they docked in Hong Kong, Fukuzawa purchased a newspaper from London. Thus, he was aware of the developments in the United States. In *Diary of the West (Seiko ki)*, he writes that America had been involved in a civil war from the previous year. The country was divided between the North and the South, and the South was steadily losing its advantage and was appealing to Great Britain for support. The South attempted to send an envoy to Great Britain aboard a British ship, but the North got wind of the plan, bottled up the ship and subsequently seized the would-be envoy. The British government protested vehemently about this breach of diplomatic protocol, upon which the American president, Abraham Lincoln, made a formal apology and a settlement was reached. The situation remained tense, however, so even though preparations for the Japanese mission's departure were completed, the *Odin* remained an extra week in Hong Kong before continuing its voyage. The ship was made ready to fight, if the necessity arose on the high seas.

The first of the Japanese party to grasp the situation was Fukuzawa. One wonders how he interpreted the news that America, where they had been warmly welcomed just two years previous, was now divided between two factions (the Union and the Confederacy) that were at each other's throats. One also wonders about his views concerning Great Britain possibly being dragged into the conflict. He may well have seen in the situation a society in which "might makes right," as described in his frequently read *Saden*.

Departing Hong Kong, the mission called at Singapore on the 17th. There Fukuzawa met Otokichi, a seaman originally from Owari province who, in 1832, was shipwrecked and drifted ashore in California. He did not return to Japan but instead became a British subject and took up residence in Shanghai. He married a woman from Singapore and fathered three children. Otokichi had once sailed on a British vessel that had entered Nagasaki harbor, but he was prohibited from landing and left on the same vessel. By coincidence, this incident had occurred during the time Fukuzawa was living with the Yamamoto family in Nagasaki.

There is no evidence that Fukuzawa showed any deep interest in the vicissitudes of Otokichi's fortunes.[13] However, he showed considerable interest in what the man told him about the Taiping Rebellion. According to the seaman, the rebellion was becoming more intense, with the area around Peking having already suffered major damage and Shanghai under siege. In the midst of these events, Otokichi explained that the Anglo-French troops stationed at Shanghai were taking it upon themselves to neither shoot at the rebels nor save Peking. On hearing this, Fukuzawa might have assumed that the Qing Dynasty's days were numbered.

Departing from Singapore on February 18th, the Japanese mission called at two ports in Ceylon from February 25th to March 1st, reached Aden on March 12th and subsequently on March 20th arrived at Suez. They then proceeded by train and reached Cairo on March 21st. When Fukuzawa visited San Francisco the previous year, the transcontinental railroad across the United States had not been completed. Thus, the overland leg from Suez to Cairo was Fukuzawa's first train journey. Describing Cairo, Fukuzawa noted in the *Diary of the West (Seiko ki)* that Cairo boasted a population of some 500,000 people, that the poor were numerous, and that the city was not prospering. He saw the inhabitants as stubborn, lazy and non-attentive to their occupations. The rule of law was strict, and because the ancient city had been a seat of government for several thousand years, there were numerous ruins scattered throughout. The city now, however, was in a state of dilapidation.

To one degree or another, most Japanese who traveled to Europe during the Bakumatsu and early Meiji periods shared this sentiment. All of the once great civilizations of antiquity seemed to have surrendered completely to Great Britain and France. Japan had not yet been taken over by Western Powers, and many Japanese resolved that such a fate should not befall their country.

On March 24th, the mission traveled from Cairo to Alexandria, from which on the following day they set sail across the Mediterranean. They anchored at Malta from the 28th through the 31st, and on April 3rd they landed at Marseilles. Being the largest port in the Mediterranean,

Marseilles, when it was busy, saw between 1,400 and 1,500 merchant ships anchored off its shore.

On April 5th, they left Marseilles for Lyon, stayed two nights, arriving in Paris on April 7th. Fukuzawa was impressed by the beautiful scenery en route to Paris and by the fact that all of the land was under cultivation.

The following is their itinerary.

Marseilles April 3rd-5th
Lyon April 5th-7th
Paris April 7th-29th
London April 30th-June 12th
Holland June 14th-July 17th
Berlin July 18th-August 5th
Petersburg August 9th-September 17th
Paris September 22nd-October 5th
Lisbon October 16th-25th
Alexandria November 17th-18th
Cairo and Suez November 19th
Aden November 28th-December 3rd
Galle (Ceylon) December 17th-21st
Singapore December 29th-January 4th
Cap Saint-Jacques (Vung Tau in Vietnam) January 7th-8th
Hong Kong January 14th-20th
Shinagawa January 29th

The Japanese had made exhaustive preparations for their travels, imagining they would experience great difficulty in obtaining provisions while in Europe. They carried with them several hundred boxes packed with white rice. They also brought along stocks of *Koshu*-style military-campaign *miso* paste. This was made according to a secret recipe handed down from Takeda Shingen, a famous feudal lord. It was believed to be able to withstand even the highest temperatures. They also brought along complete sets of several dozen metal lamp stands to light the hallways, paper lanterns, portable candlesticks, table lamps with paper shades and candles. These items, one might say, were a perfect preparation for a daimyo procession complete with all the necessary items for a large entourage on a long journey to the capital at Edo.

However, the accommodation they found in Europe was completely different from anything they had ever experienced. Since the mission had numerous members, the most senior Japanese initially requested rooms for their attendants in the neighborhood of where they were to stay themselves. However, they were told that, for a group as small as theirs, the planned accommodations could easily supply enough rooms for ten to twenty times their number. Indeed, some of the hotels where they stayed were able to handle a thousand guests a night. Moreover, inside the hotels it was bright and warm and the restaurants served delicacies of all sorts from both the land and sea. Even the most wary members of the mission couldn't resist such cuisine. Thus, there was no need for either the lanterns or the rice which had been so carefully conveyed from Japan. In fact, the carefully-prepared *miso* paste began to emit an unbearable stench shortly after leaving Hong Kong. It was subsequently dumped overboard somewhere off the coast of Vietnam.

Not surprisingly, various amusing episodes experienced by the emissaries have been handed down for today's readers to enjoy. One involved a senior daimyo of the party, who, while using the toilet, left the door wide open and posted a *hakama*-clad retainer outside to hold his sword. The hallway onto which the toilet opened was brightly lit and other guests were coming and going. Scared out of his wits by what this might lead to, Fukuzawa immediately shut the toilet door and warned the parties involved about such behavior.

The primary goal of Japan's European mission was to indefinitely postpone the opening of the designated cities and ports. The negotiations took place in London, but the Japanese request was not accepted by the other signatories. Instead a five-year moratorium on opening cities and ports was established, and in return for this concession, Japan was forced to make major reparations and lower its customs tariffs.

Another goal of the diplomatic mission was to formalize the international demarcation line between Russia and Japan on the island of Sakhalin (Karafuto in Japanese). Up until then, Sakhalin had been jointly held by Japan and Russia, with the Kurile Islands from Iturup (Etorofu) southward held by Japan, and from Urup (Uruppu) northward held by Russia. The Japanese hoped to set the point of demarcation at 50 degrees north latitude, while the Russians wanted to set it at 48 degrees. At one point, the Japanese were prepared to accept the Russian position, but the *metsuke*, Kyogoku Noto-no-kami, was strongly opposed because such a decision would exceed the power granted to the Japanese envoy by the bakufu authorities in Edo. If the truth be known, the bakufu order had been to draw the point of demarcation at the latitude of 50 degrees north; however, judging the capabilities of Japan and Russia at the time, the wisest policy would surely have been to agree to establish the demarcation at 48 degrees. However, the censor Kyogoku Noto-no-kami, in typical bureaucratic fashion, insisted that the envoys were not authorized to exceed their orders, and thus a decision was left pending.

Interest in the Social System

In terms of the official objectives of the mission, no significant goals were achieved. Nevertheless, witnessing European civilization with their own eyes proved a considerable achievement for those involved. Their observations, although falling short of those recorded by the subsequent

Iwakura Mission (1871-73), were extremely perceptive and filled with enthusiasm.

The three linguists on the mission, Fukuzawa, Matsuki, and Mitsukuri, eagerly observed everything. They were kept under close surveillance by their colleagues because they were scholars of Western learning and their ability to communicate with the local people cast a light of suspicion on them. Thus, it was difficult for them to move about as freely as they might have wished. Additionally, they were also kept extremely busy working for their superiors and in the writing of reports.

Fukuzawa in particular noted down various aspects of the social system he encountered. He witnessed government monopolies, hospitals, railroads, gas power, telegraphic systems, expositions, facilities for the blind and mute, insane asylums and tunnel constructions. Concerning military matters, he showed a strong curiosity not only about the weaponry but also about the conscription system and why France had one while Great Britain did not.

Fukuzawa was not the only member of the mission interested in such matters. However, his curiosity in them did run much deeper than most others. Most of his compatriots marveled at the speed of the locomotives, but Fukuzawa's interest went one step further. He inquired about the economic aspects of the railroads, such as the distance between Paris and Marseilles, the cost of laying track, whether the expenses of construction were born by the government or by private sector interests, the appropriate cost of freight and passenger fares, and what the differences were between France and Great Britain. As shall subsequently be noted, Fukuzawa would become a strong proponent of constructing railroads in Japan, and the foundation for such sentiment was surely laid during this period.

Fukuzawa also displayed some weaknesses. When some members of the mission were allowed to witness a surgical procedure that involved the removal of a kidney stone, Fukuzawa grew faint. On another occasion he was to observe an operation on a child's eye, but he managed to escape the operating theater just before any incision was made. He commented that he was absolutely spineless in such circumstances.

Meanwhile, the most perplexing aspect he observed was the system of elections and legislative assemblies. In *The Autobiography* he writes,

> But these were the things most difficult of all for me to understand. In this connection, I learned that there were bands of men called political parties—the Liberals and the Conservatives—who were always fighting against each other in the government. For some time it was beyond my comprehension to understand what they were fighting for, and what was meant, anyway, by "fighting" in peace time. "This man and that man are enemies in the House," they would tell me. But these "enemies" were to be seen at the same table, eating and drinking with each other. I felt as if I could not make much out of this. It took me a long time, with some tedious thinking, before I could gather a general notion of these separate mysterious facts. In some of the more complicated matters, I might achieve an understanding five or ten days after they were explained to me. But all in all, I learned much from this initial tour of Europe.[14]

As Fukuzawa comments in the introduction to his collected works this was natural, because in Japan if three or more people agree in private to something they would form factions, which was prohibited.

It was during his time in Great Britain that Fukuzawa began to thoroughly understand the West, including its politics. During the same period he began to consolidate his resolve for Japan to adopt civilization from the West.

On May 9th, while he was in London, Fukuzawa sent a letter to Shimazu Suketaro, a fellow enlightenment proponent from his home domain.

In the correspondence, he explains the significance and achievements of his travels to date.

> I am quite fortunate to be able to join this journey to the West, as it is an opportunity that will not come again. I have therefore resolved to closely research the conditions and customs of the European countries. I have already made friends in France and Great Britain and have made inquiries concerning the institutions of these countries, regulations of their armies and navies, and the collection of taxes. While not everything is clear to me, I have benefited enormously from being able to directly observe things that until now I have only known through books.

Fukuzawa in the same letter then turned to the future of Japan. "Whereas in our country there is little that can be done about the system as it developed in the past, what is essential is that we each now in our respective positions mount great reforms so that the situation will be improved." And for the time being, he concluded, the most useful method of accomplishing this is to buy a large number of books. He reports that he has already purchased a significant number of volumes in London. "Not wasting money on a single trinket, I will spend the entire sum which I was given in Edo as an allowance on the purchase of books."

At the end of his letter, Fukuzawa summed up his overall impressions and his conviction that Japan's most immediate goal should be to achieve *fukoku kyohei*, a rich country and a strong military, and that education was essential to achieving that goal. Up to this point, Fukuzawa had spoken as somewhat of a bystander, but now he had come to feel that he could not remain on the sidelines observing Japan's destiny.

One of the most impressive experiences Fukuzawa had in London involved a bill submitted to Parliament that criticized the British Minister to Japan, Rutherford Alcock. The bill harshly censured Alcock's arrogant attitude toward Japan, in acting as if Great Britain had conquered the nation militarily. On one occasion, Alcock had even gone so far as to ride on horseback into the sacred precinct of a temple, an action that constituted an unpardonable affront. Fukuzawa was deeply moved on reading the bill, writing the following:

> On reading the copy of this bill, I felt as if a load had been lifted from my chest. After all, the foreigners were not all "devils." I had felt that Japan was enduring some pointed affronts on the part of the foreign ministers who presumed on the ignorance of our government. But now that I had actually come to the minister's native land, I found there were among them some truly impartial and warm-hearted human beings. After this I grew even more determined in my doctrine of free intercourse with the rest of the world.[15]

Upon reaching Holland, the mission felt as if it had arrived in a second homeland, identifying with such things as a small country, an industrious people and fields and other lands that were kept in good condition. In contrast, they also clearly perceived the limitations of Holland's capabilities. Having visited France and Great Britain, they saw clearly that Holland suffered by comparison. There was nothing particularly novel in the country. It can even be said that this was the moment when Japanese scholars of Western learning decisively turned away from the Netherlands.[16]

In Cologne, Germany, they met Philipp Franz von Siebold's wife and children, although Siebold himself was currently in Japan. In Berlin they were lavishly welcomed by the king and warmly entertained at the opera and the theater. Because they did not understand the language, however, they found these pastimes to be of little interest. Again, after visiting France and Great Britain, the emissaries did not come away with a good impression of Germany. A decade thereafter, the Iwakura Mission would be strongly impressed by Germany, which suggests how conspicuously that country would develop in the ten-year interim.

During their visit to St. Petersburg, Russia, they were offered special accommodations in an official residence. Much to their astonishment, everything was done up in Japanese style. There were sword racks, writing implements, tableware, tobacco, bags of rice bran in the bathroom, Japanese-style pillows, plain wood chopsticks and even Japanese cuisine. They had heard that there was a Japanese man named Yamatoff in Russia and they assumed he was the one who made the preparations.

Yamatoff was actually Tachibana Kumezo, a samurai of the Kakegawa domain, who had committed some sort of crime as a young man and taken the tonsure. Assuming the name Tachibana Kosai, he traveled throughout Japan in an endless pilgrimage. When he reached the Izu Peninsula, he encountered a Russian warship which had been damaged in the wake of an earthquake. Tachibana struck up a friendship with Captain Putiatin of the vessel. When Putiatin's ship left Japan, Tachibana smuggled himself out of the country. The members of the mission were aware of his existence and that he had made the preparations, but they never encountered the man himself.

Russian dignitaries also approached Fukuzawa. Recognizing his competence, a member of the Russian reception committee invited him to give up on the small country he came from and remain in Russia. The man pointed out that there were many foreigners working in Russia, including Germans, Dutch and British, and he repeatedly tried to persuade Fukuzawa to remain and find work for himself. To Fukuzawa, Russia seemed a somewhat eerie country but he must have been impressed by its flexibility and broad-mindedness. Unable to mention this incident to any of his compatriots, he only made the episode public later when he wrote his autobiography.

Among those whom Fukuzawa befriended during his travels was Léon de Rosny, who began studying Chinese and along the way began Japanese studies as well. He subsequently developed a strong interest in Japan. Quite enthusiastic, he frequently met Fukuzawa in Paris, and then when the Japanese were in Holland staying at The Hague, he followed them and stayed there twenty days as well. After returning once to Paris, Rosny pursued the mission to Berlin, only to discover that the Japanese had left, so he followed them to St. Petersburg. Although Rosny only spoke Japanese haltingly, Fukuzawa nevertheless learned a great deal from him.

In London, Fukuzawa also became acquainted with Tang Xue Xun, a Chinese student who had come three years earlier to study at his own expense. Upon inquiring how many Chinese were able to understand Western languages, Tang responded that there were maybe a dozen or so, which left Fukuzawa astonished. It was shocking because the number of Japanese with such capability numbered in the hundreds or thousands. Despite having much longer contact with the West, the Chinese were far behind Japan in terms of Western learning. Fukuzawa later related this experience repeatedly so it obviously made a deep impression on him.

From about the time the Japanese mission returned to Paris from St. Petersburg, the attitude of the French government towards their guests rapidly cooled. In his autobiography, Fukuzawa says that the Second Tozenji Incident, which occurred on June 26th, 1862, resulted from the Richardson Incident *(Namamugi Jiken)*, but that is a mistake on his part. The cooling actually resulted from a second attack on the British Legation at Tozenji Temple by a fanatical anti-foreign extremist.

The emissaries departed for Japan from Rochefort. Fukuzawa noted in his diary, quoted in the autobiography, that an escort of over one thousand soldiers lined the sides of the mile-long road leading from the train to the harbor. It officially formed an honor guard but nevertheless adding a menacing air to the send-off. This experience also stuck in his memory and in his later years (1898) during a speech he delivered at Mita, he took out his *Diary of the West (Seiko ki)* and cited the aforementioned incident from it.

The Decision to Introduce Western Civilization

In summing up Fukuzawa's experiences in Europe, the following points are important. First, there can be little doubt that he developed an even deeper sense that the world is a place in which the strong prey upon the weak. Looking at the Taiping Rebellion, the American Civil War and the tragic demise of the ancient civilizations together with the development of Great Britain, France, Prussia and Russia, Fukuzawa saw the world filled with constant harsh competition. He must have felt that an immediate ruinous fate awaited anybody who was left unprepared. On the other hand, as evidenced in the criticism of Rutherford Alcock in Great Britain, his faith in civilization must have deepened further.

Second, during this period he was constantly anxious about the activities of the "expel the foreigners" advocates back in Japan. "What hope is there for the future of Japan as long as our people show this foolish pride, keeping aloof from the rest of the countries of the world. The louder the voices are for expelling the foreigners, the more we lose strength as a nation. When I think about where their actions would ultimately take us, I am dismayed."

Third, he was impressed by the complexity of international relations. The attitudes of the European nations were quite amicable, but things changed when it came to foreign policy rights and interests. On the other hand, he was also impressed by the varieties of exchange that were carried on behind the confrontations between nations. Surely he must have felt this as a result of his encounter with Otokichi who had been shipwrecked and unable to return to Japan, with Yamatoff who went to Russia, with Rosny who had such an ardent interest in Japan and even with his own experience in being encouraged to stay and work in Russia.

Not only did the journey to Europe deepen his understanding of Western civilization, but it also allowed him to perceive with more depth the severity and complicated nature of international relations.

The advocates of Western enlightenment, including Fukuzawa, believed that Japan had to be guided toward increasing national wealth and military strength. To do this, they felt the need to introduce Western civilization as rapidly as possible.

During their travels, Fukuzawa, Matsuki and Mitsukuri repeatedly debated Japan's future among themselves. When Fukuzawa commented, "If things were to go as we would like, we would receive a stipend of two hundred *hyo* of rice per year from the shogun to serve as instructors, spreading the ideas of civilization and opening the country, creating a major reform," Matsuki was strongly in agreement. They were all that enthusiastic.

One of the other members, Fukuchi Gen'ichiro, was also extremely eager to make use of their newly-acquired knowledge in some major undertaking. As things worked out, however, they were not appointed to positions of high status. Fukuchi later reflected on how they had never been as disheartened and despondent before as when they were passed over for high office (*Kaiojidan* [Reminiscence]).

The reason why they were not given important posts was because during the year that they had been away, Japanese politics had undergone a transformation. The bakufu's credibility was shot, and now there were bloody confrontations between those advocating opening the country *(kaikoku)* and those calling for expulsion of the foreigners *(joi)*.

As Fukuzawa was on the point of departing Japan on February 13th, 1862, the senior councilor Ando Nobumasa was attacked and wounded (in the Sakashitamongai Incident). In May, Shimazu Hisamitsu led a force of one thousand men to Kyoto where he presented a memorial to the Court calling for a reform of the shogunal administration. The Imperial Court accepted the memorial and decided to dispatch an imperial envoy together with Hisamitsu to Edo, where he elevated Hitotsubashi (Tokugawa) Yoshinobu and Matsudaira Yoshinaga. As a result, Yoshinobu was appointed shogunal regent *(kokenshoku)* and Yoshinaga was appointed shogunal head minister *(seijisosaishoku)*, and the system of alternative residence *(sankin kotai)* was eased. As a result, the relationship between the bakufu and the Court was improved, but at the same time the bakufu's prestige was significantly weakened.

Moreover, on Shimazu's way back to Kyoto, the Richardson Incident occurred, during which members of his retinue killed an Englishman whom they thought had failed to show proper respect to their lord. In the light of domestic laws, their action was understandable; in the light of the rules of international affairs, however, it was unacceptable. To make things worse, the parties involved were the world's greatest power Great Britain and Japan's strongest domain Satsuma. Further, the Court, which had gained prestige, was in the camp of the expel-the-foreigner advocates. In November, the Court issued a mandate expelling foreigners and in December the bakufu was forced to abide by it. This was the Japan to which Fukuzawa and the other emissaries returned.

Chapter 5

Conditions in the West

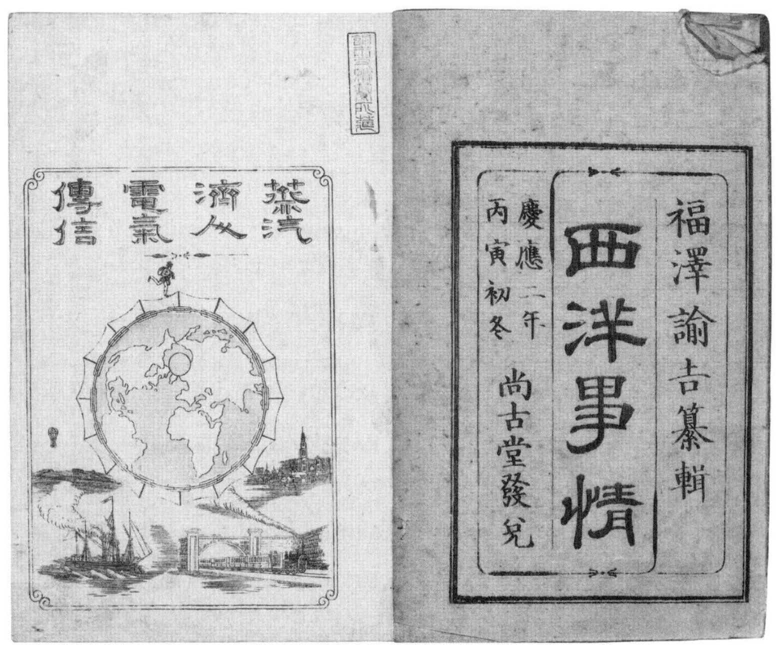

Conditions in the West, first pamphlet. (Courtesy of Keio University Fukuzawa Memorial Center)

The Storm of Anti-foreign Sentiment

Upon the mission's return from Europe, a storm of anti-foreign sentiment was raging throughout the country. Up until that time, a doctrine of expelling foreigners had existed in principle, but when he was in Osaka, then after arriving in Edo and even after returning from America, Fukuzawa had not felt personally endangered in any way. In 1863, however, merchants engaged in foreign trade were attacked and a Western Studies colleague of his was assaulted.

Fukuzawa became doubly cautious. When a visitor he did not know called on him, he refused to meet the person. One day his maid announced that a caller was at the entrance asking to see Fukuzawa. When she asked for his name, the man replied that Fukuzawa would know him. Fukuzawa asked the maid what he looked like and she described him as tall, with one eye, and wearing a long sword. When he nervously took a peek at the man, he discovered it was an old friend. "You damned fool! Why didn't you give your name?" Fukuzawa blustered. "I was scared out of my wits!" They then shared a big laugh of relief.[17]

Fukuzawa was also apprehensive about walking the streets alone. Although he avoided going out at night, on one occasion he had to do so alone. As he walked down a particularly dark road, he became aware of a man coming toward him from the opposite direction. There was no way to escape. Thinking that it would be even more dangerous to betray a sense of vulnerability to the oncoming figure, instead of continuing along the left side of the road, Fukuzawa purposely drew close to the center of it, so that he would encounter the stranger face to face. But the approaching figure did exactly the same thing, and the situation became even more desperate. If necessity arose, Fukuzawa had a degree of skill in the art of drawing his sword, so he braced himself to dispatch the would-be assailant. But when the two men passed each other, the stranger did not draw his sword and neither did Fukuzawa. Instead, at the same instant, both men started running away at full speed until they were out of range of each other's sword blade. Once they were some ten meters apart, Fukuzawa looked back and saw that the other man was now in full flight. Undoubtedly, the stranger had been as terrified as Fukuzawa. This particular episode occurred sometime in February or March of 1863.

Ironically, Fukuzawa's first job on return to Japan was to deal with the fallout of the Richardson Incident (*Namamugi Jiken*). The British demanded an indemnity of 100,000 pounds from the bakufu authorities; and from the Satsuma domain an indemnity of 25,000 pounds. They also sought the execution of Richardson's murderers. The British demanded a reply within twenty days. The demands were received by the bakufu authorities on April 6th, 1863, and Fukuzawa was summoned in the middle of the night to translate the document by daybreak. Prior to this event, however, on March 31st, the shogun, Tokugawa Iemochi, had departed Edo for Kyoto, and unfortunately the deadline for a reply to the demands was to fall before his return to the city. There followed a flurry of exchanges in which the bakufu asked for a postponement of the proceedings, to which the British refused to budge. When all this was happening, one of the senior councilors *(roju)* absented himself from council meetings citing ill health and the situation degenerated into a complete lapse of responsibility.

Fukuzawa felt that war was inevitable and to prepare for the opening of hostilities, he ordered thirty *hyo* of rice from the family's regular dealer and asked the dealer to store it. He also purchased a barrel of *miso* paste and placed it in his shed. As time passed and tensions rose further, however, he began to realize how foolish he had been because, if it became necessary to flee, it would be impossible to carry along such huge quantities of rice and *miso*. He could not help being amused by the needless trouble he had gone through. On the other hand, what cash Fukuzawa had on hand was divided into several bundles. This would allow his wife, his live-in students and himself to escape if such a course of action became necessary. Thus equipped, his household was ready for war if it should break out the next day or soon thereafter. On June 24th, however, Ogasawara Iki-no-kami, a senior councilor from the Karatsu domain, suddenly and on his own authority, paid the indemnity demanded of the bakufu authorities. The war crisis had passed.

The outcome of this settlement with the bakufu was that the British next moved against the Satsuma domain. A fleet proceeded to Satsuma and on August 15th, the Bombardment of Kagoshima began. The Satsuma troops made good use of initial British overconfidence and they fought bravely, killing several commissioned officers, and seizing a British ship's anchor when the crew had to cut it loose to escape. Overall, however, Satsuma was not Great Britain's opponent.

During this period, Fukuzawa's close friend Matsuki Koan became entangled in the war and was captured by the British. From that point onward, he was particularly in danger of being killed by Satsuma samurai for having been taken prisoner by the barbarians, so it was best to lay low. *The Autobiography* describes their reunion more than a year later.

The British demands resulting from the Richardson Incident were quite high-handed and even the American envoy hoped that the bakufu would not knuckle under. However, the French envoy took advantage of the hard-line British stance, and as a result, it may have been inevitable that the bakufu would concede. Fukuzawa was extremely dissatisfied with the conduct of the British. To demand and receive 125,000 pounds for the murder of a private citizen was an excessive claim and he wrote, "We Japanese still feel the injustice of that demand and settlement."[18]

From the British view, the bakufu's foreign policies seemed to offer no concrete options for the short term and were simply a means of delaying any form of response. It was especially unacceptable to give as an excuse the fact that the person in charge was absent due to illness. By contrast, even though the outcome was conflict, Satsuma's actions were swift, and immediately after losing the so-called Anglo-Satsuma War (the Bombardment of Kagoshima), the domain candidly submitted a request to purchase weapons from Great Britain. As a result of the Richardson Incident and the conflict that followed, Great Britain changed its negotiating stance toward Japan, attaching greater significance to the Satsuma domain. The situation that resulted from the international negotiations over the Richardson Incident is described in great detail by Ernest Satow in *A Diplomat in Japan* and Hagihara Nobutoshi's *Toi gake—Aanesuto Satou nikki-sho*.

Fukuzawa's record of this period of negotiations, however, is based on his recollections of the events, which he wrote down at the end of each day after he returned home. If these private written recollections had become known at the time, they would have had serious consequences for Fukuzawa. In fact, a certain acquaintance wrote a letter to his family which was stolen. In it he reproached the bakufu leadership saying that he hoped that a wise ruler would appear who would solve the issues that had arisen. When the content of this letter was discovered and seen to cast aspersions on the shogunate—indeed, to be treasonous—the acquaintance in question was forced to commit *seppuku*, ritual suicide by disembowelment. Frightened by this development, Fukuzawa burned all copies of the correspondence he possessed, and because he had previously shown some of it to others, he was beside himself with worry.

Prior to the Anglo-Satsuma War, and under pressure from the Imperial Court, the bakufu had established a deadline of June 1863 for the expulsion of foreigners from Japan. However, while the bakufu itself had no real inclination to drive the foreign presence from the country, its hand was forced in that from June 25th the Choshu domain had commenced bombarding any European or American ship that approached Shimonoseki.

On July 25th, Ogata Koan suddenly passed away. He had been employed in work that had not inspired him. Fukuzawa had just visited him two or three days earlier and was stunned by a report that Ogata had suddenly vomited blood. Fukuzawa ran from Shinsenza to Ogata's residence in the Shitaya District, but he did not arrive in time.

Several dozens of Ogata's followers arrived that night, staying for a wake. Fukuzawa met with Murata Zoroku, who had been the head student before him, initiating the conversation by asking, "What do you think about that mess at Shimonoseki? Wasn't Choshu crazy to do such a thing?" *(The Autobiography)*. Murata's outburst in response stunned him. He refused to forgive the behavior of the high-handed Westerners and declared that Choshu would expel all the foreigners, even if it cost everyone their lives.

Fukuzawa was concerned that such reckless expulsions would, to the contrary of what they hoped to achieve, weaken the country. The negotiations surrounding the resolution of the Richardson Incident had left him acutely aware of the dangers involved in such political maneuverings. Yet he felt the same barely suppressible anger that Murata had openly exhibited.

The disagreement between the two was a reflection of the differences in their respective positions, but Fukuzawa, as a proponent of *yasegaman* (greater self-restraint), was not that different from Murata. Nevertheless, Fukuzawa was unable to find a government that would express this dissatisfaction with the West.

Publication of *Conditions in the West*

Amid this storm of anti-foreign sentiment, Fukuzawa began to pour his energy into education. Beginning in approximately the spring of 1863, he made the changeover from Dutch Studies to English Studies and launched full-fledged school operations. In the section entitled, *Rireki no koto*, which he himself wrote in *Keio Gijuku Kiji* [The History of Keio Gijuku] in 1883, he noted that the school opened in 1858, but because there were frequent changes of location and because the scale of the school was small, the earlier years should be ignored, and instead, the founding of the school should be recorded as February 1863. This was the true beginning of Keio Gijuku.

In April 1864, Fukuzawa returned to Nakatsu for the first time in many years. It had been six years since he had last seen his mother. His visit lasted two months and one of his goals was to gather promising young men for the school. On July 29th, he returned to Edo with six of them, including Obata Tokujiro.

The school was still not fully equipped, especially in terms of teaching materials. This situation would not be remedied until Fukuzawa returned from his second trip to the United States.

Furthermore, from October 1864, Fukuzawa was employed by the bakufu as a translator for the magistrate of foreign affairs. The prescribed salary was listed as one hundred fifty *hyo* of rice, though it actually amounted to only one hundred *hyo*, with an allowance of fifteen *ryo*.

Most of Fukuzawa's effort now went into writing. Following his return from Europe, he organized the notes that he had written and submitted them to Kimura Settsu-no-kami on January 15th, 1864. In addition, it is known that a more extensive version of these notes in a transcribed form with the title *Conditions in the West (Seiyo Jijo)* began to circulate by at least June 1864. It was a much simpler version of the printed *Seiyo Jijo* and was partially the same as *Seiko ki.*

The first edition of *Conditions in the West*, comprised of three volumes, was published in 1866. The second three came out in 1868 and there were four more in 1870.

Conditions in the West became a major best seller and in a single stroke Fukuzawa's name became widely known. The book was not simply an introduction to foreign countries. It was Fukuzawa's first, even modern Japan's first, attempt at a true understanding of the West. In insight, it anticipates the ideas that Fukuzawa would subsequently put forward in *An Encouragement of Learning*, so let us look at it in some detail.

The book's purpose, as shown in the opening of the first volume of the first set, is made clear when Fukuzawa comments that previous works had introduced Western countries' physics, geography, military strategy and navigational techniques. However, Fukuzawa added, without knowing about each country's politics and customs, one could not grasp how such scholarship would relate to understanding the foundation of the administration of the country. Since previous volumes had started out with an inadequate goal, not only would such knowledge be of little practical use, it might even be detrimental. Therefore, the current volumes, he said, would introduce each country's politics and customs. In order to do that, reading history would be the best approach, but the present state of things was such that one would simply busy oneself in absorbing scholarship and the gains would be small for the effort expended. Therefore, he himself would read several books on Western geography and history, and then introduce four subjects: geography, politics, military affairs, and public finance.

Fukuzawa placed in the first volume the following brief accounts, entitled *biko* or preliminary remarks:

(1) Politics
(2) Taxation
(3) National bonds
(4) Paper currency
(5) Trading companies
(6) Diplomacy
(7) Military affairs
(8) Literature and technology
(9) Schools

(10) Newspapers
(11) Libraries
(12) Hospitals
(13) Poor houses
(14) Homes for the dumb
(15) Homes for the blind
(16) Insane asylums
(17) Homes for mentally-disabled children
(18) Museums
(19) Exhibitions
(20) Steam engines
(21) Steamships
(22) Steam locomotives
(23) Telegraphs
(24) Gas lampposts
(25) Appendix
(The author has added the numeration to the original for the convenience of the reader.)

Conditions Leading to Enlightened Politics

Of these *biko*, "politics" was of special significance. In this section of *Conditions in the West*, Fukuzawa described three types of government: government through monarchy, government through aristocratic council and government through republicanism. He further distinguished between two types of monarchy: despotism (or absolute monarchy) and monarchy built around a constitutional framework.

Moreover, Fukuzawa was not simply making mechanical distinctions. In Great Britain, he noted that the government was administered by three institutions: the titular monarch, an upper house comprised of aristocrats, and a lower house with a republican form of government. Russia, on the other hand, had what would appear at first glance to be a despotic monarchy but national government was not carried out by a single individual's will. Republican government, by comparison, was on occasion completely lacking in substance. In 1848, the harshest laws of the Republican government in France and elsewhere were to some degree even more severe than those of a professed absolute monarchy such as Austria. Of the republican governments, the American government was most clearly the one in which representatives of the people set aside personal views to decide on national administration. Fukuzawa dealt with these realities of foreign governments.

Fukuzawa also commented that there were six basic conditions for enlightened government administration.

The first is autonomous discretion, in which the national laws are lenient and the individual is not restricted. The individuals select their social station, with those seeking to be gentlemen becoming gentlemen, those desiring to become farmers becoming farmers, and there is no distinction made between *shi-no-ko-sho* (the Japanese feudal statuses of warrior, farmer, craftsman, merchant). No one pays attention to familial lineage, no one with court rank looks down on others, high and low each have their place, and no one interferes with the freedom of the others, each contributing from their own natural talents.

The distinction between the high and low social standing that results sets a high value on court rank for those in public service, but there is no other rank between citizens like the four statuses of feudal Japan. The emphasis should be on a person of noble character who learns to read and write, to debate on the basis of reason, and to take initiative. To not know how to read and write turns a person into a small being who can only perform physical labor. This description reminds us of the opening passage of *An Encouragement of Learning*.

In an explanatory note Fukuzawa adds,

> The terms, 'autonomous discretion' and 'freedom,' do not mean doing just as one likes, ignoring the laws of the country. Rather they refer to having relations with all of the people of the country without constraint or deference, employing one's abilities to the utmost. In English, this is referred to as 'freedom' and 'liberty'. There is not yet an appropriate translation in Japanese.

Such sentiment is also repeated in *An Encouragement of Learning*, and from about this time Fukuzawa begins commenting that defining the concept of freedom is difficult.

The second condition for an enlightened government is freedom of religion. The third is broadening the path toward new inventions by encouraging technology and literature. The fourth is to build schools and educate capable people. The fifth is having people observe the laws and stabilizing the fundamentals of livelihood. The sixth is to relieve the suffering of people by constructing hospitals and poor houses in order to aid the indigent.

Seen from the modern perspective, these are deeply interesting conditions. The first is a guarantee of freedom; the second, a freedom of religion; the third, an advancement of higher learning; the fourth, an enrichment of education; the fifth, measures to stabilize the country's livelihood by improving justice and public finance; and the sixth, social welfare. To have accurately grasped these as vital aspects of government is truly impressive.

It is also intriguing that "politics" should be followed by "taxation" in Fukuzawa's writings. Traditionally, the point of government was to collect taxes, and until that time, Japanese taxation centered on agricultural income. By contrast, Fukuzawa raises the issue of taxes levied on ports (in the form of customs duties), taxes levied on licenses (in the form of liquor and tobacco), taxes on documentation, land and house taxes, and family property taxes. At the end of the discussion of taxation, there is a section on the "express messenger" seal, and this is a reference to the phenomenon of postage stamps. At that time, foreign nations did not have courier services, so the government provided such services instead, and here Fukuzawa introduces the system of postage stamps in some detail.

The third condition explained by Fukuzawa deals with "government bonds." A government issues bonds so as to secure public funds, and while it does not often redeem them, it does regularly pay interest. He also added an appropriate explanation that where confidence in the government is high, the value of the notes is high, whereas where confidence is low, so is the value. The fifth condition Fukuzawa discussed was the nature of mercantile companies, which represented an unfamiliar institution in Japan at the time. Thus, he explained the way in which capital was accumulated and put to use in carrying on an enterprise.

With regard to military conscription, a survey of the history of the development of military technology was provided, followed by a description of how the military system evolved. The facts included here were comparatively well known in Japan.

Concerning schools, Fukuzawa explained how the various countries were putting their energies into education. One wonders how he felt about these developments as somebody who already had a significant number of students in his own school.

With regard to newspapers, Fukuzawa wrote, "to Westerners, reading a newspaper is one of the pleasures of life. It can be said that reading a paper even makes one forget to eat. While there are many books from overseas and from one's own country, from ancient times to contemporary times, with the goal of clearly grasping what is occurring at present, and as a path to belonging to the world at large, there is nothing to compare with a newspaper." He appraised the newspaper's effectiveness highly. To be sure, during the stopover in Hong Kong on the European mission, Fukuzawa bought a newspaper from London and read about the Civil War that had broken out in the United States, thus, he was somebody who had become interested in print media early on. He commented that newspapers were thriving in London and New York, taking note of their massive circulations and the speed with which information was conveyed. In one instance, he noted that a legislative assembly continued debating until four in the morning, yet by noon of the same day, the content of the deliberations was published in newspapers and available to be read some hundred kilometers away. Further, as to the impact of these publications, there was a bias depending on the country and the individual. Nonetheless, because publications had to be approved by the authorities, "controversies were to be fundamentally impartially conveyed and there were no hindrances to criticizing the government's policies or stating the good and the bad points of the persons involved. In other words, if one took fairness as a fundamental stance, it was acceptable to question the rights and wrongs of government administration and to laud or censure the individuals concerned. Therefore, newspapers had great influence and on occasion might change a government's policies. Fukuzawa would begin publishing the *Jiji Shimpo* in 1882 for different reasons, but it must have been a long-term ambition of his to publish what he saw as the ideal newspaper.

Fukuzawa showed great interest in libraries, museums and exhibitions. While in London and Paris, he also eagerly observed first-hand the goings on of hospitals, poor houses, homes for the dumb, homes for the blind, insane asylums and homes for mentally-disabled children. At first glance, it may seem paradoxical that Fukuzawa as a libertarian would have an interest in social welfare, but that is not the case. It is natural for a proponent of competition to advocate the need for a social safety net.

Fukuzawa also remarked on steam engines, steamships, steam locomotives and telegraphic services. He would repeatedly expound upon the advantages of transportation and communication as the greatest driving force for enlightenment. If he were alive today, Fukuzawa would undoubtedly be an assertive proponent of the advancement of information technology. Throughout *Conditions in the West*, Fukuzawa's explanations are extremely precise and forceful. His commentary on steam power, for example, requires little amending: "Steam is vapor. One can understand the power of steam by watching water boil in a pan, a pot or an iron kettle. When it comes to a boil, it forces the lid upwards. If one brings a certain quantity of water to a boil and keeps the heat up, it will turn all of the water into vapor, producing a certain measure of steam. That is, it fills a space 1,700 times that of the original volume of water. A steam engine uses this expansion of volume by means of a precision mechanism that provides the driving force that moves the engine."

Diligence in Translation

While writing *Conditions in the West*, Fukuzawa had to create many new Japanese words. The "Preface to The Collected Works" *(Fukuzawa Zenshu Shogen)* describes his travails as follows: first, he would look through various books written in Chinese, but in the end, the individual ideograph was only a symbol of the concept underpinning the thought. Nevertheless, there were many cases in which the concept itself that Fukuzawa was trying to convey through his translation did not exist in either Japanese or Chinese. In such cases, he had to actively invent new terminology. For example, when he had to translate the word "steam" into Japanese, he looked through the *Koki jiten*, a comprehensive multi-volume dictionary, and discovered the character 汽 (ki) and the annotation *mizu no ki nari*, and believing that it was what he was looking for, he adopted it as the translation. A second example is "copyright," for which there was no corresponding concept that meant a written work which was the exclusive possession of an author. The word 官許 already existed in Japanese, but all it meant was to avoid a legal challenge. As a result, Fukuzawa translated the word literally and used the term *hanken* (版権), whose two characters mean "copy" and "right" respectively.

The second section of the First Volume of *Conditions in the West* took up as its topic the United States. In it he wrote that the Declaration of Independence of the thirteen states of America was issued on July 4th, 1776, and that it was based on the universal principle that all men are endowed with equal rights. "According to this principle, men have the right to ensure their own lives, pursue freedom and hope for happiness, and these rights may not be taken away from them by anyone. The reason that governments are established by men is to enforce this principle. Only when government satisfies the people does it possess true authority. If the government does not act in accord with the spirit of this principle, the people have the right to seek reforms or abolish the government. Further, on the basis of this great principle, it is the fundamental right of the people to establish a new government that seems most likely to guarantee their safety and happiness. The justification for our argument is clear."

This translation of the Declaration of Independence is quite well done. Professor Matsuzawa Hiroaki lauds Fukuzawa's translations of the Declaration of Independence and the United States Constitution as masterpieces in the history of Japanese translation. Furthermore, the discussion of the relationship between government and the people in *An Encouragement of Learning* comes, for the most part, from this.[19]

In this same section, in addition to the United States, Fukuzawa also writes about Holland. His original plan was to introduce Great Britain in the third section, Russia in the fourth, France in the fifth, Portugal and a general overview of Germany in the sixth, with particular attention to Prussia. However, he did not complete the project and brought it to an end with Russia in section four. This is understandable. In the *biko* section and the section on the United States, he had already fully discussed the relationship between a nation and its citizens. Having already introduced Great Britain, the strongest and most prosperous country, to his readership, he may have thought that there was no particularly significant country left to deal with.

Competition and Progress

Although the Extra Volume *(gaihen)* of *Conditions in the West* (1868) came a bit later, let us consider it here. After returning from his second journey to the United States in 1867, Fukuzawa translated the first part of William and Robert Chamber's *Political Economy*. Rather than a translation, what Fukuzawa produced by going far beyond the scope of the source was closer to an original work. He only worked on the first half of the source because he later heard that the second half had already been translated.

The table of contents is as follows.

Chapter 1
Social organization
The family circle
Individual rights and duties
Civilization and enlightenment around the world
Distinction between high and low social status, wealth and poverty
Mutual effort and competition among people
The life and work of Watt
The life and work of Stephenson
Comments on how people are divided in each country
Relations among various countries
Comments on the basis of government

Chapter 2

Varieties of governments
National laws and customs
Duties of government

Chapter 3
Education of the people
An introduction to economics
On the basis of private ownership
Distinctions in labor, differences in merit and experience
  Licensing of inventions
  Copyrighting of books
Guaranteeing private property
Protecting the interest of private property

Of these sections, "Individual rights and duties" gives advance notice of what Fukuzawa would later set out in *An Encouragement of Learning*. The essence of the rights of the people is contained in the passage which states, "the principle of independence and freedom bestowed by heaven is neither to be sold nor bought. If a person carries this out properly and does nothing to interfere with what is carried out by others, that freedom cannot be taken from him by his nation's laws." Meanwhile, the essence of the duties and obligations of people is conveyed in the passage that contends: "If each person gives free rein to this universal principle without restraint to what is inborn, each as a consequence must carry out his duties, just as one carries out the family business and pays one's taxes."

In the section, "Mutual effort and competition between people," Fukuzawa writes that competition is the dynamic force that drives the progress of society, and this is one of the fundamental tenets of his thinking. On one occasion, an official in the bakufu noticed the word "competition" in the table of contents of *Conditions in the West*, and feeling it was inappropriate, asked Fukuzawa to replace it with a "more suitable" expression. Unable to reach a suitable compromise, Fukuzawa said that he simply deleted the word. This passage is probably the one that was referred to.

In the section entitled, "Relations among various countries," while stating that the fundamental method of achieving security is for a nation-state to possess military force; he also discusses the significance of international law. Due to the fact that when a country breaks international law, it inevitably creates an enemy, he notes, nations tend to observe such laws. Further, Fukuzawa comments that the "balance" of national powers serves as a major impetus for protecting peace.

In Chapter 2, he interestingly describes the "Duties of government" as having three goals: calmly ruling the people, firmly protecting the nation's laws, and maintaining international relations.

As we can see from the partial introduction above, it is not easy to write a book such as *Conditions in the West*. Fukuzawa, in the preface to his collected works, modestly reflects that its popularity resulted from the fact that there was no other book like it, so it was "like a bat in a countryside where there are no birds." However, that is far from the truth. As we have noted regarding the terms he used in the translation, the introduction of concepts that did not exist in Japan or any other region under the influence of Chinese civilization, was nothing less than pure creativity on Fukuzawa's part. It was something a person could not achieve without a deep understanding of the subject.

Second Visit to the United States

Fukuzawa departed on his second voyage to the United States on February 27th, 1867. This trip was his third overseas journey.

Back in 1862, the bakufu had decided to order and import three warships from the United States to enhance its military preparedness. Further, it had proposed to send students to America. Due to the outbreak of the Civil War, however, the students were instead sent to the Netherlands (Enomoto Kamajiro, later Enomoto Takeaki, was among them) and one warship was also purchased from the Dutch. Following the Civil War, the United States sent one of the previously-ordered ships to Japan; however, $500,000 of a prepaid sum from the bakufu remained on account with Washington. With the intention of using what money remained in Washington to purchase warships, the bakufu appointed Ono Tomogoro as comptroller, the official bakufu representative who would handle negotiations. Compared with the second mission that Fukuzawa had joined to Europe whose objective had been diplomatic, this third mission to the United States had just eleven members in total: eight vassals of the shogun, two retainers and one British expert in government service.

Ono, the official bakufu representative, was an expert in mathematics and measurement who had sailed on the *Kanrin Maru*. Thus, he and Fukuzawa were acquainted. Fukuzawa of course had previously traveled to San Francisco, but had no experience on the East Coast, so hoping to join the mission, he pushed himself as a candidate and Ono accepted his services. Fukuzawa's position was official deputy translator for the magistrate of foreign affairs.

There is an interesting episode regarding the payment of funds. Fukuzawa planned to acquire bills of exchange for both the mission's funds and his own private resources. He had an American merchant in Yokohama arrange for three sets of bills to be drawn on the Bank of England. Of course, it was the most money Fukuzawa had ever handled, amounting to several thousand *ryo*. He asked one question after another about the transactions (three people were to carry one set of bills each for reasons of safety, with one of them actually taking passage on a separate steamship). The bills could be cashed only when all three sets were assembled. Fukuzawa also wanted to know why the bills were drawn on the Bank of

England even though the party was traveling to the United States. After discussing the details for two hours, Fukuzawa was finally persuaded. The clerk of the company that arranged for the bills laughed, saying that Fukuzawa was a fast learner because it had taken him only two hours to comprehend the situation, whereas another person who had come with a similar request took a half-day to negotiate and ultimately left without having understood how things worked. Another part of this episode is that the ship carrying the third set of bills was delayed in reaching San Francisco so Fukuzawa had considerable trouble exchanging them for cash once they reached New York.

Comptroller Ono and his deputy Matsumoto Judayu, however, were exceedingly old-fashioned regarding the bills of exchange. They called a Mitsui clerk to their accommodations in Yokohama. The current exchange rate against the dollar was high, they said, and they thought Mitsui must have some dollars that they had obtained at a better rate at an earlier date. They asked if the clerk would exchange their silver for dollars, in what they thought would be a beneficial exchange. The Mitsui clerk prostrated himself before agreeing to do so, and then returned later with Mexican dollars at a somewhat discounted exchange rate. Whether Ono and Matsumoto were completely ignorant of financial matters or took advantage of their superior status is hard to determine, but Fukuzawa was dumbfounded at Mitsui's subservient acceptance of what they knew to be an unreasonable demand.

Fukuzawa's principal purpose in traveling to America a second time was to purchase an enormous number of books, because his school still had relatively few.

Scraping together his own cash, he had some 2,000 *ryo*. He also had 2,500 *ryo* from the Sendai domain to purchase weapons on their behalf. Along with other sundry sums, he was to carry close to 5,000 *ryo* with him. Staff members from a prominent New York bookseller came to Washington,

D.C., to meet with him and arrange to select the books he wanted. Fukuzawa purchased several dozen copies of each textbook he intended to use. This would be a breakthrough in Japan, because it was the beginning of each student having his own textbook to study with.

Comptroller Ono also decided to buy books, but it seemed that his plan was to sell the books in Japan for the profit of the bakufu. Fukuzawa opposed this idea head-on, and the relationship between the two men grew strained. If the government would sell such books to the public at cost, Fukuzawa would make every effort to select the best books available and beat down the purchase prices as much as possible. However, if the government intended to profit from such purchases as a business deal, Fukuzawa said he would expect a commission for selecting the books on their behalf and arranging the transactions. Such caustic remarks continued even after they returned to Japan and because he openly professed the need to overthrow the bakufu, things became even more complicated. At least that was how Fukuzawa portrayed the situation.

Comptroller Ono, on the other hand, griped that Fukuzawa had made repeated mistakes in the handling of funds, such as the bills of exchange matter mentioned earlier, that he did not tend to his assigned duties, that he spent all of his energies in purchasing books for his own use, and that he did not pay for shipping the books back to Japan as he should have done.

During the return voyage, Ono prepared an accusation against Fukuzawa and soon after landing he submitted it to the government. As a result, Fukuzawa was placed under house arrest and his books were held at the customs office. Fukuzawa refuted the charges and, in the end, he was released from house arrest in late November and was able to retrieve the books he had purchased at the beginning of the following year (1868).

From the perspective of common ethics, Comptroller Ono may have been right about the matter. Shipping would normally be free of charge, but in Fukuzawa's case the amount of freight was excessive. Furthermore, although Fukuzawa claimed that his other activities had not interfered with the carrying out of his proper duties, since he had been so enthusiastically purchasing books for his own use, it is not hard to understand why he could have seemed to be inattentive to his official work.

But it seems that Fukuzawa had already given up on the bakufu and saw no other way to enlighten Japan than to do it himself. From this position, the idea of devoted service to the bakufu must have seemed meaningless to him.

"The Tycoon's Monarchy" and Its Collapse

In the period between the European mission (1862) and his second visit to the United States (1867), Fukuzawa's views on Japan's domestic politics underwent a major transformation. Upon returning from Europe in the autumn of 1862, Fukuzawa wondered whether it would be possible for Japan's various daimyo to form a confederation like that of Germany. On this point, it must be noted that Germany had not yet formed the German Confederation, so Fukuzawa's recollections might have been slightly off, but nevertheless around that time what he had in mind was a union of the influential clans gathered around the shogun. When he returned from the United States in 1867, however, he had begun to declare openly that it was necessary to break up the shogunate.

What happened was that during this period another major change had occurred in Japan.

As we have seen, anti-foreign sentiment grew even more intense after the Richardson Incident in September 1862, before subsequently peaking in June 1863 with the bombardment at Shimonoseki. At that point, however, the exclusionist movement hit a particular barrier. Learning of Great Britain's military prowess as demonstrated during the Anglo-Satsuma War, the coup of September 30th [August 18th according to the traditional calendar] occurred. This development saw bakufu and Satsuma forces combine to chase the exclusionist Choshu and the allied nobility from the imperial capital of Kyoto.

The result of this coup was that, through January and February 1864, an assembly was established within the Court to create a system similar to a confederation. This system saw the prominent domains being promoted by those political forces who wanted a union of the Imperial Court and the shogunate.

In April 1864, French Minister Léon Roches assumed his post and began to actively court the government. In response to this, within the bakufu, pro-French bureaucrats gathered strength and they launched a movement to once again strengthen the bakufu with active French support.

In August of that year, because Choshu forces attacked Kyoto, the bakufu allied with Satsuma forces in the city to repulse them. This incident became known as Kinmon Incident (the Palace Gate Incident or the Hamaguri Gate Incident). Immediately a decision was made to launch a punitive expedition against the Choshu clan. In retaliation for the previous year's events, a combined fleet of British, French, American and Dutch warships attacked Shimonoseki and Choshu subsequently surrendered. In November, Choshu signaled its allegiance to the bakufu.

In October 1864, Fukuzawa became a retainer of the bakufu, just as it was reinforcing its authority. Also at approximately the same time, the pro-French faction within the bakufu was gaining the ascendancy.

From this period on, Fukuzawa was quite zealous in his actions on behalf of strengthening the bakufu.

In November 1865, for instance, he wrote "A proposal regarding duties that must be carried out at present." Therein he criticized the fact that anti-foreign sentiment was being roused because certain exalted personages in the capital were not acquainted with the ways of ordinary people, saying that efforts toward unification of the Court and the shogunate should be abandoned and the bakufu alone should bear responsibility. He emphasized the need for a resolute stance in dealing with the actions of the daimyo.

"At long last the time has come," he wrote, "to Westernize all military preparations and armaments." The cost of doing so might prove immense, he stressed, but that should be offset by profits from overseas trade.

Sometime around August 1866, he wrote a "Petition regarding the Second Expedition to Choshu." The exact date of authorship is unclear, but because he showed it to Kimura Settsu-no-kami on September 7th, he must have composed it prior to that date. The petition begins as follows:

> Since treaties were signed with various foreign nations several years ago, voices among the people have been asserting baseless, irresponsible theories regarding revering the emperor and expelling the foreigners. As a result, various disputes have arisen around the country. While the Court is not a little anxious, in the end, the purport of this way of thinking has nothing to do with reverence for the emperor or expulsion of foreigners. It is simply a group of rowdy characters with no means of subsistence seeking a livelihood. Or else it is an intrigue by daimyos with ambition seeking an excuse to free themselves from the control of the bakufu.

To sum matters up, Fukuzawa denounced the idea of *sonno joi* (revere the emperor and expel the foreigners) as a simple baseless slogan which emerged from political intentions.

Consequently, it was necessary to completely denounce the central Choshu group, and another Choshu Expedition would be a thoroughly pleasurable event. The first Choshu Expedition, as a result of taking internal and external factors into account, had not inflicted sufficient punishment, which was unfortunate. The Second Expedition, "a fortunate event resulting from an unfortunate event," however, "would provide an extremely welcome opportunity." "With one fell swoop, it would allow the bakufu to simultaneously suppress other daimyo as well, quelling the disturbances in Kyoto. In regard to foreign relations, it is desirable that the people of Japan have no opportunity to interfere."

With regard to war, Fukuzawa presented the following suggestions:

First, Choshu talks about expelling the foreigners, but that is a total falsehood. The domain sends students abroad to study and carries on smuggling activities, both of which must be completely prohibited. It is essential to dispatch several warships to the seas surrounding Choshu to prevent contact with foreign ships. During the American Civil War, Great Britain sent ships to the South (the Confederacy) causing major trouble for the North (the Union). (This comment was touched on in the earlier passage regarding Fukuzawa's reading of news articles about the Civil War.)

It was of particular importance to suppress the idea of "a confederation of daimyo." The idea of forming such a league of domain lords as the one found in Germany was supported by Parkes and others, but in order to prevent the establishment of such a union, the bakufu should send ministers without portfolio to the various Western countries, maintaining exclusive control of international relations by the bakufu and preventing the involvement of any other Japanese party.

Second, he asserted that there should be no hesitation regarding the employment of foreign troops in crushing Choshu. While there might be various views on this matter, the government should not waver on the issue. If Choshu were to win, Choshu would march into Kyoto and transform itself from being enemies of the Emperor to being imperial loyalists, and the imperial forces (the bakufu) would suddenly be termed enemies of the emperor. "Superficially the terms 'enemy of the emperor' and 'imperial loyalist' may both refer to a legitimate party, but depending on the degree of military force it has, an imperial mandate, as with the command of the Romanish Pope, simply gives the title to a military force and fixation of such an issue knows no bounds." Elaborating on what he said earlier, Fukuzawa felt the government should dispatch military forces in pursuit of any daimyo who raised an objection. "With a single stroke, the bakufu should be capable of exerting its influence over the entire country, and it would change the entire system of feudalism in Japan."

Covering the expenses for such action would not be problematic. Choshu domain's income, he estimated, was one million *hyo* per year, or some two million *ryo*. Using Choshu's income as collateral, he estimated that even if they borrowed twenty million *ryo* to pay expenses, they would be able to repay everything within twenty years. Japan did not at that time have national bonds, but the issuance of such instruments was common in various foreign nations. (The concept of national bonds was introduced in *Conditions in the West*.) Fukuzawa's proposal for an expedition against Choshu was resolute.

His emphasis on going so far as to borrow foreign military force to use in suppressing Choshu was especially inconsistent with his views in later years. Furthermore, his analysis of the financial dimension of such an audacious proposal was optimistic to the point of being fanciful.

The Second Choshu Expedition ended in complete failure. Under unfavorable conditions, the shogun Tokugawa Iemochi died on August 29th and Hitotsubashi Yoshinobu (who succeeded as head of the Tokugawa clan in September and officially took the position of shogun in January) decided temporarily to proceed with the expedition but shortly thereafter abandoned the idea, ultimately concluding a peace with Choshu in November.

Even at that stage, Fukuzawa was hoping to strengthen Tokugawa control, and in a letter addressed to Fukuzawa Einosuke (the pseudonym of Wada Shinjiro) he wrote the following.

> Advocacy of a league of prominent clan lords continues to be popular. If the idea of such a union becomes widely favored, the nation will become considerably freer, however, this freedom is in effect only the freedom of the Japanese to fight among themselves. No matter how one looks at the situation, without a monarchy of the shogun, the results will be that the daimyo will simply dispute among themselves and our nation will make no progress toward civilization and enlightenment.

In other words, under the current conditions, those who advocated a league of daimyo were opposing civilization and enlightenment, and Fukuzawa was criticizing them as culprits on a world scale, guilty of offending the law of nations.

From approximately October 1864, when he became a vassal of the shogun, until at least December 1866 (in other words, until just prior to his second journey to the United States), Fukuzawa was a fervent advocate of strengthening the bakufu. He must have written many of the items in *Conditions in the West* with the hopes that a reinforced bakufu would implement them. In *The Autobiography*, he writes that from the time he returned to Japan in 1862 until the beginning of the Meiji era, he lived as discreetly as possible for several years, but this does not correspond with the known facts of his life. Nakajima Mineo, in *Bakushin Fukuzawa Yukichi* [Bakufu Loyalist Fukuzawa Yukichi], comments that Fukuzawa in all probability did not want to make public that period of his past.

At any rate, following the humiliating failure of the Second Choshu Expedition, Fukuzawa gave up all faith in the shogunate. However, he did not for a moment believe in the Satsuma-Choshu anti-foreign forces either. Having strongly committed himself to politics only to be plunged into despair, the only path Fukuzawa could find was to devote his energies to the education of the rising generations.

It might be the case that Fukuzawa's insistence from this point onward to be distant from politics was due to his initial deep commitment to the debate which was followed by a subsequent loss of faith. Taking such a reaction into consideration, it becomes easier to grasp why, at the time of the battle against the Brigade of Righteousness *(Shogitai)* at Ueno on July 4th, 1868, Fukuzawa admonished his students not to allow themselves to be distracted and told them to devote themselves to their studies.

Chapter 6

Keio Gijuku

Painting by Yasuda Yukihiko of Fukuzawa Yukichi lecturing on Francis Wayland's *Elements of Political Economy.* (Courtesy of Keio University Fukuzawa Memorial Center)

From Imperial Restoration to the Abolition of the Domains

Tokugawa Yoshinobu formally surrendered the reins of national government to the Emperor on November 9th, 1867. The direction the new government was to take was made clear later, on August 29th, 1871 with the Imperial Edict that abolished the feudal domains and established the prefectures. The transformation that occurred between these events was rapid and requires explanation.

First, in restoring the reins of power to the Emperor, Tokugawa Yoshinobu of his own accord abandoned the bakufu system and entrusted responsibility for governing the country to the Imperial Court. That being said, however, he actually sought to secure real power for himself. The Court possessed almost no practical capacity to govern in its own right; thus, it would be obliged to depend upon a government through a council system comprised of the prominent domains. It seemed quite obvious that given its extraordinary stipend of 8,000,000 *koku* of rice, the cumulative experience it possessed in adapting to Western civilization, its experience in international affairs, the exceptional leader it possessed in Tokugawa Yoshinobu and the support it received from France, the Tokugawa clan would play a central role in such a new form of government.

Consequently the Satsuma-Choshu Alliance was desperate to halt such a development. On January 3rd, 1868, the alliance assembled the nobility who belonged to the faction that favored imperial rule. This party then issued the Decree for the Restoration of Imperial Rule *(Osei fukko no daigorei)*, and subsequently at an audience chamber in the Imperial Palace, it demanded that Yoshinobu seek a pardon for his crimes, resign his official post, and surrender all Tokugawa lands. Further, the alliance instigated incidents of arson and robbery in Edo to undermine the Tokugawa in their home base.

The infuriated Tokugawa confronted the combined alliance. This led to the Battle at Toba-Fushimi on January 27th, 1868. The clash lasted just a single day and although the Satsuma-Choshu forces were only slightly stronger, they were able to settle the dispute.

It still took time for things to quiet down after this. Saigo Takamori, a representative of the alliance, and Katsu Kaishu, former commander of the bakufu land forces, agreed to a capitulation of Edo Castle without resistance on April 6th, 1868. The fortress was not actually handed over until May 3rd. In that the new government did not move to immediately quell the pro-shogunate force called the Brigade of Righteousness *(Shogitai)* that had entrenched itself at Ueno, complete control of Edo was not achieved until July 4th.

In Japan's other regions, on June 22nd numerous pro-shogunate daimyo in the Tohoku region formed a group called the Northern Alliance *(Oetsu Reppan Domei)* to oppose the forces of the new government. Elsewhere, Enomoto Takeaki, vice commander-in-chief of the former bakufu navy, escaped from Shinagawa near Edo with eight warships on October 4th. He then headed north to Hokkaido to continue his resistance.

Resistance in the Tohoku region came to an end on November 6th, 1868 (Meiji 1) with the fall of the besieged castle at Aizu Wakamatsu. By the end of the year, all the pro-shogunate domains in the region had been suppressed by the new government. Enomoto Takeaki, who had taken shelter at the Goryokaku fortress at Hakodate, in Hokkaido, surrendered to government forces on June 27th, 1869.

The Imperial Court issued the Charter Oath of the Emperor Meiji *(Gokajo no goseimon)* on April 6th, 1868, the same day Edo Castle's surrender was agreed. On May 22nd, the British Minister Plenipotentiary to Japan, Harry Smith Parkes, presented his credentials to the Emperor, becoming the first representative of a foreign power to recognize the new imperial government.

On October 23rd, 1868, the Grand Ceremony of Accession was held to enthrone the Emperor, and the era name was changed to Meiji. On March 2nd, 1869, the four domains of Satsuma, Choshu, Tosa and Hizen submitted a request to be allowed to return the domain registers to the Meiji Emperor. The Imperial Court accepted this request and on August 5th, 274 former daimyo were appointed to serve as governors of their respective territories. This took place one month after the Goryokaku fortress was handed over and the Boshin Civil War came to a complete end.

On its path to establishment, the new government thus crushed resistance by the former bakufu powers. At a glance, because it was the former daimyo who governed the provinces, it was not really clear how much of a change had actually been introduced. In February 1868, samurai from the Tosa domain fought and killed some French sailors in the Sakai Incident, while in March of the same year the British envoy Parkes was attacked. In October 1869, the Vice Minister of War in the new government, Omura Masujiro, was assassinated, and the turbulence of politics continued for some time.

A truly surprising development occurred on August 29th, 1871, with the Imperial Edict that abolished the feudal domains and established the prefectures. In a narrow sense, this act brought to a close the drama that was the Meiji Restoration.

Developments at Keio Gijuku

During the period from the restoration of political power to the Imperial Court through until the abolition of the feudal domains and establishment of the prefectures, Fukuzawa turned away from politics and began to focus more closely on educational matters. This was the period in which Keio Gijuku (Keio University) came into being. At this point, let us review how the early school evolved into what later became Keio Gijuku.

Fukuzawa was sent to Edo under orders from the Nakatsu domain in

1858. He then opened a school of Dutch Studies at his home, a row house he rented. The house itself was located within the grounds of the Okudaira clan secondary residence in Edo's Tsukiji Teppozu District. When he started the school, he taught three to five boys who were sons of samurai from his own domain as well as five or six boys from other places. Within the house, the first floor had a six-mat room that Fukuzawa and a houseboy *(shosei)* shared, while on the second floor was a fifteen-mat room which seven or eight students had access to. It is said that during this period Fukuzawa would sometimes come running upstairs to ask his young charges how to write a particular Chinese character. He would then go back downstairs to resume his translation work. This is a telling episode. Fukuzawa originally intended to stay in Edo only three or four years, so he failed to make records of things, but in fact there was a considerable turnover among the students who came, and there were always several dozen students.

Following this initial period, although the exact dates are unclear, between his first trip to the United States (1860) and his trip to Europe (1862), Fukuzawa relocated the school to the Shiba Shinsenza District. Then being employed by the bakufu, he became occupied with translation, and the reason for moving was probably so that he would be closer to work. Furthermore, having gotten married, he needed a larger place to live. Yet, the school itself remained pretty much the same.

As we have seen, Fukuzawa's school hit full-stride at the beginning of 1863 just after he returned from Europe. Letters that he penned from London reveal that he felt strongly that the training of capable people was of urgent necessity. Immediately upon his return to Japan, he devoted his energies to operating a fully-fledged school. He also began keeping records of those who came to study with him as well as converting the curriculum from Dutch Studies to English Studies.

In autumn of the same year, the school returned once again from the

Shiba Shinsenza District back to the Nakatsu domain secondary residence at Tsukiji Teppozu. This time, however, Fukuzawa was able to borrow five row houses that were connected to one another. In 1862, the bakufu authorities had loosened their control over the various daimyo, relaxing the system of alternate residence *(sankin kotai)*. This development had allowed the dependents of the daimyo to return to their home domains. Thus, the number of people living in the various Edo residences of the daimyo decreased dramatically. Perhaps that is why the school was able to obtain the use of the vacant row houses. Two of the five were for Fukuzawa's family residence and the students' dining hall. The others were for student residences. The toilets that had been in each of these were eliminated and relocated outside.

Having said this, the school was not immediately transformed into a large-scale educational institution. Fukuzawa was busy with his own work, and some of the students were engaged all day in observing the state of political affairs, so not everyone was an out-and-out student.

In April 1864, Fukuzawa returned home to the Nakatsu domain for the first time in six years. One purpose for returning was to recruit people who could guide students in his place and to whom he could entrust the operations of the school. He returned to Edo with six candidates including Obata Tokujiro. As a result of this development, the school for the first time brimmed with a pervading spirit of there being an earnest dedication to learning.

The records for those who registered as students from spring 1863 through July 1864 list some 28 students, including the six he brought with him from Nakatsu. We can safely refer to this group as the first cohort of students at the new institution. However, Fukuzawa privately persuaded the Obata brothers and the others to come back to Edo with him, so he could not rely on the domain to cover their expenses. He had to struggle to support them on his own.

Before long, the reputation of the Fukuzawa's school spread. When a number of applicants from the Kishu domain applied to join, Fukuzawa responded that there were insufficient quarters for them, but they were welcome to commute as day students. The Kishu domain subsequently agreed to build a lodging house for their students, so they were accepted. These nine additions are indicated in the records for 1866.

One of those who entered that year from the Tosa domain was Baba Tatsui, who later became known as a political thinker who was active in the Freedom and People's Rights Movement. According to Baba, education within the school was still not fully organized, with the senior students instructing those who entered the school slightly after them, and so on down the ladder. The English textbook was a simple grammar book about thirty pages long and the students' pronunciation was for the most part haphazard. Once they completed the grammar text, they would go on to books on physics or geography, because there was not a single book on history, philosophy or political science. *(Kosho)*

Keio Gijuku in the Midst of Unrest

It was Fukuzawa's second trip to the United States that significantly improved the situation. His main purpose in joining the mission was to purchase a collection of English texts. We have already seen the dangerous ground he trod so as to accomplish his aims.

Upon returning in 1867, Fukuzawa immediately relocated the school. The Tsukiji Teppozu District was scheduled to become a residential area for foreigners, and the Nakatsu domain had already agreed to vacate its holdings there. He considered various options until he heard that the Arima clan was about to put its secondary residence in the Shiba Shinsenza District up for sale and he subsequently decided to buy it.

The payment for the property was to be made on January 19th, 1868, which turned out to be the day of a major political uprising in the city. By way of response, the top echelon of the Tokugawa shogunate took a hard line and set fire to the Satsuma domain residence in Edo.

The city was thrown into an uproar by rumors of war. A steward of Kimura Settsu-no-kami, who had exercised his good offices to facilitate the transaction with the Arima clan, warned Fukuzawa against making the purchase under the current circumstances, but Fukuzawa, saying that a promise was a promise, made the payment as prearranged. This episode is well known for it highlights Fukuzawa's scrupulousness. However, during his second visit to the United States, Fukuzawa was not always fastidious about finances. There was a difference between the Fukuzawa who lived as somewhat of a parasite while low in the pecking order of the bakufu, and the man who subsequently to some small degree attempted to establish his own independence.

Because those living in the Satsuma domain residence in Edo had made preparations for escape, they put up no resistance to its burning and thus no major confrontation resulted. However, when Tokugawa Yoshinobu was defeated at Toba-Fushimi and returned to Edo on February 5th, 1868, within Edo Castle there were voices calling loudly for a further rallying of the bakufu forces.

Against this backdrop, Fukuzawa remained composed. Kato Hiroyuki, a colleague of his in the bureau dealing with foreign countries, and other bakufu officials put on their ceremonial *kamishimo* robes and attempted to meet with Yoshinobu to plead their case. By contrast, Fukuzawa declared publicly that all he wanted to know was whether there was going to be a war so that he could escape if it broke out. When he was asked how many of his retainers he would take with him, if fighting did occur, and how much food he would need to prepare for everyone, he casually replied that they would escape promptly so there would be no need for provisions.

However, his attitude regarding Keio Gijuku was entirely different.

When imperial forces closed in on Edo, no small portion of the Edo populace escaped to the outskirts of the city. Some of them assumed that there would be no violence against the foreign enclaves, so they headed to Yokohama. Still others thought that if they had a certificate showing one was an employee of a foreigner it would guarantee their safety. Similar actions occurred at Keio Gijuku and when Fukuzawa asked his opinion on the matter, Obata Jinzaburo responded adamantly;

> As a proud, dignified Japanese, rather than forgetting the noble cause of patriotism and escaping into the protection of foreigners, I would rather be cut down by a blade in the hands of someone from my own country. Together we have founded this Gijuku and we have repeatedly struggled to determine what the purpose of learning is. It is nothing other than to read foreign books although we are Japanese, to aim for individual independence, and as a consequence we have strongly emphasized the authority of the country. That is the single point. To weaken in our support of this noble cause at a time such as this would be to say that we were mistaken in our purpose from the outset and our school is destroyed. Such documents as these certificates that purport the holder to be employed by foreigners can be cast into the flames.

This passage from the words of a deceased member of the school staff remains one of its fundamental precepts *(Fukuzawa Yukichi Zenshu, Volume 8)*. This was reported to be at the time when rumors were circulating that imperial forces had left Kyoto and were crossing the Fujikawa River, which would have been in March.

Fukuzawa was deeply moved and pleased by Obata's response *(Fukuzawa Zenshu Shogen)*. However, in comparison with his prior detachment from the authorities at Edo Castle, this is considerably nationalistic and zealous. Fukuzawa was not the nationalist he superficially appeared to be. His base was his strong commitment to the values he himself had chosen.

Completion of Keio Gijuku

With the coming of 1868, Fukuzawa initiated the building of a new dormitory at Shinsenza. Completed that April, the building could accommodate some one hundred students. According to Kimura Settsu-no-kami, the lodgings were both "large and magnificent." It was at this time that the school started to be called Keio Gijuku, the name by which it is now well known. It was the fourth year of Keio, and although in October the Imperial era name was changed to Meiji, it was decided that the Keio name should remain.

The pronouncement that accompanied the founding of the school was truly magnificent. It began by declaring that the school would be involved in the study of Western Studies. There was also an attestation as to the school's public character.

> We have gathered together as a corporation to found a school, to collaborate with and cultivate each other in the study of Western learning. Our purpose is not by any means private. We have opened the doors of the school wide to the public to allow all men, regardless of their status as samurai or commoner, to come and participate in our program.[20]

After touching on the translators who had been active in Nagasaki, Fukuzawa then mentions how scholars such as Aoki Kon'yo, Maeno Ranka, Katsuragawa Hoshu and Sugita Genpaku contributed to the development of Western Studies in Japan. He then affirms that the very existence of Keio Gijuku is due to the legacy of such predecessors. After commenting on the excellence of Western learning, and at the same time noting how difficult it was to attain, Fukuzawa then went on to state,

> Our group has pursued Western Studies for many years, but we have had but a glimpse of the whole. Hundreds of subjects still untouched are so extensive that we are ever lured with the vision of the ocean of wisdom before us. It is indeed a tremendous work that we have undertaken.[21]

But to hesitate just because the task seems so formidable was not, to Fukuzawa's way of thinking, "the way of the courageous person" and to fail to take on the task when there are benefits to be had contradicted the ideal of "service to the country." In order to spread Western learning, it was deemed essential to create a school that is disciplined in order to guide students. Consequently, the cohort built a school and named it temporarily Keio Gijuku, after the era in which it has been established *(Fukuzawa Yukichi Zenshu, Volume 19).*

Considering the aforementioned pronouncement that accompanied the founding of the school, it seemed an attempt to place Keio Gijuku within the historic tradition of Western learning in Japan. It also tried to tie such learning to the interests of the nation. From such conviction, the reader can grasp a view of learning that fundamentally differs from a superficial worship of the West. By this time in the school's development, Fukuzawa had lost faith in the bakufu and had absolutely no hope for the aspirations of the Satsuma and Choshu domains. Rather his burning passion for what Japan could and should be constituted the foundation on which the pronouncement was made.

The Battle of Ueno against the Brigade of Righteousness (*Shogitai*) was fought on July 4th, 1868. At daybreak, the government forces commenced an offensive sweep against the brigade. By evening, the remnants of the brigade had fled. Ironically, the officer commanding the government troops was Omura Masujiro, Fukuzawa's predecessor as head student at Ogata's *Tekijuku*.

There is a well-known story about how classes at Keio Gijuku carried on as usual during the Battle of Ueno. The book under discussion that day was Francis Wayland's *Elements of Political Economy*. Fukuzawa wrote that this volume was hard to read the first time he attempted it, but after rereading it several times, he finally began to understand its contents. He was astounded by how each phrase seemed so vivid, the prose so masterful, and the ideas so original. Reading the work was so impressive that he forgot to eat meals.

On the day of the battle, Fukuzawa intellectually challenged those students who remained at the school by comparing Keio Gijuku to the Dejima settlement at Nagasaki. In the Napoleonic Wars, the Netherlands had lost its independence, and the territories of the Dutch East Indies were occupied by France's enemy, Great Britain. There remained only one place in the world where the Dutch flag was still flying, and that happened to be the Dutch trading house located at Dejima in Nagasaki. After the defeat of Napoleon, the Netherlands were revived, and the Dutch pointed to the Dejima settlement as evidence that they had never entirely lost their independence. Fukuzawa noted that the bakufu schools had collapsed, that scholars and students had scattered, and that the new government was in no position to be concerned about schools.[22] The only place in Japan where books were being used in lectures was at Keio Gijuku. Just as the Dejima settlement was to the Netherlands, Keio Gijuku was proof that the spark of life placed in Western learning in Japan still existed. As long as the school continued, Japan would be a civilized country. In modern times, the anniversary of that momentous day is commemorated annually as Wayland Day at Keio University, and it is marked by a memorial lecture.

The Establishment of a Tuition System

Because society had been thrown into utter confusion, the pervading spirit of the school remained unsettled. Nevertheless, Fukuzawa made efforts to improve the situation. Within the school regulations there were rules that stated such things as: "in all daily activities from sleeping through to eating, care shall be taken to maintain cleanliness," and "residents shall rise early each morning, put away their bedding and sweep their own quarters."[23] These rules contrasted interestingly with the uninhibited lifestyle that Fukuzawa had experienced at Ogata's *Tekijuku.*

The school gates were closed at nine in the evening, a development that is said to have been instituted because some students slipped out at night to investigate the current state of political affairs. The drawing of swords was also prohibited, even at a student's own desk. If a student felt it absolutely necessary to practice with a sword, he would make a written notification prior to practicing and do his training somewhere outside the lecture hall where no one would be endangered. That such a regulation was necessary indicates how firmly entrenched the custom of sword practice actually was. The same was also true for regulations that prohibited the lending and borrowing of money and also the restrictions that were placed on the scribbling of graffiti. There was no small number of young men who returned to the school from participating in bloody battles. Thus, these regulations remained in place until 1871 when the school was relocated from Shinsenza to Mita. Such regulations called on all the members of the school to cooperate in providing a quiet, orderly atmosphere that was conducive to learning.

Fukuzawa was the first to institute a tuition system.

At Keio, the young men who came to learn were not referred to as students but rather as "colleagues" *(shachu)*. Entrance to the school was called an "initiation" *(nyusha)* with individuals joining the corporation formed of colleagues which was comprised of students and teachers. Rather than becoming "disciples" of the teacher who operated the school, new entrants became colleagues in a common endeavor.

In 1868, tuition fees were one *ryo* with another two *shu* being paid to the servant in charge of the dormitory. According to documents dated September of 1869, initiation into the corporation was three *ryo* as an entrance fee, with two *bu* [half a *ryo*] paid for tuition each month. Around the Obon period (mid-August) and at the end of the year, one thousand *hiki* (approximately one *ryo* and one *bu*) were to be paid. However, no ceremonial cords *(mizuhiki)* or ceremonial strips *(noshi)* were to be attached to the sums involved. If payment was in excess of what was owed, change would be returned to the person making the payment. *(Kosho)*

The Autobiography describes the system:

> Until that time, almost all the private schools in Japan imitated the Chinese system, in which upon entering, the students gave the head of the school an entrance fee *(sokushu)*. Out of respect for the sensei, they brought presents to him twice a year—once at Bon in summer and once at the end of the year. Sometimes this was money and other times it was a gift, taken to the sensei's house in traditional wrapping with cords and formal *noshi* attached....It seemed to me that no teacher would do his utmost under such a system. Instruction is work and a man should be paid for his work. Whatever others may say, we would openly charge a set fee for our instruction. We created a new term, *jugyoryo*, for "tuition" and charged each student two *bu* per month. These fees were divided among the advanced students who had been designated to carry on instruction.[24]

"At that time a teacher boarding in the school could live on four *ryo* a month; so if we had this amount for each from the tuition collected every month, we would have sufficient to keep ourselves alive. Any amount over and above that was to be used for the maintenance of the buildings."[25]

Whether in China or Japan, under the traditional system of education, the financial burden on students was light and depended on the beneficence of the teacher. In return for the limited expense incurred, it was expected that students would continue to respect their sensei forever. In other words, students were not materially independent but at the same time they were spiritually subordinate. However, respect received through such material subordination does not constitute true respect.

Under the new system, students bore some degree of the material burden but at the same time they were not forced to respect their instructors. In his *Science as a Vocation*, Max Weber wrote that in the United States paying tuition to study was in effect purchasing learning, which was entirely different from the system in Germany. A similar thing could be said of Fukuzawa's new school when compared to traditional education.

An additional point that deserves attention is that it would have been difficult for Fukuzawa to develop the school without modern management practices. As a result of competition between such organizations, schools would have developed. In developing his institution, what Fukuzawa arrived at might be described as the polar opposite of Ogata's *Tekijuku.*

The gist of the aforementioned tuition system is recorded in the New Order for Keio Gijuku *(Keio Gijuku Shingi)* dated September of 1869. This was a document which confirmed the essential framework of the school, at the time when Keio Gijuku established a branch school in a rented row house on the estate of the Okudaira domain primary residence in Shiodome. Thus, it might be assumed that this plan of action existed prior to 1869.

Strategies for Enlightenment

Fukuzawa's actions during this period were both anti-bakufu and anti-new government. They were, however, stimulated by a sense of patriotism.

Although invited to take a post within the fledgling government on numerous occasions, Fukuzawa declined each time. On March 27th, 1868, Fukuzawa also received from the bakufu a formal letter appointing him to the position of *Otsukaiban*, a kind of domestic inspector. However, in citing ill health, he again declined to act. On July 27th Fukuzawa submitted his resignation from his post as interpreter and translator, to which he had been appointed for the European mission, and his resignation was accepted in September. On July 29th, Fukuzawa was ordered to come to the capital by the new government, but he again failed to do so citing ill health. He was criticized for this as showing lack of respect in not acceding to these orders.

Fukuzawa's attitude in denying the advances of both sides was only natural. On one hand the bakufu seemed to have little vitality left, while on the other, Fukuzawa saw the new government as promoting the expulsion of foreigners.

For a short time following the Meiji Restoration, Fukuzawa refrained from actively speaking in public. One clear exception, however, were his efforts to extricate his old friend Enomoto Takeaki from difficulties.

Fukuzawa did not yet have a firm idea concerning the form Keio Gijuku was to take. In a letter he wrote in 1869—the date of which is not clear, but it seems to have been written in May or thereafter—Fukuzawa himself proposed the idea of making Keio Gijuku into a government-owned institution.

According to the letter, Keio Gijuku had only two hundred students at that time, a number considered insufficient to bring enlightenment to the country. It also stated that Fukuzawa had already proposed making the school both government-owned and operated, thus allowing the state bureaucracy to tend to the majority of the syllabus. Such a development would have allowed the instructors (seven or eight advanced students together with Fukuzawa) to travel throughout the country giving lectures.

From the perspective of Fukuzawa's consistent view that education be independent, the sentiments expressed in the letter seem a complete contradiction. We can only assume that, given the uncertainty of the situation in the government, Fukuzawa was contemplating various means by which he could conduct activities to promote social enlightenment.

The government conceived the idea of having the land and population registers of the domains returned to the Meiji Emperor *(hanseki hokan)* and the lords of Satsuma, Choshu, Tosa and Hizen requested permission to comply on March 2nd, 1869. The government subsequently accepted their request on July 25th. It also appeared that the new government would assume a stance that favored enlightenment.

Even as such developments occurred, what might have happened if the government had acceded to Fukuzawa's proposal? Perhaps his ideas would have been more widely reflected in public policy. Or perhaps he would have been discarded along the way. If that had happened, Fukuzawa's personal standing, without the foundation of Keio Gijuku, would have weakened. In hindsight, it is fortunate that what he proposed at the time never came to pass.

Because the government did not respond to this proposal, Fukuzawa could pay special attention to the development of Keio Gijuku. He could also disseminate the cause of enlightenment through his writings.

There is another interesting comment from Fukuzawa on his strategy for further extending the cause of enlightenment during this period. It comes from a letter in which he declined an offer of work in Wakayama for a stipend of 6,000 *koku*. The letter is addressed to Matsuyama Toan, and it was dated March 14th, 1869.

In the letter, Fukuzawa wrote that he was not merely flattering the ethos of Wakayama in saying that within the exchanges he had had with the people of many different provinces, the only ones who seemed amiable and broad-minded were the inhabitants of Kishu (Wakayama). However, Fukuzawa argued that the people of Kishu suffered because "their education is insufficient and therefore they lack a foundation." Thus, they are "swept along by the trends of the times."

Fukuzawa explained to Matsuyama Toan that school education was difficult, particularly when it came to the reading of English materials. He wrote that it was impossible to encourage students to abruptly launch forth and attempt to read books in Western languages when they could not sufficiently read books in Chinese or Japanese. Fukuzawa also stated that it was difficult to employ instructors, commenting that even the government was eagerly seeking people who could teach. However, not many qualified teachers seemed eager to ply their trade in the provinces.

Therefore, in addressing Matsuyama, Fukuzawa suggested that the first thing to do was to have temple school *(terakoya)* teachers within the domain not take up Confucius' *The Analects* or the *Teikin-orai* as texts for instruction, but instead to study materials on subjects such as geography, physics and national history, before moving to books that explained foreign languages, ethics and philosophy. Once this was done, students could take on works in the original languages.

> I venture to say that if the individual is independent, his family is independent; if the family is independent, the country will be independent and so shall everything be. In order to make the individual independent, it is essential to first extend to him knowledge. In order to extend that knowledge, it is essential that people be able to read Western books. To prepare to read Western books, it is first of all important to inspire people through learning that broadens their point of view. To

do that, it is essential to increase the number of Western works translated into Japanese, to immediately reform the instruction provided by the *terakoya*. It is my hope that through conversations day and night they will naturally learn about all things in the universe and all the nations of the world.

Fukuzawa foresaw this as the proper order necessary to realistically expand education.

Determination of Copyright

It was a period when up-to-date knowledge was in great demand, so Fukuzawa published translations and his own writings one after another. To accomplish this, he created his own publishing business. It is said that when he purchased paper, Fukuzawa normally paid 200 *ryo* or 300 *ryo* a batch; however, on one occasion he purchased a batch of particularly fine quality worth 1,000 *ryo*.

In 1869 Fukuzawa published in succession *Shochu bankoku ichiran* [Pocket Dictionary of the World], *Eikoku gijiindan* [British Parliament], *Shin-ei kosai shimatsu* [Anglo-Chinese Relations] and *Sekai kunizukushi* [All about the World]. Of these, *Shochu bankoku ichiran* was a handbook on human geography while *Eikoku giji indan* explained the British parliamentary system, the latter work being written at the request of the Kishu domain. *Shin-ei kosai shimatsu* was an explanation of the details of the Second Opium War, the subsequent negotiations between China and Britain, and the Treaty of Tianjin. According to Tomita Masafumi, the original text that Fukuzawa used when writing this book might have been one that he purchased in London. *Sekai kunizukushi* was an enlightening work that, by using a clever seven-and-five-syllable meter, introduced to the reader the geography of the world. Although difficult to mimic the rhythm of the original Japanese text in English, the content may nevertheless be simply explained. “The world is wide and the countries are many, but it is divided roughly into five parts—Asia, Africa, Europe, North and South America, and another island in the southern seas called Oceania.” Tomita felt the flowing rhythm of such Japanese text to be a form of martial song. Reflecting on this work in later years, Fukuzawa commented that such phrasing was overly-simplified. Thus, he purposely put a difficult passage in the opening section of the book to counterbalance such simplicity. This action proved that an extraordinary person like Fukuzawa could sometimes feel a bit embarrassed *(Fukuzawa Zenshu Shogen).*

These books, with *Conditions in the West* at the top of the list, all sold well. So did numerous pirated editions, particularly in the Kyoto-Osaka area. The pirating of published works has a long history, but during the period that saw the end of the bakufu and the subsequent imperial restoration, the phenomenon was rampant. Such circumstances stemmed from the combination of a strong desire for new knowledge and the state of social upheaval. Fukuzawa was perhaps its greatest victim.

In a letter to Yamaguchi Ryozo dated May 31st, 1868, Fukuzawa wrote,

> In the countries of the West, counterfeits and fake articles are strictly banned and there are laws protecting what is called copyright. In the Kyoto-Osaka area, however, there is absolutely nothing that hinders such practices and disreputable characters simply do it for their own profit. Carefree and enjoying themselves, they steal the hard work of others. Unknowledgeable themselves, they rob others of their knowledge. Circumstances as they are, I have suspended writing and am resigned to finding another way of making a living.

Fukuzawa protested against this illicit use of others’ work in November 1868, and he called for strict enforcement against infringements.

In June 1869, regulations regarding published works were established that prohibited illicit publishing. Provisions were also made for fines. However, the reality was that the regulations were not enforced. Thus, a large number of pirated copies of *An Encouragement of Learning* circulated in the market when the book was first published in 1872. It would take approximately ten years before the concept of copyright spread in Japan.

Fukuzawa had confidence in knowledge and because he had made back-breaking efforts to realize and disseminate it, he made copyright a priority issue. The government had an obligation to protect the proper rights of the nation's citizens and the citizens also had the right to demand such protections from the government. This conceptualization was a fundamental principle of the modern nation-state and it was one that Fukuzawa frequently asserted. Over the copyright issue, Fukuzawa keenly felt the need for establishing this principle.

Chapter 7

An Encouragement of Learning

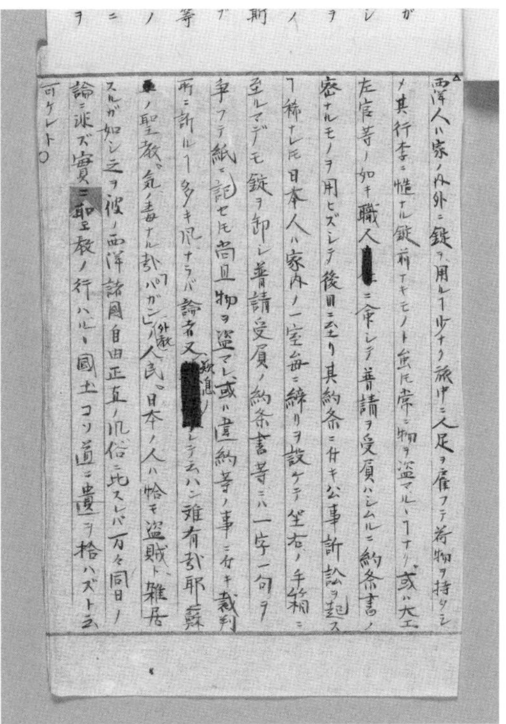

Manuscript of the 15th installment of *An Encouragement of Learning.*
(Courtesy of Keio University Fukuzawa Memorial Center)

When Was *An Encouragement of Learning* Actually Written?

In June 1870, Fukuzawa came down with typhus and at one point was critically ill. By early autumn, however, he had fully recovered. In October, he took his family to the hot springs at Atami in order to recuperate, and this trip led to what would become a sort of family tradition.

Around this time, the gap between the views held by Fukuzawa and the new government gradually contracted. This was because the government showed itself to be on track with respect to its promotion of civilization and enlightenment. In November, Fukuzawa called on Iwakura Tomomi to request permission to use the former Shimabara domain residence in Mita, and approval was received the next month. In February 1871, he relocated his household to Mita, and this was followed by the school in May. In 1872, the land, which Fukuzawa had until then rented from the government, transferred its ownership to Keio Gijuku. In exchange for the land, at the request of the Tokyo government, Fukuzawa investigated the details of a policing system, and thus he became one of the contributors to the modern policing methods later introduced to Japan.

In November 1870, Fukuzawa returned to Nakatsu to get his mother. At the time, scholars of Western learning were still not safe. In Osaka, Fukuzawa's life was targeted by Asabuki Eiji, who would later become a confidante, while in Nakatsu, Masuda Sotaro had intended Fukuzawa harm.

With the abolition of the domains and establishment of administrative prefectures in 1871, the revolution that constituted the imperial restoration reached its climax. In some regions of the country, feudal families who had exercised power for several centuries were uprooted. The government, which had until that time been considered a Satsuma-Choshu duopoly, was suddenly transformed when those domains disappeared along with the rest. In *Fukuo hyakuyowa* [More Discourse of Fukuzawa], around this time, Fukuzawa wrote that when he and his cohorts gathered in small groups they always commented that they were willing to face their graves at any time because at the very least they had witnessed a grand transformation in the fortunes of the new government. Within a short period of time, half of the central figures of the government left the country on a long-term inspection tour of the United States and Europe. This odyssey was known as the Iwakura Mission. It offered decisive proof that the new government did actually intend to bring about the introduction of Western civilization to Japan. *An Encouragement of Learning* was written in the midst of Fukuzawa's enthusiasm.

Although not planned at the outset, *An Encouragement of Learning* ended up being comprised of some 17 installments. In all likelihood, Fukuzawa only intended to write an initial piece, but because that was so well-received, he continued to add installments one after the other. The initial piece was published in March 1872, while the seventeenth and final installment appeared in November 1876. The titles of the pamphlets which formed the different installments or sections along with their publication dates are shown below:

Installment one
  March 1872
Installment two
  November 1873
  The equality of men
Installment three
  December 1873
  The equality of nations
  National independence through personal independence
Installment four
  January 1874

Installment fourteen
- March 1875
- A criticism of people's thoughts
- The meaning of the word *sewa*

Installment fifteen
- July 1876
- Methodical doubt and selective judgment

Installment sixteen
- August 1876
- The spirit of independence in everyday affairs
- The compatibility of intention and activity

Installment seventeen
- November 1876
- On popularity

At a glance, one can see that about a year and eight months elapsed between the publication of installments one and two. Following on, installments two through eleven appeared over a period of seven months. Thus, these ten may be considered to constitute a series. Five months later, installments twelve and thirteen appeared, followed three months later by installment fourteen. Then, after a long break of one year and four months came installments fifteen through seventeen.

The above timeline coincided with some of the major events of the early Meiji period. The initial installment of *An Encouragement of Learning* first appeared just after the abolition of the domains and the establishment of the administrative prefectures. The departure of the Iwakura Mission also fell around this time. Although Fukuzawa appeared to have completed the work at one stage just after the government became divided during the debate over sending a military expedition to Korea *(seikanron)*, he resumed writing and did not get finished until just prior to the outbreak of the

Satsuma Rebellion of 1877. Indeed, *An Encouragement of Learning* was written in the final stages of the Meiji Restoration.

In the foreword to the work, Fukuzawa comments on how widely the book had been read. Including pirated editions, it sold 220,000 copies, and considering that Japan's population was 35 million, that meant one copy for every 160 people. Fukuzawa referred to this as "the trend for literature to spread rapidly." Literature normally suggests the novel, but in those days, it indicated a broad range of writing including history, essays and other genres.

Equality of Opportunity and Inequality of Circumstances

Installment one of *An Encouragement of Learning* opens with the famous line, "Heaven, it is said, does not create one person above or below another."[26] As the caveat "it is said" implies, the origins of this argument do not lie with Fukuzawa. Fukuzawa's thinking was deeply influenced by the ideology of the American Revolution. This passage here may have been suggested by the Declaration of Independence; however, it does not lack merit simply because it is not original. Its intense message of demolishing deep-rooted, outmoded customs surely had an impact because Fukuzawa remembered it and wrote it down.

In the first section of *An Encouragement of Learning*, Fukuzawa then continues, "Nevertheless, as we broadly survey the human scene, there are the wise and the stupid, the rich and the poor, the noble and the lowly, whose conditions seem to differ as greatly as Heaven and Hell."[27] In short, his argument is that although everyone should be equal, the reality is that they are not. Fukuzawa posits that the cause of this inequality has to do with learning.

Of the work that people do within society, there are both difficult and easy occupations. Those who undertake difficult tasks obtain a high social status, while those who complete easier work are viewed more modestly. Professions that require care such as medicine, academia, the bureaucracy, high commerce or agriculture are viewed as noble pursuits. What determines whether or not an occupation is considered thus is the power that comes from learning.

Some readers might be dissatisfied with such observations, pointing to the perceived unfair advantage of children of wealthy families. In contemporary society, they might note the fact that parents whose children attend the University of Tokyo tend to have higher average incomes.

Such arguments are certainly valid. However, compared to the period prior to Fukuzawa and his writings, an age in which almost everything was determined by birth, the social mobility that was offered by learning definitely represented a major change. In recognizing this development, Fukuzawa both places learning to the forefront of his arguments and welcomes the change it brings.

So what did Fukuzawa actually mean by "learning"? What was the nature of the beast? In laying out his arguments, he referred to the study of obscure Chinese characters, the reading of difficult texts and the composition of poetry as being impractical pursuits. Within Fukuzawa's mind, learning was to be applicable and responsive to everyday life. Thus, as a first step he exhorted his compatriots to obtain both literacy along with numeric proficiency, with the aid of an abacus. Next he suggested a syllabus comprised of geography, physics, history, economics and ethics. Once such steps had been completed, Fukuzawa felt his compatriots were ready for Western books. With such knowledge he contended, individuals could go about their duties and manage their family businesses, armed with an independence that contributed to the individual, to the world and to the nation.

In the pursuit of learning, however, it is important to recognize "responsibility." Individuals are equal in that they are free to act as they wish, but there is a difference between freedom and selfishness, and the fine line between the two lies "at the point where one does or does not infringe upon the freedom of others."[28] Such an interpretation is not just avoiding direct infringement upon the rights of others. Rather it also includes pleasures and dissipations that might harm social morality, even if such involve a person using his own funds. Thus, in addition to the ideas Fukuzawa expressed regarding the individual, his conceptualization of freedom possessed a public persona.

Freedom and its accompanying responsibilities accrue not only to an individual but to a nation as well. Fukuzawa felt that Japan could not remain the only country closed off from the rest of the world. He felt that what one has one should share with others, and what one does not have one can receive from others. His argument was that nations should mutually teach each other and learn from each other.

> Such an attitude, based on reason, implies acknowledging one's guilt even before the black slaves of Africa; but it also means standing on principle without fear of the warships of England and America. It further implies that if this nation is disgraced, every Japanese citizen, to the last man, must sacrifice his life to prevent the decline of her prestige and glory. National independence entails all of these things.[29]

This is arguably the most significant passage in *An Encouragement of Learning*.

To reiterate, the freedom and equality of the individual is, by necessity, firmly bound to the independence of a nation. The first half of Fukuzawa's life can be seen as challenging convention, while the second half became constructive; yet throughout his life, the theme of national independence occupies a central position.

All men are equal, and no rank comes from birth. It is appropriate that one not treat a government official with disrespect, but this is not due to the dignity of that person's status. Respect should be accorded to him because he deals with the nation's laws. This is entirely different from the former bakufu period when even the physical possessions of the shogun had to be treated with awe and deference.

In continuing his arguments, Fukuzawa stated that people were free to learn, and that opportunities to do so were more widely available than ever before. Despite this, he felt that some people failed to notice their own ignorance and that it was outrageous that they then blamed others for the fact that they had fallen into poverty. He felt it was only natural to say that "there must be a harsh government over stupid people." If people pursued learning and advanced toward a pervading spirit of civilization, Fukuzawa felt that government would naturally become more broad-minded and magnanimous. He believed that those who think of their country should diligently pursue learning, broaden their knowledge and attain virtue.

The preceding discussion is an overview of the pamphlet first published. It later became Section One of *An Encouragement of Learning*. It spelt out what were then Fukuzawa's learning aims. Namely, he hoped to open a school for the Nakatsu domain. However, he considered the possibility that the work might reach a broader audience in the future, so he noted in a postscript that the pamphlet was printed at Keio Gijuku so as to make his thoughts available to colleagues.

National Independence through Personal Independence

After a hiatus of almost two years, at the end of 1873, Fukuzawa began publishing the second and subsequent pamphlets of the series. This continuation probably resulted from the success of the first pamphlet and the demand that arose for more detailed discussions. Fukuzawa had also given matters deeper consideration and must have felt there was some value in the dissemination of his ideas.

In his foreword to the second pamphlet, Fukuzawa stated that learning could be divided into "immaterial spheres" (including theology and philosophy) and "material" spheres. Regardless of this distinction, being able to read was essential, but even beyond that, one had to learn how to discern the principle of things *(monogoto no dori)*. This argument was Fukuzawa's criticism of the time-honored tradition of rote memorization. What good was it to learn the laws of commerce and not be able to execute a transaction? What value was there in devoting one's energies to mastering Western learning and then not being able to earn an independent living? Rather than becoming a "wholesaler of letters" or a "food-consuming dictionary," Fukuzawa felt that one should aim to realize learning that could be put to practical use.

Following his forward to the pamphlet, Fukuzawa then discussed his belief as to "the equality of men." For Fukuzawa, equality did not mean equivalence in state or circumstance. Rather it meant an equality in essential human rights, a universal principle. In his Japanese translation of the Western principles of "human rights," Fukuzawa originally used the term *kenri tsugi*. The character *ken* was used to imply "authority or "strength," while *ri* was used to denote "reason" or "logic." Meanwhile, *tsugi* was not related to ideas of "justice" or "rights" that would differ from person to person and situation to situation, rather it offered the contextual underpinnings of the sentiment of "human rights" that would apply universally to all situations. In other words, "human rights" were seen by Fukuzawa as a form of universal justice that was consistent under all circumstances, regardless of a person's status. Such holds true for all human beings. His translation is close to the English word "right." Shortening the expression from *kenri tsugi* —the latter term referring to universal justice— Fukuzawa used the term *kengi*. He explained this decision, thus: instead of the character 利 (*ri*, interest) in *kenri* (権利), as the translation for "right." I believe that it would be better to use *kenri tsugi* or *kengi*.

In other words, the rights one has at birth are the same for all human beings. The class distinctions observed during the period of the bakufu were disgraceful. The distinctions between samurai and commoner were bad enough, but even worse were the distinctions between the government and the people. Ultimately all the people were equal. The peasants grew rice to feed the people; the townspeople sold things as a business; the government established laws to control evil people and protect the good. There was no inherent difference in the human rights they possessed. Fukuzawa saw the fundamental relationship as a contract between the people and the government that carried out its duties which were entrusted to it by the people.

In the third volume, Fukuzawa defended the "equality of all nations." Just as all men are equal, so are all nations. He felt that nations may differ in their outward appearance but they possessed the same inherent rights. The powerful nations should not be allowed to unjustly oppress the weak. And in much the same way that the external differences between people vary according to whether or not they had pursued learning, Fukuzawa felt that nations differed according to whether they made efforts to advance themselves or not. There were numerous examples from ancient times of poor nations becoming prosperous through the diligent efforts of the people; the reverse also occurred.

"If we Japanese begin to pursue learning with spirit and energy, in order to achieve personal independence and enrich and strengthen the nation, why would we need to fear the power of the Western nations?"[30]

In the second half of this third installment, Fukuzawa discusses as a topic the idea of "National independence through personal independence." In opening his argument, he conveys the view that "persons without a spirit of personal independence will not have deep concern for their country." In other words, unless a person possesses a spirit of independence and is capable of realizing that their own destiny is tied to the destiny of their country, they shall not give serious thought to that country's fate. Individuals capable of seeing the fate of their state as their own are called the nation (*kokumin*). Without numerous such citizens, a state cannot be maintained, and persons who are strongly reliant on the power of others will not support it. In Japan's Period of Warring States, with the mere defeat of Imagawa Yoshimoto at the Battle of Okehazama (1560), his family's powerbase in Suruga Province completely collapsed. By contrast, in the Franco-Prussian War, even though Napoleon III was defeated and subsequently capitulated after the Battle of Sedan (1870), France still remained France. Fukuzawa used these events to illustrate this point: while the people of Suruga were entirely dependent on Imagawa Yoshimoto and his fortunes in war, the French people fought all-out to defend their country.

In expanding his arguments further, Fukuzawa then stated that "those without the spirit of independence within themselves will also be unable to exercise their right of independence when in contact with foreigners outside." Thus, it follows that those without a spirit of independence themselves shall grow to rely on others. People who grow to rely on others also come to fear them. Such relationships become habitual in that the fearful seek to curry favor with the feared. Fukuzawa felt that the excessive sycophancy that some of his compatriots exhibited towards government officials was typical of such relationships. Under the rigid government of the Tokugawa bakufu, having a populace in such a state was undoubtedly convenient. However, in the "new world" that confronted Japan, with its formal relations with foreign nations, such people were detrimental to the country's welfare.

> For example, if a merchant from a rural area plucks up enough courage to dare to engage in trade with the foreigners at Yokohama, he will first be frightened at their physical size, then at the amount of their money,

> the size of their trading houses, the speed of their steamships. He may utterly lose heart.... However, this will be the loss not only of that person, but also of Japan.[31]

Moving on, the third issue that Fukuzawa sought to address under the topic of "National independence through personal independence" was as follows: "those who lack the spirit of independence rely on the power of others and sometimes perpetuate evil deeds."[32] In expressing this sentiment, Fukuzawa argued that if a person does not have confidence in his own power, he cannot actualize his own strength but will rely on others to try to protect his rights. As an example of this phenomenon, he referred to the days of the bakufu, and the unscrupulous merchants who used their influence with the *Go-Sanke*—the three branch families of the Tokugawa shogunate—in order to threaten the other daimyo. In contemporary times, Fukuzawa claimed that such people might well attempt to utilize the prestige of foreigners in order to realize their own agendas. With these three points, Fukuzawa argued that the spirit of independence represented the foundation upon which national independence must be established.

The "Spirit" of the People

The pamphlet that came to be recognized as installment four of *An Encouragement of Learning* sought to discuss the relationship between the government and the people. In this section, Fukuzawa declared the importance of the private sector. An equilibrium of power was needed to maintain any system, and here we refer to "balance." The same principle obtained within a state, in which governmental power must be balanced by the power of its people.

What Japan was lacking, in comparison with the West, was scholarship, business and law. The reason for this was the ignorance and illiteracy of its people. Even if the government gathered common [universal] knowledge and encouraged initiative, things would not be rectified easily. "The government is as despotic as it was before, while the people continue to be ignorant, spiritless and powerless." This resulted from a lack of balance between the government and the people. Consequently, no progress could be made toward civilization.

What was needed was a new spirit. The government's despotic and oppressive spirit continued unchanged and the people remained obsequious and insincere. It was the scholars of Western learning who had to play the role of eradicating the old spirit of the people. Yet many of those scholars entered the government, humiliating themselves with servile petitions to the administration. The situation was such that Japan had a government but did not yet have a nation. For that reason, Fukuzawa says, he would not enter government service but will stand outside it and devote himself to carrying out his responsibility to change the spirit of the people.

This opinion naturally attracted the attention of many scholars of Western learning. The issue was debated in the *Meirokusha* [Meiji Six Society], which was founded in Meiji 6 [1873] and in which he participated, and the debate continued in the *Meiroku zasshi*. While there was partial refutation, there was little direct counterargument.

The fifth in the series of pamphlets which later became installment five of *An Encouragement of Learning* was titled "Speech delivered January 1st, 1874." Its basis was the written record of a lecture Fukuzawa had delivered to his Keio Gijuku colleagues. In the speech, Fukuzawa expressed joy that Japan has been able to maintain its independence as had Keio Gijuku, and once again he asserted that such independence could only be maintained if the people further develop their own independent outlook.

It was fine that the government had recently promoted reforms in education and military affairs, but that was precisely what is unsettling, because the foundations of education and military affairs are that spirit of independence. In Japan, from ancient times, the government had firmly held all authority and power and had intervened in all important matters. In Japan currently, he pointed out, the people bustled about following the directions of the government, but the independent spirit of the people was in retreat. The reason for this was that the government not only had power but it also had a monopoly on knowledge, taking the initiative in everything from schools, military affairs, and railroads to telegraphic communications.

In putting forward his argument, Fukuzawa expressed the view that civilization could not arise only from the government, nor could it come from small people. It must arise from something in-between, the middle-class that would serve as the pillar on which government would stand. To demonstrate his argument, Fukuzawa referred to James Watt, Adam Smith and George Stephenson whom he described as "great scholars belonging to the middle class." "They were neither government administrators nor the laboring masses."[33]

At present, he wrote, "the only Japanese in the middle class who can advocate national independence and modern civilization are the scholars. But most of these same scholars are unsatisfied with their present positions. They are going into government service instead."[34] Keio Gijuku, however, had not lost its independence, and—Fukuzawa encouraged his followers—they should continue their studies, put what they learned into practice, and in concert with the government promote the advancement of Japanese civilization.

The fourth and fifth installments that became sections of *An Encouragement of Learning* employed somewhat abstract concepts and their contents were rather theoretical. This makes them considerably different from the preceding three and following twelve installments. It is perhaps likely that Fukuzawa was hoping to engage in a sort of theoretical debate with intellectuals who were close to the government. The content of what was discussed in these pamphlets began to approach what Fukuzawa hoped to broach in *An Outline of a Theory of Civilization*.

With the sixth pamphlet in the series which later became a section of *An Encouragement of Learning*, the tone employed by Fukuzawa returned to a simpler style. However, both the sixth and seventh installments invited public criticism because of their provocative content.

Given the titles "The importance of national laws" and "The duties of the citizens of the nation," respectively, these two works effectively formed a single treatise. Fukuzawa argued that the nation had two roles to play. As sovereign, the nation brought people together to form a country, enact laws and implement them. The second role was as subject of the government. Because the nation entrusted the government with the responsibility to administer the affairs of the country, it must obey the laws and not resort to taking the law into its own hands. Actions such as the revenge taken by the retainers of Ako for the death of their lord were out of the question, and with this in mind, Fukuzawa emphasized that anyone who plotted the assassination of a political opponent was absolutely unforgiveable.

What course of action was open to the people when the government illegally exceeds the powers delegated to it? Fukuzawa posited three choices. One was to simply obey the government at the cost of the people surrendering their integrity and violating their duties as men, but Fukuzawa viewed this as undesirable. It simply promoted apathy. The second recourse was to resist the government by force of arms. Fukuzawa considered this extremely dangerous because it led to the formation of political cliques and could give rise to civil war. The third path was for the people to be prepared to sacrifice their lives in order to uphold their just principles. Through non-violent civil disobedience, they could resist the government, and if they sacrificed their own lives to uphold these righteous claims, Fukuzawa felt their acts would eventually win over the hearts of the government officials.

We cannot help wonder about the realistic nature or effectiveness of Fukuzawa's suggestions. It seems that he had retreated from the contract theory of government that he had pushed since the publication of *Conditions in the West*. The reason for such an impression lies with the fact that the arguments set forth in the pamphlet were written at the beginning of 1874. In other words, as a result of the political disturbance that arose regarding the debate that raged over sending a military expedition to Korea *(Seikanron)*, the government split into two factions, with five of its members deciding to withdraw: Saigo Takamori, Itagaki Taisuke, Goto Shojiro, Eto Shimpei and Soejima Taneomi. Fukuzawa probably felt that such a development was a serious matter, in that it might well lead to the collapse or disintegration of the Meiji government and all it had achieved.

In "The duties of the citizens of the nation," Fukuzawa described the parable of a servant named Gonsuke, who lost one *ryo* of gold whilst on an errand for his master. At a loss as to how to apologize, he removes his loincloth, ties it to a branch and proceeds to hang himself. It is a truly pitiful incident. However, the story of the so-called loyal retainers who accomplished their vendetta and thus salvaged the honor of their lord was similar. Neither of these self-sacrifices was of benefit to the advance of civilization. They did not die for the cause of justice. The only one who did was a man named Sakura Sogoro, who petitioned the shogun on behalf of the peasants for tax relief.

The argument Fukuzawa wanted to make was clear; however, the method he employed invited a storm of criticism. There was criticism that his views insulted someone like the warrior hero Kusunoki Masashige. For certain readers there was the implication that Kusunoki's name was being associated with that of Gonsuke, a mere servant. However, Fukuzawa made no mention of the warrior hero at all. He responded with a long diatribe in the *Choya Shimbun* (a newspaper). The combined pseudonym he employed for this purpose, Keio Gijuku-Gokuro Senban, also raised eyebrows. The literal English equivalent of Gokuro Senban might be "you might have spared yourself the trouble." Without mincing words and filled with fight, Fukuzawa went on the attack. As Koizumi Shinzo explains, Fukuzawa was not one to avoid saying something that might cause offense. Fukuzawa's view was "if something had to be said, there was no point in saying it unless it provoked a debate." *(An Encouragement of Learning—Comment)*

One Should Not Control Others with One's Own Beliefs

"Respect for the independence of others" was the title of the eighth installment of the series that later became *An Encouragement of Learning*. In this pamphlet, Fukuzawa discussed freedom and criticized certain aspects of feudal morality. In particular, he targeted those aspects that placed men over women and superiors over their subordinates.

Every human being was independent but could not live alone, and that meant that human relationships develop. However, as long as one did not infringe on the rights of others, one was free to conduct oneself as one pleased. Some claim, however, that one should act in obedience to the will of others and not express one's own mind. The shogun should surmise the will of the emperor; the daimyo should surmise the will of the shogun; the chief retainers should surmise the will of the daimyo; and the stewards should surmise the will of the chief retainer. If one followed this argument, there is no sovereign independence at all.

The principle of "triple obedience" for women—in Kaibara Ekken's *The Great Learning for Women*—receives special scorn from Fukuzawa. According to these principles, a woman was "to obey her parents when young, to obey her husband when married, and to obey her children when old."[35] In this scheme of things, asked Fukuzawa, where did the woman exercise her own will? He asserted that such thinking should be abandoned and that people should be independent and self-respecting.

As is evident here as well, Fukuzawa paid serious attention to the status of women. He strongly opposed the view that women were in some way inferior to men. This undoubtedly resulted from his view of his own mother. Fukuzawa was frequently faulted for not being progressive enough, but some of the more militant thinkers were often rather contemptuous of women.

The ninth installment was a continuation of its predecessor, and in it, Fukuzawa took what he had discussed in the eighth installment and then painted a picture as to how these ideas might be applied to the lives of people in society.

The work of human beings was first and foremost to provide themselves with clothing, food and shelter. Yet if that is all one did, one was only "a pupil of the ant," who has not fulfilled the true aim of being human. Humans existed as participants in human intercourse. Law, learning and politics all served the purpose of human intercourse. They brought forth progress of civilization, and it was the duty of human beings to carry out their respective roles in the promotion of civilization.

This discussion was continued even further in the tenth installment. To pursue learning, Fukuzawa says, was to improve one's mind. One should aspire to learn not just to provide a livelihood for oneself and one's immediate family, but also to contribute to the security of one's own country and the world as a whole. Fukuzawa promoted practical learning and at the same time contends that such learning should aim not simply at an individual's success in life but at something far broader.

The eleventh installment entitled "The falsity of the idea of moral subordination" was intimately connected with the eighth installment. Furthermore, it strongly criticized the Confucian view of human relationships.

Fukuzawa asserted that one ought not to introduce the analogy of the

Confucian view of parent-child relationships into the conception of how the ruler and the ruled interact. The monarch, in Asian countries, had been called the parent of the people, but that notion was patently false and completely undesirable. Fukuzawa offered an illustration to demonstrate this belief. If the master of a shop tightly controls all the decision-making authority within his shop and does not allow either the head clerk or any of the shop attendants to have any role in deciding things, they will simply carry out their tasks in a way that avoids displeasing the shopkeeper. Morning and evening the head clerk will keep watch over the master's moods, while at the same time embezzling money from the shop coffers. The problem is not that men are untrustworthy, but that the master is despotic in the shop's management. One can easily agree with Fukuzawa that a sense of responsibility can come into being only if responsibility is divided.

Among the samurai who proclaimed their loyalty to their lord at the cost of their lives, cases where these same men took bribes were not rare. Fukuzawa referred to such men as "accomplished pseudo gentlemen." On the surface, they wore the logic that has been provided to them, but they have not internalized it, so they could not be relied upon at all.

The actions of Fukuzawa during his second trip to America are a case in point. He was not given proper status as a member of the mission, and consequently he felt no shame at having the bakufu pay the shipping costs for the books that he purchased and brought back to Japan. Yet needless to say, there is a difference between "affected moral subservience" *(kyoshoku no meibun)* and "true professional duty" *(jitsu no shokubun)*. It was this difference between ostentatious names and actual responsibilities that Fukuzawa emphasized here.

The Method and Attitude of Learning

In the twelfth installment, Fukuzawa took up the method [the way, the plan and the means] of learning. First, he encouraged "speech" *(enzetsu)*, meaning public speaking. On one occasion in the *Meirokusha*, there was a discussion about whether or not it was possible to deliver a true speech in Japanese, and Fukuzawa stood up and gave an off-the-cuff presentation to prove that it could be done. Fukuzawa had previously done some research on how Rennyo Shonin, the Buddhist priest, had delivered his sermons. Based on what he found, Fukuzawa concluded that such discourses were just one step away from full-fledged speeches in that the style Rennyo used to deliver his addresses could be easily understood.

The essence of learning, Fukuzawa asserted is "observation" (the perceiving of things) and "reasoning" (the construction of logic). In my own view, these issues have remained points of weakness within Japanese scholarship until the present.

Fukuzawa further stressed the importance of "refinement of conduct," that is, attaining more lofty views on the topic being studied. At the level of the individual, the person should not be focused solely on gaining high social status. It was regrettable, he wrote, that in the selection of a school, parents were often concerned only about issues such as the influence of school discipline over a student's moral life. In the final analysis, the decline of India and Turkey were due to the fact that the minds of the people were introspective in that they focused only on their own country. Fukuzawa believed that one's view should be outward in order to see the rest of the world.

"The damage caused by envy," the thirteenth installment in the series, is extremely interesting in that Fukuzawa contended that immorality was generally simply the negation of morality. There is only a paper-thin difference between stinginess and thrift, bravery and recklessness, and boorishness and being frank. However, Fukuzawa felt that envy was a vice through and through, with no positive dimension to it. This was because of the shadow that envy casts over behavior. For example, people compared their own situation with that of others and became dissatisfied, but instead of endeavoring to better their own circumstances, they find fault with the other party. This seriously undermined social relationships.

What brought about such feelings? They resulted not from poverty but from a kind of impasse which impeded human communication and limited a person's ability to act; this sensation in turn resulted in resentment. The most obvious instance of this, Fukuzawa added, occurred during the Edo period in the inner palaces where women of the feudal lords' entourages resided.

Some readers may feel it peculiar that Fukuzawa purposely singled out envy as a target for his criticism, but the British philosopher and political theorist Thomas Hobbes also devoted considerable space to discussing "envy" in *Leviathan* (1651). Many prominent philosophers of political ideology constructed their arguments upon a foundation of intrinsic human nature, and the power exerted by jealousy and envy was even greater in Japan than it was in the West. Fukuzawa, who was by no stretch of the imagination resentful, regarded resentment with a great aversion.

In the fourteenth installment of the series, Fukuzawa first took up the idea of "taking stock of motives." People were not as capable of carrying out business affairs as they would like to think. In business, it was important to take stock and settle accounts on a regular basis. Fukuzawa advised his readers that it was also necessary to take stock of their own life.

The second part of this installment was titled "The meaning of the word *sewa*." The term *sewa* was a composite of two meanings: protection and direction. One should not simply protect another without providing direction or, in reverse, provide counsel without offering protection. Fukuzawa warned against this, saying that it was like giving money to a prodigal son.

What Fukuzawa called for was independence. Providing the absolute minimum of protection together with instruction or counsel is desirable, but one should not go beyond that. Within the binding human relations of Japanese society, there are more than a few instances, he noted, where a person meddled in another's affairs under the pretext of providing assistance *(sewa)*, or where a person sympathized excessively with another person's feelings and prevented that person from developing naturally and manifesting his own capabilities. Fukuzawa strongly denounced such behavior.

Fixing One's Gaze on Japan

The fifteenth pamphlet of the series began the process of bringing *An Encouragement of Learning* to a close. Titled "Methodic doubt and selective judgment," it argued that "the course to truth in human affairs" is limited to "zigzagging through the disputations of rival theories."

However, a person should not lightly believe things or uncritically doubt things. They ought not to believe in the new with the same type of faith they once had in the old. Examples of those who adopt this mistaken behavior are people who cast aside Japanese civilization entirely and become obsessed with the West. Fukuzawa, writing paradoxically in the following, raised multiple examples of aspects of Japanese civilization that were superior to those of the West.

If Westerners bathed every day, while the Japanese bathed only once or twice a month, the teachers of enlightenment would undoubtedly claim this was because the Westerners had a superior understanding of hygiene. If Japanese kept chamber pots in their bedrooms to use at night or did not wash their hands after going to the bathroom, these same reformers would probably claim that it was because the Japanese had a poor understanding of hygiene. If Westerners used disposable paper tissues to wipe their noses while Japanese used cloth handkerchiefs, these teachers would say it was because the Japanese were poor. If Japanese women wore gold rings in their ears and wrapped tight girdles around their waists, these reformers would probably claim that it was some barbaric custom that endangered the health. They would say that because Westerners do not lock their doors, the West is safe and secure. They would add that because Westerners agree to simply stated contracts, Westerners have high moral standards. If Westerners wore *geta* and Japanese wore shoes, they could say that the primitive Japanese did not understand how to use their toes to put them on. If Westerners had tofu, grilled eel or *chawanmushi*, these teachers would praise these dishes as the finest in the world. If a Saint Shinran was born in the West while a Martin Luther was born in Japan, these people would chant Shinran's praises to the heavens.

Over several pages, Fukuzawa continued this reversal of Japan and the West to show how superb many aspects of Japanese culture actually are. He probably did this in order to show how abominable it was to credulously worship the West and because he had a strong affection for Japan. For Fukuzawa, Western civilization was not simply something that should be superficially imitated but something that should be grasped deeply. Further, the introduction of Western civilization was ultimately an endeavor that should be carried out for the benefit of Japan.

We begin to feel Fukuzawa is approaching his epilogue when we reach the sixteenth installment. In "The spirit of independence in everyday affairs," he promoted a solid way of life that does not depend upon others. Drawing on the proverb "A man drinks the first cup of saké, but the third cup drinks the man," he warned that a desire for things can impede a person's judgment. This he later reproached as *wakudeki*, the continued valuing of things that are irrelevant to the existing facts of life.

In the latter half of the sixteenth installment under the title "The compatibility of intention and activity," Fukuzawa encouraged people to balance words and actual deeds. This was a discrepancy in the relative scale and weight of the doings of men and it is the will that makes the difference. By elevating one's mind and one's intentions, one could avoid exerting oneself to no purpose. Further, it was important to determine the right time and place for action.

On the other hand, there were examples where people have lofty aspirations but no practical ability. This was problematic because such people are always frustrated. They did not like to do work which they were actually capable of, because they believed it did not measure up to their ideals. Another might be of noble mind but poor practical ability. Their work was inferior to that of others, but they found fault only in others, not in themselves. They became like a person who reproached someone else for not promptly returning money that was in fact never lent in the first place. In the end, all such sentiments were related to envy.

The seventeenth and final installment was titled "On popularity," and here popularity was used by Fukuzawa in the sense of trustworthiness and integrity that was accumulated gradually by actively employing a person's intelligence in whatever calling the person pursues. Phony doctors enlarged the entrances to their clinics and prospered, while pharmacists decorated their store signs with gold-painted writing that expanded their sales. Such behavior should be condemned, said Fukuzawa, but true popularity was a worthy goal.

Reputation and fame in the proper sense were to be sought. Confucius taught that the true gentleman should "not grieve over not being known by others, but grieve that he does not know others." This precept calling for detesting public vanity was not a contemplation of withdrawal from the world.

To accomplish this for personal and private good, the first thing one should do was to learn language and develop the ability to explain things to others in simple terms. The second is to wear a cheerful expression on one's face. While it is detestable to wear an obsequious smile, it was just as bad to wear a scowl or look as if one has just imbibed something bitter. "A cheerful and lively countenance is one mark of a man of true virtue; in social intercourse it is quite essential." The third was to communicate with people from a broad spectrum of society. Fukuzawa was a person who believed that intercourse between people yielded meaningful results. His easily comprehending, strong-mindedness contrasted significantly with the nervous, wan intellectuals so common among the Japanese. Fukuzawa continued writing *An Encouragement of Learning* much longer than he intended to, but he finished it with a statement that very much represented who he was.

Chapter 8

An Outline of a Theory of Civilization

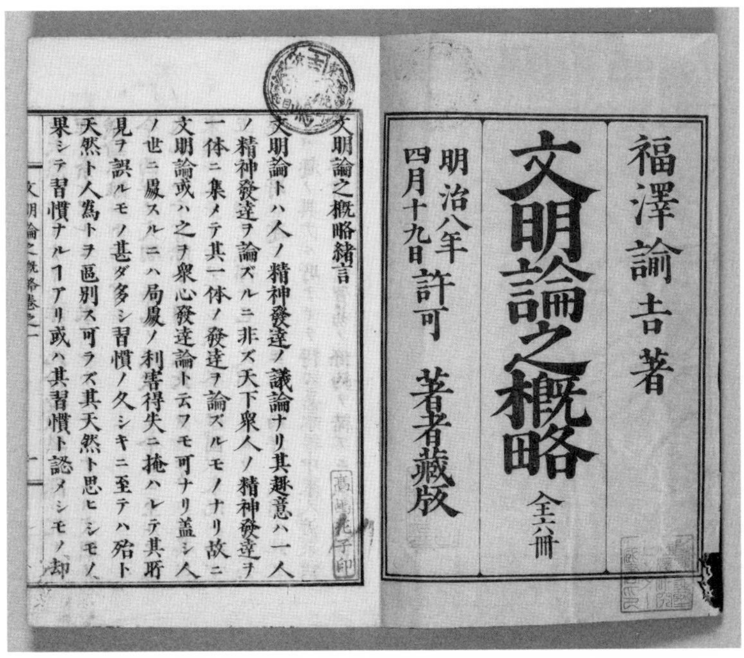

福澤諭吉著

文明論之概略　全六冊

明治八年四月十九日許可　著者藏版

文明論之概略緒言

文明論トハ人ノ精神發達ノ議論ナリ其趣意ハ一人ノ精神發達ヲ論ズルニ非ズ天下衆人ノ精神發達ヲ一体ニ集メテ其一体ノ發達ヲ論ズルモノナリ故ニ文明論或ハ之ヲ衆心發達論ト云フモ可ナリ蓋シ人ノ世ニ處スルニハ局處ノ利害得失ニ掩ハレテ其所見ヲ誤ルモノ甚ダ多シ習慣ノ久シキニ至テハ殆ト天然ト人爲トヲ區別ス可ラズ其天然ト思ヒシモノ果シテ習慣ナルヿアリ或ハ其習慣ト認メシモノ却

文明論之概略巻之一

An Outline of a Theory of Civilization (Courtesy of Keio University Fukuzawa Memorial Center)

Resolved to Write

Written around the same time as *An Encouragement of Learning*, *An Outline of a Theory of Civilization* also represents a monumental achievement. Fukuzawa failed to write any other fully-fledged theoretical works during his lifetime. Nevertheless, compared against all the works of other Japanese thinkers, *An Outline of a Theory of Civilization* remains one of a handful of masterpieces.

The ideological underpinnings of this volume go back at least as far as a memorandum titled *Plan for a Theory of Civilization*, which was dated February 8th, 1874. In a letter dated the twenty-third of the same month, to a trusted colleague, Shoda Heigoro, Fukuzawa wrote, "I have lost the desire to continue translating, and this year I intend to set everything else aside and devote myself to reading and study. Although I am gradually returning to health, if I let down my guard, what knowledge I currently possess will gradually become insufficient, thus I plan to spend a year in the pursuit of learning." Discontent with introducing fragments of knowledge as he had done in the past, Fukuzawa conceived a plan to write a scholarly work of a coherent and theoretical nature. As mentioned previously, in *An Encouragement of Learning*, Fukuzawa had written about the need to "take stock" of one's own ideas and advocated how important it was to lay out a plan and check one's actual achievements. He now planned to do just that by examining his own knowledge.

Much later in 1898, Fukuzawa wrote the following when recalling *An Outline of a Theory of Civilization*.

> What I have published to date has been aimed at importing Western things and ideas and expelling old and evil practices that have existed in our country since ancient times. They were a piecemeal introduction of Western Civilization. However, between 1874 and 1875 social

> conditions finally began to settle, and people's ideas began to mature. I decided to extend my writing by outlining Western Civilization for the public. Thinking it most peculiar to attempt to obtain the approval of the old Confucianist types, I decided not to treat them as enemies but rather to try to pull them over to my side in what became all six volumes of *An Outline of a Theory of Civilization*.

It is true that by around 1874 or 1875, Japanese civilization had reached a point where it needed to broaden and deepen. It is certainly interesting that Fukuzawa intended that the work be read by "the old Confucianist types." In actual fact, *An Outline* is unique among Fukuzawa's works in that it employs an abstract style of expression. The fact that the book was printed in a larger typeface than usual also suggests he hoped it would gain a somewhat older readership.

The work was completed in April 1875, slightly over a year from the time he penned the aforementioned letter to Shoda Heigoro. In another piece of correspondence, this time to a friend from Nakatsu named Shimazu Yutaro, dated April 24th, Fukuzawa wrote,

> I have recently completed *An Outline of a Theory of Civilization*, but it will take another three or four months to have it printed, so I will describe how it came about. Around March of last year, I resolved to write this volume, but to tell the truth, because I had only read a limited number of Western, Chinese and Japanese books, I depended on various sources, so along the way, I began to take turns reading a while and then writing, reading and then writing. While I am not thoroughly confident regarding the fate of what I have written, I do believe that the attempt is of value. If I have made mistakes, then it is only due to my lack of skill. Deciding that I will leave the difficult things to the younger generation, I have simply expressed my own foolish opinions based on

> the limited knowledge that I now possess. Undoubtedly, three to five years from now, when my learning has advanced further, I will be embarrassed by what I have published. When that time comes, I will have to beg forgiveness for my faulty understanding and write something that is an improvement.

Taken at face value, these comments sound like simple modesty, but Fukuzawa was undoubtedly sincere when he wrote them. He was already forty years old, and a younger generation had emerged who had studied abroad and seriously delved into Western Civilization. Furthermore, Japan had successfully passed a particular point on its road to modern civilization and enlightenment. With an eye to carrying out further activity, Fukuzawa must have felt the need to once again solidify his intellectual footing before proceeding.

An Outline of a Theory of Civilization is comprised of six volumes with ten chapters. Professor Maruyama Masao has already published a three-volume commentary in the Iwanami Shinsho collection entitled *Bunmeiron no Gairyaku o yomu* [Reading 'An Outline of a Theory of Civilization']. To be sure, interpreting Fukuzawa's work requires such depth of treatment. Here we do not have the luxury of space, and a detailed interpretation would also present an obstacle to the overall flow of my argument here. Having said that, even though we have to be briefer than we were in considering *An Encouragement of Learning*, we should at least outline the contents of *An Outline of a Theory of Civilization*.

First, in the preface to the work, Fukuzawa defines what a theory of civilization deals with. According to him, it is concerned with the development of the spirit of people. By that, he does not mean an individual but rather the spiritual development of "the people as a whole."

He writes that Western civilization has developed for over a thousand years since the fall of Rome. The civilization of Japan, on the other hand, has ancient roots to which have been added the influences of Buddhism and Confucianism and, more recently, the influence of the West. Fukuzawa explains that this most recent influence has deeply shaken the minds of the Japanese people. The initial manifestation of this spiritual disturbance came with changes external to the individual involving the restoration of the emperor. They then continued with the abolition of the feudal domains and establishment of the prefectures. The internal upheavals within the minds of the people, however, are ongoing. Japan is rushing to elevate its civilization to that of parity with the West, or even to surpass it. Meanwhile, Fukuzawa writes, Western civilization is constantly moving, so it is difficult to see in which direction Japanese civilization is actually progressing.

Japanese scholars nonetheless have a certain advantage. Western scholars view things from within their already established culture, while the Japanese are witnessing the historical changes in their own culture as they occur. "We have, as it were, lived two lives; we embrace within ourselves two completely different patterns of existence." (This is a frequent expression that he employs.) As a result, Japanese scholars are able to carry out a reliable discussion of the subject at hand. In this sense, Fukuzawa commences the discussion that follows with great confidence.

Establishing a Basis of Argumentation

The title of chapter one of *An Outline of a Theory of Civilization* is "Establishing a Basis of Argumentation." In it, Fukuzawa set out his argument as follows:

> Light and heavy, long and short, good and bad, right and wrong are all relative terms. If there were no light, there could be no heavy; if there were no good, there could be no bad. Thus light is light relative to heavy, and good is good relative to bad. If there were not such relativity

> between one and the other, we would not debate over light and heavy or good and bad. The criterion in terms of which something is judged relatively heavy or good may be called the basis of argumentation.[36]

Maruyama Masao, in *Fukuzawa Yukichi no tetsugaku*, wrote that this passage was as equally important as Fukuzawa's opening sentence in *An Encouragement of Learning* which reads, "Heaven, it is said, does not create one person above or below another." The crucial argument being set forth is that all things are relative. Through comparison, humans judge something to be relatively heavy or relatively good. Fukuzawa calls this process the "basis of argumentation." He later uses this same expression with slightly modified meanings, so it is difficult to define it as having a single meaning. Generally speaking, however, it refers to "the grounds for argument" or "the purpose of argumentation."

According to Fukuzawa, unless one first establishes a basis of argumentation, one cannot discuss the advantages and disadvantages, the merits and demerits, of an issue. A castle is an advantage to a defender, but a disadvantage to one who attacks it. Therefore, one should first establish a basis from which one will argue.

When the original points of departure in an argument differ between people, even though the conclusions drawn from the argument may nevertheless end up being the same, the objectives of the parties may differ. Concurrently, if the perspectives from which the parties argue differ, in extreme cases, the act of argument in itself may be absolutely pointless. In that constant social intercourse within society is vital, it is important to hold discussions with many people so as to avoid such unnecessary conflict.

Fukuzawa adds that in every country there are very few people who are extremely foolish or extremely intelligent. Rather, the majority of the populace falls somewhere between these two extremes. Moving with the times, with neither blame nor merit, the majority spend their whole lives blindly following the crowd. They are the so-called "common people." They serve as the source of what is called "public opinion." Such opinion is in no way capable of leading society. Indeed, he asks the reader to consider how "since ancient times, progressive steps in civilization were considered unorthodox when they were first proposed."

Both Adam Smith's economic theories and Galileo's theory of the earth's rotation were considered heretical in their day. But the unorthodox theories of yesteryear grow to be accepted. Thus, scholars should not be afraid of criticism or charges of heresy. Rather, they should courageously state their beliefs. Even when another's argument does not square with one's own, a person should try to grasp the rationale behind it, accept what they can accept, and let the points which cannot be admitted simply stand as they are. They should then wait for a time when matters can be reconciled.

When it comes to whether Japan should progress or turn back, acquire civilization or return to a primitive state, Fukuzawa says, it is clear that we must move forward. It is from this standpoint that he launches into his discussion.

The Spirit of Western Civilization

The title of chapter two is "Western Civilization as Our Goal." As earlier argued with respect to the relativity of light and heavy, right and wrong, Fukuzawa points out that the construct of "civilization and enlightenment" is something to be understood in relative terms. Looking at the world that surrounds him, Fukuzawa sees the nations of the West as being the most civilized, the Asian states such as Turkey, China and Japan being semi-developed, while Africa and Australia (hard to imagine in our day) remain primitive.

Fukuzawa defines these terms as follows: In "primitive" (uncivilized) lands, neither dwellings nor food supplies are stable. Even if the people have enough of both, they do not yet know how to make tools, and even if they possess a written language, they have no literature. They are still in a state of fearing nature and being dependent on good fortune. The "semi-developed" nations have commenced agriculture and urbanization, and they have created the outward semblance of a state. Yet, they still lack many things. Book-based learning flourishes, but few within society devote themselves to learning that is of a practical nature *(jitsugaku)*. "Though in human relations the sentiments of suspicion and envy are entrenched, when it comes to discussing the nature of things, people lack the courage to voice doubts and ask questions." The people are skilled at crafts but their production lacks originality. "They grasp the cultivation of the old, but not ways to improve on it." They recognize rules that govern society, yet they are constrained by their customs and never form rules in the true sense. The third definition of being "civilized" contrasts with the other definitions in every respect. The people of such nations grasp the principles of heaven and earth but are not bound by either of them. "Their spirits enjoy free play and are not credulous of old customs." They act with autonomy and are not dependent upon the kindness of others. They cultivate their virtues and refine the knowledge that they possess. "They are neither nostalgic for the past nor complacent about the present." Fukuzawa at length describes the many spiritual attributes and attitudes he previously discussed in *An Encouragement*. We can plainly see that for him, civilization was a spiritual foundation upon which the concept of *fukoku kyohei* (a rich country and a strong military) had to stand.

To Fukuzawa, the terms "civilized" and "primitive" are relative. Japan ought not to be satisfied with the level of civilization achieved by the West, yet in the short term, it serves as a benchmark. The world is divided into various countries, each with its own sentiments and social customs. If a person is to introduce civilization into a country, what exactly is one to introduce? It is essential to decide upon certain standards for what is to be introduced.

Fukuzawa makes a distinction between the visible trappings of civilization and its internalized and spiritual aspects. The trappings of civilization include matters such as clothing, food, machinery, housing, government regulations, laws, armies and cannons. Of these elements, tangibles such as iron bridges and stone buildings are easily constructed, while non-tangibles such as government institutions and laws prove more difficult. Far more difficult still is the matter of the inner spirit of civilization. It is possible to select which visible trappings of a material civilization shall be introduced. However, the incorporation of spiritual aspects is not so easy. The march of civilization cannot be advanced without the spirit that accompanies it. Fukuzawa declares that obtaining that fundamental spirit is the hardest part of this process. He poses and answers the following question: "What then is the spirit of civilization? It is a people's spiritual makeup." What makes Fukuzawa's insight outstanding is he has not looked at Western civilization for the wealth or military strength it promises, but for the spirit or sentiment that it offers.

In terms of the conditions necessary for the pursuit of Western enlightenment, Fukuzawa contrasts Japan and China. His view is that "the spirit of freedom can only exist in an atmosphere of diversity of ideas and contending views." Toward the end of the Zhou period, China experienced a time of conflicting teachings and a sense of freedom occurred within such a diversity of thought, but this phase was followed by a period of despotism. Because Japan had a dual form of government, comprised of the Imperial Court and the military bakufu, it possessed a spirit that was more receptive to Western enlightenment.

In putting forward his arguments, Fukuzawa makes distinctions between the terms, *kokutai* (national polity), *seito* (political legitimization) and *ketto* (blood lineage). *Kokutai*, he says, refers to what is called "nationality" in the West. People with a common race, religion, language or geography—and particularly those who share a common history—are bound as a single people who establish a country. The maintenance of nationality is dependent on not losing sovereignty. It means not losing political legitimacy or political authority. Therefore, when it was defeated at the end of the Song dynasty by the Yuan (Mongols) and again when the Ming dynasty was defeated by the Qing (Manchu), China lost its nationality. When India fell under the rule of the British, it too lost its nationality. In contrast, Japan has constantly preserved its nationality.

In contrast, by *seito* Fukuzawa means what is called in English "political legitimization." He argues that the monarchies of both China and France have changed their forms of political legitimacy. Holland, which once had a republican form of government, is today a monarchy. In Japan, the Fujiwara had at one point held the reins of power with respect to the Imperial Family, as later did the Hojo regents with respect to the Minamoto. In this sense, a change in political legitimacy, Fukuzawa claims, is unrelated to the rise or fall of nationality.

Thirdly, *ketto*, is called "blood line" in the West. A change in the blood line does not mean that political legitimacy will change, and it certainly does not mean that nationality is lost. Yet even if the line of the ruling family continues, as it did in India under the British, one can only conclude that nationality can still be lost.

There was an ulterior motive in Fukuzawa's argument. Some of his contemporaries contended that it was not possible for civilization and enlightenment to coexist with Japan's nationality; Fukuzawa was eager to defeat their arguments. Japan had never lost its nationality. Compared to the maintenance of nationality and independence, the arguments of political legitimacy and blood line are of secondary importance. In fact, changes in political legitimacy had previously occurred in Japan. There had been periods when the Imperial Court had actually governed in its own right and others when the military classes had been ascendant.

Fukuzawa uses the notion of *wakudeki* (fixation on the irrelevant) to describe these circumstances. *Wakudeki* refers to a method for achieving a certain outcome that is completely separate from its original application. To wit, it becomes an end in itself. He clarifies this idea with a reference to the two swords that the samurai once wore for self-protection. Despite peace, this custom was not abandoned. To the contrary, the samurai spent their money foolishly decorating their swords. The same sort of credulity toward outdated customs *(wakudeki)* applies to the government. Fukuzawa argues that the introduction of Western civilization is an effective way to maintain Japan's nationality, while remaining addicted to outdated customs endangers that polity.

Needless to say, the pre-World War II interpretation of *kokutai* differed from what Fukuzawa had earlier espoused. More than anything else, the term referred to Article One of the Constitution of the Empire of Japan (1889), which read, "The Empire of Japan shall be reigned over and governed by a line of Emperors unbroken for ages eternal." By contrast, an opinion that this should be modified, or even a simple suggestion to do so, was made a punishable crime under the Peace Preservation Law of 1925. Considered from this perspective, Fukuzawa's assertion in *An Outline of a Theory of Civilization* that political legitimization and blood line were elements of only secondary importance, while the central issue was the maintenance of Japan's independence, would have been a rather dangerous view to have in the early Showa period prior to World War II. As shall be explained, Fukuzawa strongly denounced the interpretation of *kokutai* that would later take hold in the early Showa period. This later interpretation attempted to intertwine the Imperial Household with political ends.

Progress toward the Comfort and Dignity of the People

The title of chapter three is "The Essence of Civilization" and in it Fukuzawa continues to define his topic. Stated simply, he sees civilization not just as a "comfort in daily necessities but also the refining of knowledge and the cultivation of virtue so as to elevate human life to a higher plane." In short, his argument is about progress toward comfort and dignity. What makes this possible is knowledge and virtue. Consequently, civilization for Fukuzawa means the advance of knowledge and virtue.

What is the relationship between the advancement of civilization and the system of government? The opening lines of *An Encouragement of Learning* famously proclaim the equality of all men, thus one might expect that Fukuzawa would set forth democracy and democratic institutions as his ideals. The character of the "Gentleman of Western Learning" who appears in Nakae Chomin's treatise *A Discourse by Three Drunkards in Government* strongly argues that the course of development proceeds from monarchical autocracy (despotism) to constitutional monarchy then finally onto a democratic state. Fukuzawa's views, however, do not follow such reasoning. While he recognizes that the first stage of reform in the West is often the overthrow of the nobility, and that in Japan's case reform has involved the abolition of the domains and establishment of the prefectures, he also notes that the status of samurai households has been endangered. In *Conditions in the West* we detect early indications of Fukuzawa's belief that there may be good monarchies just as there are bad republican governments. In other words, the evolution of systems of government has differed from country to country. Thus, separate pivots govern the trajectory of civilization and the development of knowledge and virtue.

How are we to judge the virtue and knowledge not of the individual but of an entire country? Chapter four, "The Knowledge and Virtue of the People of a Country," and chapter five, "A Continuation of the Preceding

Chapter," consider this matter.

According to Fukuzawa, the West has some stupid people just as Asia has some outstanding talent. The fact that the West is advanced is because the foolish people do not hold sway over public opinion; the counterpoint to this argument is that it is unfortunate that in Asia the outstanding people have not held sway. Fukuzawa claims that the reason for this situation is the spirit that is inherent to the individual countries.

Fukuzawa uses the term "spirit" in multiple contextual settings but he fails to offer an exact definition of what it means. Rather, he interprets factors that have determined history as constituting "spirit," and he then attempts to illustrate his reasoning through historical examples.

Confucius was not influential during the end of the Zhou dynasty because his ideas were not in tune with the trends of the times. The plans of Emperor Go-Daigo and Kusunoki Masashige also failed for a similar reason. By "trends of the times," Fukuzawa simply means the predominating spirit of the people at certain junctures in history. In the case of Emperor Go-Daigo, his failure resulted from not being able to overturn the rule of the warrior class. When contemplating something like loyalty to the emperor, Fukuzawa does not believe one can impose a criterion on history that goes beyond the realities.

At any rate, an observer can appreciate the circumstances of a country's civilization by learning about the virtues and knowledge of its common people. Such traits that are keeping with the times are exhibited far and wide throughout the populace. In regard to this argument, Fukuzawa raises two pertinent points.

The first is that the power of public opinion does not always depend upon the number of people involved in its formulation. It is said that what brought about the Meiji Restoration was the nation's general intellectual power. While the number of people exercising such power may have been rather small, the arguments that they posed were highly convincing and ultimately brought about change. Fukuzawa adds that the arguments for reform on a whole tend to emerge from those who possess intelligence but who lack wealth. Conversely, those who are satisfied with the status quo do not exhibit reformist tendencies. This argument parallels the expectations of the middle class which Fukuzawa offers in *An Encouragement of Learning*. Indeed, his own self-confidence in studying Western learning and his attempting to influence the times in which he lived rests on this argument.

The second point that Fukuzawa raises is that even if people are intelligent, unless they coordinate their activities, they will be unable to shape public opinion. In highlighting this point, he comments on the fact that within the native Japanese tradition there were strict prohibitions against the formulation of what might be construed as constituting factional cliques. However, if a group of interested people gather to engage in discussion, they will attain a higher level of wisdom, and that is why Fukuzawa emphasizes social intercourse. In general, Fukuzawa argued that discussions carried on in the West tend to elevate the thinking of the people of a particular country, but in the East, the reverse tends to occur. Fukuzawa points out the reason for this is that people in the East are hindered by custom from actively participating in both public discussion of issues in an open-minded fashion and broad social intercourse.

In chapter six, "The Distinction between Knowledge and Virtue," and chapter seven, "The Proper Time and Place for Knowledge and Virtue," Fukuzawa distinguishes between knowledge and virtue, and he also defines knowledge as intellect. Virtue in the West is called "morals" and it means a person's internal good behavior that "enables a person to feel ashamed within his heart and to do nothing shameful even when no one else is around." It is typical of Fukuzawa to provide an explanation of these terms so that anyone can understand and then add to it an abstract explanation addressed to the Confucianist. For the latter reader, he employs terms drawn from the classical *The Great Learning* (Ch: Daxue, Ta-Hsueh) and *The Doctrine of the Mean* (Ch: Zhongyong, Chung-yung).

Fukuzawa further divides knowledge into the private and public, or lesser and greater, while also segmenting virtue into the private and public spheres as well. Private virtue includes the traits of fidelity, purity, modesty, integrity and alike, and it pertains to an individual's own heart. Public virtue, on the other hand, includes a sense of honor, fairness, impartiality and courage, and these traits are manifest in a person's dealings with others. Private knowledge refers to the capacity to grasp and respond to the principles of things. Public knowledge means the ability to evaluate human affairs and events, giving priority to the greater, and being able to judge proper time and place. This public knowledge can also be called the greater knowledge of wisdom.

For Fukuzawa, the most important of these spheres are public virtue and public knowledge. In Asia, he argues, emphasis has traditionally been placed on private virtue. Private knowledge refers to whether a person is skilled at playing go or shogi or using an abacus. Figures such as Adam Smith and James Watt, however, are good examples of people who possessed public knowledge. Among those who illustrate public virtue are Thomas Clarkson, who attacked the system of slavery, and John Howard, who stood up for penal reform. By providing illustrations, Fukuzawa stresses the importance of knowledge over virtue, public knowledge over private knowledge, and public virtue over private virtue. As we can see from his holding private knowledge in low esteem, Fukuzawa had little interest in theater, music or artistic pursuits in general.

The Difference between Western and Japanese Civilization

In chapter eight, "The Origins of Western Civilization," Fukuzawa discusses the origins of Western Civilization by introducing parts of François

Guizot's *History of Civilization*. The central thesis of this work is that the origin of Western Civilization lies in its plurality, and through this plurality freedom was able to develop. Meanwhile, in chapter nine, "The Origins of Japanese Civilization," Fukuzawa writes,

> Now in the first place, the freedom of civilization cannot be bought at the expense of some other freedom. It can only exist by not infringing upon other rights and interests, other opinions and powers, all of which exist in some balance. It is only possible for freedom to exist when freedom is limited.[37]

After the introduction of Guizot in chapter eight, some critics hold that the next two chapters of *An Outline of a Theory of Civilization* are somewhat heavier. However, Maruyama in *Reading 'An Outline of a Theory of Civilization,'* contends that such a view is misguided. As he correctly points out, Fukuzawa does not argue that the origins of European civilization are grounded in the traditions of Greece and Rome. Rather, he claims that contemporary Western civilization began with the fall of centralized control in Rome. He also praises highly the Germanic notion of freedom. "The spirit of seeking the independence of the individual and the full development of his aspirations first originated in the Germanic tribes." He points out that it was within the context of the feudal lords establishing bases in their own territories, the opposition between religious power and secular power, and the rise of the "free cities" and the competitive coexistence of a plurality of elements that freedom was born and society underwent dynamic development. When that happened, it was as always the middle classes that provided the driving force.

Chapter nine, "The Origins of Japanese Civilization," is the most well-known chapter of the book. In it Fukuzawa discusses the plurality of the West in contrast to the single dimension of Japan, and asserts that an imbalance of power pervades Japanese society. Such a disproportionate emphasis is the opposite of equilibrium and it is, in short, an imbalance. Fukuzawa argues that this lack of balance is especially apparent in various human relationships within Japan.

Japan has a proper order for everything. In human relations, between man and woman, parent and child, older and younger brother, the former always has primacy. But that is not all. There is an imbalance between rich and poor, elder and younger, teacher and student, master and servant, high status and low status, veteran and novice, main household and branch household.

In Japan such relations are weighty. The administrator browbeats the subordinate, the subordinate browbeats the village headman, and the headman then browbeats the minor figures under his supervision. "A is oppressed by B, B in turn is oppressed by C; and in this way there exists an unending cycle of pressures and controls. Truly an amazing phenomenon, indeed!" This author believes that Maruyama Masao's concept of *yokuatsu ijo* ("the transfer of oppression") is derived from this construct.

The imbalance of power in Japan commenced with its consolidation within the imperial household during ancient times. Regarding an anecdote about the Emperor Nintoku, who upon seeing smoke rising from the houses of the common folk is said to have identified with them, Fukuzawa comments that such sentiment was less a manifestation of an affectionate attitude and more about the Emperor viewing everything as his private domain.

Over time, the exercising of authority shifted to the warrior class. Fukuzawa comments that from that time onward, regardless of whether there was a change of government, authority itself only shifted within the ruling class. There was no change in the fundamental relationship between rulers and the ruled. There was no major upheaval involving the general populace, so the people completely lacked any awareness that they actually were the sovereigns of the country. He concludes, "in Japan there is a government, but no nation *(kokumin)*."

From the groundwork of chapter nine comes the central tenet of chapter ten, which is entitled "A Discussion of Our National Independence." Fukuzawa states that the greatest task Japan faces is to become a full member of the modern international community, to survive and to develop. To achieve this, Japan must establish its status as a sovereign state, becoming a nation-state *(kokumin-kokka)* whose foundation is the people *(kokumin)*.

Until that time, Fukuzawa argues that Japan had been bound by various concepts such as "true relations of sovereign and subject," "the traditions of one's ancestors," "the obligations of lord and vassal" and "the relationships of traditional discrimination." Despite this, however, what has allowed the Japanese to achieve their civilization is "the strength of the ethical customs" that have governed its society. Fukuzawa concludes that it is this mentality that prevents the people from becoming a real nation *(kokumin)*.

The international community is a harsh environment. Fukuzawa draws on an article written by his colleague Obata Tokujiro, which comments that when Commodore Perry came to Japan, he called for communication and trade to follow. According to Obata, the gist of Perry's argument "was that all men on this earth are brothers, sharing the same sky above and the same earth beneath, that if we turn a man away and refuse to deal with him we are sinners against Heaven, and so, even if it means fighting, trade relations must be opened." "How beautiful Perry's words, and how unseemly his deeds!" In other words, Fukuzawa adds, while the West talks about justice and humanitarian reasons, in actual fact, it is all a matter of self-service. Fukuzawa harshly criticizes the West's actions and one can clearly see how different he is from those who worship the West.

On the other hand, the social intercourse of the various countries is based on a universal moral principle[38] *(tenchi no kodo)* and is not usually aimed at doing damage to the other party. In this view, therefore, one should let things progress as they naturally will, free trading and coming and going at will. Yet this can be a major mistake. In the Edo period, such a relationship between individuals was possible. However, when it became a matter of relationships between the domains, it was not possible. Every state invariably has its own variety of *henpashin*, irrational biases, and one has to survive within such competition.

Thus, "relations with other countries pose an intractable problem for us, and to address them, we must rely upon the people of our country." Where Japanese society once centered on principles such as "the obligations of lord and vassal," "the traditions of one's ancestors," "the moral obligations between superiors and inferiors," and "the distinction between main trunk and branch households," Fukuzawa claims, it is now becoming ever more important to focus upon "loyalty toward one's own country," "the traditions of one's own country," "domestic and foreign obligations," and "distinctions between domestic and foreign."

Regarding the size and breadth of the issues Japan faces, Fukuzawa writes,

> The fact that England has one thousand warships does not mean that she has one thousand warships only. If there are one thousand warships, there have to be at least ten thousand merchant ships, which in turn require at least one hundred thousand navigators; and to create navigators, there must be naval science. Only when there are many professors and many merchants, when laws are in order and trade prospers, when social conditions are ripe—when, that is, all the prerequisites for a thousand warships—only then can there be a thousand warships.[39]

Thus, more important than developing a strong military is developing a rich country, even more important is establishing government and laws, and still more important is a revolution in the spirit of the people.

Chapter 9

Leaders of Meiji Restoration and Fukuzawa Yukichi

Photo of Fukuzawa Yukichi in 1876 in Western-style clothes. From middle age onward he ordinarily wore only Japanese clothes. (Courtesy of Keio University Fukuzawa Memorial Center)

Empathy with Kido Takayoshi

As already noted, Fukuzawa wrote both *An Encouragement of Learning* and *An Outline of a Theory of Civilization* between 1871 and 1876. The first volume represented a practical application of the latter's ideas; while the latter gave the former its theoretical foundations. Fukuzawa commenced work on *An Encouragement of Learning* in the autumn of 1871, and while doing so he felt the need to place it on a solid theoretical footing. Thus, in 1875, he turned his hand to completing *An Outline of a Theory of Civilization*. He then returned to finish *An Encouragement of Learning*. This period spanned the years between the abolition of the domains and establishment of the prefectures, and the eruption of the Seinan War (the Satsuma Rebellion) of 1877.

Naturally enough, Fukuzawa's frenetic activity attracted the attention of politicians both in and out of office, and he was noticed by businessmen as well. Thus, in due course, Fukuzawa began to participate in the forming of the Meiji state, and we now turn our attention to his activities.

In addition to the persons with whom he had maintained relationships since the days of the bakufu, Fukuzawa began meeting prominent political figures around the autumn of 1873. The Iwakura Mission which had departed in 1871 had finally returned to Japan, and this in itself had created a rift. On one side of the rift there were members of the just-returned mission. On the other were representatives of the caretaker government who had remained in Japan. The disagreements between them centered on perceptions of the current circumstances and on other policy matters.

The debate over sending a military expedition to the Korean Peninsula *(Seikanron)* was then raging. Two camps of opinion had formed with respect to diplomatic relations because Japan's policy towards Korea had been allowed to lapse in the wake of the Meiji Restoration. One group argued that Japan should dispatch an expedition to conduct forceful negotiations. The other, some of whose members had returned from the Iwakura Mission painfully aware of the gap between Japan and the West, worried that sending such an expedition to Korea could develop into military conflict. Instead they argued that priority should be given to domestic improvements and reforms.

Fukuzawa first met Kido Takayoshi on September 4th, 1873. Kido, who had served as vice-envoy, had just returned in July with other members of the Iwakura Mission. He later recorded in his diary that he and Fukuzawa had "together deplored the trend of the times." Along with his colleagues, Kido had probably also read *Conditions in the West* as a reference during his travels. Furthermore, they probably hoped to meet and share opinions with the pioneering travel author.

The two men next met on September 16th, and this time it was Kido who called on Fukuzawa. He stayed from seven in the morning until two in the afternoon, the men also lunching together. They met once again less than two weeks later enjoying a conversation of seven hours. It was as if each had found a kindred spirit in the other. A follower of Fukuzawa may have referred to this occasion when he recalled later that, during Kido's visit, Fukuzawa had given instructions to get some refreshments. Unfortunately, due to a heavy rainstorm the local caterer was closed, so they made do with some boiled potatoes and pickled vegetables. From this we can imagine how close their friendship had become.

Kido deplored the *Seikanron* controversy. To dispatch a special envoy had been decided at two separate cabinet meetings on August 17th and October 15th. However, due to the forceful leadership displayed by Okubo Toshimichi and Iwakura Tomomi. The Emperor decided to postpone the dispatch indefinitely on October 24th.

But political crises did not end there. Many people were already frustrated with the reforms since the Restoration and under these circumstances the majority who had formed the nucleus of the new government abandoned it. A particularly shocking event was when Saigo Takamori, the most popular of the new leadership, resigned his post. For its own part, the fledgling government found it necessary to devise a vision of how the new Meiji state would be formed. It then had to present its vision to the public.

Immediately after the government fractured over the issue of the Korean expedition, a reform movement began within the remaining leadership and, on November 20th, 1873, Ito Hirobumi and Terashima Munenori were charged with investigating how to form the new system. Okubo Toshimichi then submitted a draft of an opinion regarding a legislative form of government to Ito and recommended adding Fukuzawa as a member of the committee that would deliberate over this draft.

In his draft, Okubo touched on the relative merits of democratic government and constitutional monarchy. While contending that the democratic form was in principle superior, he concluded that the conditions it required to function in Japan were lacking. Thus, he expressed the opinion that the country should pursue a system in which the monarch and the people governed together, which is similar to a constitutional monarchy. Okubo and Fukuzawa were not too different on this point.

Regarding the matter of appointing Fukuzawa to the deliberations committee, Ito did not show opposition to Okubo, but after seeking the advice of Kido, he did not invite Fukuzawa. If Fukuzawa were to be included, it would be necessary to reflect his views to some degree, and if Fukuzawa's views were not adopted, it would invite more criticism.

As this author sees it, however, such an assumption seems somewhat far-fetched. To interpret the circumstances differently, there was perhaps the apprehension that if included, Fukuzawa rather than Ito would come to dominate the deliberations. Fukuzawa's arguments would be strengthened by the fact that Terashima Munenori, a close friend of Fukuzawa, was also to be a committee member.

In January 1874, the Public Party of Patriots *(Aikoku Koto)* was founded, and it petitioned the government to establish a national assembly whose members would be selected by popular vote *(Minsen giin setsuritsu kenpakusho)*. The *Aikoku Koto* was Japan's first political party. The document establishing it was signed jointly by nine founding members, and the accompanying petition was signed by eight of the nine. It was little more than an assembly and a declaration proposed by a small group of prominent figures. Moreover, one of its members, Eto Shimpei, soon returned to Saga to lead an insurrection now known as the Saga Rebellion *(Saga no ran)*, and shortly thereafter the party was disbanded.

We have no way of knowing how Fukuzawa felt about the Public Party of Patriots and its petition *(kenpakusho)*, but we do know that the *Meirokusha* members discussed the matter of an elected legislative assembly at some length. None of its members was opposed to the idea in principle, but it appears that more than a few believed it was too early to carry out such a plan. Fukuzawa's stance was that awakening the spirit of the people had to precede a reform of the system, and as a close friend of the anti-Korean expedition advocate Kido, he was in favor of an elected legislature but was probably not deeply committed to it.

In February 1874 it was decided to send a punitive expedition to Taiwan *(Taiwan Shuppei)* and carried it out in May. As overseas adventurism, it was of the same character as the proposed expedition to Korea. Thus, as a consequence, Kido opposed it and withdrew from the government in protest. However, Okubo, who adopted the policy, had his reasons for doing so. He was particularly concerned about the possible actions of Saigo in Satsuma. Consequently, he felt it necessary to decisively crush the Saga Rebellion and then divert the energies of the Satsuma forces overseas. He did this by recruiting soldiers primarily from the former Satsuma domain and deploying them under the leadership of Saigo Tsugumichi, the younger brother of Saigo Takamori.

Okubo's action left Kido with the impression that Okubo would try to do anything to achieve his goals, and this caused an estrangement between the two.

It is unclear where Fukuzawa's sympathies lay with respect to this incident. He appeared to be somewhat opposed to the Taiwan Expedition, but not strongly so. Toward the Saga Rebellion, he was neither strongly opposed nor was he supportive. His stance was perhaps closest to that of Kido. However, he could also appreciate Okubo's motivations. It must have been the case that Fukuzawa was focusing his efforts on his writing and education activities.

In March 1875, Okubo, Kido and Itagaki Taisuke met in Osaka. The meeting's purpose was to convince Itagaki (who had left the government over the Korean issue) and Kido (who had left over the Taiwan Expedition) to return to the fold. Kido and Itagaki demanded that the excessive power of the oligarchs be restrained and that a constitutional government be established. On April 14th, Emperor Meiji issued an Imperial Edict to proclaim a gradual transition to a constitutional government. It included such important plans as those to establish a Genro-in (senate) as a step toward a parliament, the Supreme Court for judicial independence, an assembly of prefectural governors in an attempt to establish regional autonomy, and the separation of Councilors and state ministers. Fukuzawa favored this Imperial Edict proclaiming a gradual transition to a constitutional system (as per his letter to Tomita Tetsunosuke dated April 29th), and at the gathering of the *Meirokusha* on May 1st, he opposed Kato Hiroyuki's view that it was premature to establish a popularly-elected legislative assembly.

However, following these developments, Itagaki differed with Okubo and left the government again. He was accompanied in political exile on this occasion by Shimazu Hisamitsu, the former leader of Satsuma domain, who had been Minister of the Left. Now isolated, Kido was exposed to considerable criticism. During this period Fukuzawa apparently encouraged Kido in a variety of ways. In his journal, in an entry for November 14th, 1875, Kido writes,

> Fukuzawa called. According to him, at present public opinion is in discord over various issues and the hostility is focused on me alone. He has regularly conjectured what my intentions might be but could no longer bear simply observing from the sidelines, so he spoke at length about sharing the same feelings. I expressed my heartfelt gratitude. Today I realized that I could not betray the understanding of so many people. Unable to refrain from speaking my mind, after a day in peace, I am once again determined, without regard for reputation or life and limb, to dedicate myself once more to serving the state.

The content of their discussion is not stated, but it is clear that Kido was deeply moved by Fukuzawa's kindness, and from his comment that there was no other choice but to do his utmost for the state, it is obvious that he felt a strong bond with his friend. *(Kosho)*

Fukuzawa's Human Rights *(jinken)*, Okubo's Political Power

As we have seen, Fukuzawa's stance was close to that of Kido in acting as a moderate inside the government. Now we turn to Fukuzawa's relationship with the most influential figure in the drama, Okubo Toshimichi.

Fukuzawa first met Okubo on June 13th, 1875. He then renewed his acquaintance on February 27th, 1876. The first encounter involved several other guests, but on the second occasion, Fukuzawa was the main guest and it seems that both men enjoyed an extended conversation. Okubo later noted in his journal, "At five, Samejima Naonobu turned up. Fukuzawa also came and we discussed a variety of issues. A very interesting chap. No wonder he is well known." Fukuzawa later recalled this visit, saying Okubo had said to him, "The talk of people's rights, that is so prevalent in current public debate, is all well and good, but if the people argue with the government over rights, then they must be prepared to take on some responsibilities." Fukuzawa inferred that Okubo was tacitly referring to him as a sort of "ringleader of the advocates of people's rights." In responding to Okubo, Fukuzawa stated that the nation *(kokumin)* possesses both political rights and human rights, and that the government is free to tend to political affairs but is not free to dictate what are human rights *(jinken)*. For a government official to regard the masses with scorn is just as unforgivable as the samurai of the feudal era who looked down on the farmers and townspeople. Fukuzawa was merely defending the idea of human rights. However, controversies over government will in all likelihood arise and develop into a major commotion. When that happens, Fukuzawa says, he will not participate. Fukuzawa writes, "Today the Fukuzawa you judged to be an advocate of people's rights somehow has become a trustworthy figure. Rest assured, this new figure may be considered as a reliable one for your purposes, too." *(Fukuzawa Zenshu Shogen)*

That Okubo to some degree recognized the legitimacy of the people's rights is interesting. It is clear that Fukuzawa strongly stressed human rights, especially the dignity of man. We can also see from other written sources that Fukuzawa took a cautious attitude toward government, in other words, toward popular participation in political administration. Thus, there was not such a huge gap between the two as might have been expected. Okubo poured his efforts into the establishment of government. Meanwhile, Fukuzawa focused his own efforts in securing human rights that form the basis of government. Rather than contradicting and opposing one another, the two men simply differed in the fields in which they were actively participating. It would be nice to imagine that assuming the difference between their fields of activity, there might have been a profound discussion between one of the most influential people of the Meiji era and one of the era's most prominent intellectuals.

Bunkenron: The Separation of Powers

In November 1876, Fukuzawa wrote an essay entitled *Bunkenron* [Separation of Powers]. This is an important treatise in which he discusses the relationship between the centralization of government and the decentralization of administrative power. He also discusses the moral force of the samurai. The essay was written in a period when dissidence among members of the samurai class was growing. The greatest upheaval of the period, the Satsuma Rebellion, broke out in February 1877. As is shown below, the subject of the essay was somewhat delicate considering the broader political climate. Thus, it was not immediately published.

Fukuzawa observes that the power to change things is not created overnight. A person who possesses the ability to read Chinese works may also develop an outstanding ability to read Western books. A merchant may change his business, but he will still be able to get by somehow. The same thing can be said of government. Fukuzawa argued that until that time, it had been the samurai class that had dealt with affairs of state. Others had been involved, but eight or nine out of ten had come from the samurai class. In this essay, Fukuzawa reexamined the role that this group played in national government.

The radical change of the Meiji Restoration was a reformation of government. The pillars of that change were to be the samurai. Fukuzawa notes that in his day the members of that class were divided into three types. One followed the path toward civilization and enlightenment, entered government service and occupied an appropriate office, or remained outside the government and was active in an occupation he had taken up. The second type lived on the boundaries of civilization and enlightenment, but things did not go well for him, so he either quit or tried to enter government and failed. This is the person who was "ready and capable but who was unable to find a position in which he could fulfill his ambitions and, as a result, he became dissatisfied." Fukuzawa commented that the advocates of people's rights fell in this category.

There were some scholars in this group and Fukuzawa felt that the arguments they put forward were *kan'i shojiki*, or "simple and sincere." He stated that, while their arguments may not have seemed significant, one ought not to dismiss these scholars out of hand. Indeed, I believe what Fukuzawa said even holds true today.

The third type of samurai maintained the spirit of their class *(kiryoku)*, but were nonplussed by the social changes occurring about them. Instead, they preferred to protect the long-established social conventions. Fukuzawa saw such people as lacking an astuteness to handle their new circumstances, but lacking for neither spirit nor strength. He felt this third type perhaps accounted for 70 to 80 percent of the samurai class. Moreover, some such samurai were influential and in possession of a superior moral character. Their personal principles gave them considerable power, which garnered the admiration of others. "Within the laws of human affairs," wrote Fukuzawa, "those who possess physical strength, without much education or superior intelligence, inevitably gather around personal virtue." (This too, I believe, is a message worth taking seriously.)

In expressing such views, the figure that Fukuzawa had in mind was Saigo Takamori. As shall be discussed, Fukuzawa held warm feelings toward Saigo. Many samurai unable to find a future congregated around Saigo, whom they saw as the very embodiment of moral character. These arguments as to the division of the samurai class into three types were set out by Fukuzawa a mere two months prior to the outbreak of the Satsuma Rebellion.

Considering the social tensions swirling about him, Fukuzawa wrote that in the final analysis, the forces of conservatism would probably be suppressed, and that with such a suppression, the foundations of government would become even firmer. But would such developments be to Japan's benefit? Fukuzawa's characteristic view was that it was the independent spirit of the people that would maintain the state's independence. From such a perspective, therefore, it was not at all desirable that the force of will of the descendants of the samurai families be buried and forgotten. Fukuzawa's suggestion was that the energy of the samurai could be best employed in the provinces.

Fukuzawa advanced the concepts of *seiken* and *chiken* as prerequisites for the employment of the samurai in the provinces. By *seiken*, or government power, he meant the power required to equitably establish across the entire country unified functions such as law, the military, taxation, diplomacy and currency. By *chiken*, he refers to such functions as the police, roads, bridges, levees, schools, shrines and temples, playgrounds, sanitation and the collection of local taxes, which would benefit the local area and work for the happiness of the local people.

In his arguments on the undesirable impact of government power upon private industry, Fukuzawa cited the works of Okura Nagatsune (an agriculturist of the later Edo period). Meanwhile, when commenting on the importance of local autonomy, he quoted Alexis de Tocqueville (who had been translated into Japanese by Obata Tokujiro, one of the most senior students of Fukuzawa). The exercising of government power at the time meant holding elections for ward chiefs *(kucho)* and headmen *(kocho)*. These elections would place those elected over the commoners. Fukuzawa argued that this was completely different from decentralization and was little more than an atomization of central authority. "When these *kucho* and *kocho* return to their village offices, it is a case of 'where there is no one of significance, the person of minor significance makes a broad path.' In other words, the chief puts on the airs of being an "official" and takes an arrogant attitude toward the poor people. He gives tedious instructions about how documents should be worded and the form of the characters that should be used, criticizes the paper used either because it is Mino-style paper or common writing paper, has three or four exact copies prepared, and has his subordinates make several trips to complete one single task. Surely one could not call this 'decentralization.' To the contrary, in my opinion, this has the reverse effect of making centralization even more thorough." Might we not in our own day apply this as a humorous critique of bureaucratic government?

Regarding this centralized control over local areas that Fukuzawa raised, the people's rights faction of the contemporary Japanese polity also did not show a deep enough interest. There was an enthusiastic debate over a popularly-elected legislature, but that was an entirely different issue from the arguments for local autonomy. Regardless of whether or not a legislative assembly materialized, it was essential to centralize some powers and delegate others to the local regions. In this way, Fukuzawa criticized both the government and the people's rights advocates for focusing too much on the center and paying insufficient attention to a decentralization of power to the periphery.

Appreciation for Saigo

The Satsuma Rebellion broke out in 1877. It seems that Fukuzawa stood in the camp of those who opposed the sending of a military expedition to the Korean Peninsula. However, he continued to revere and have affection for Saigo. Fukuzawa's sentiment seems to have arisen from the influence that Saigo wielded in abolishing the domains and establishing the prefectures. He also recognized Saigo's lenience when dealing with the defeated Tohoku domains of the Boshin War (1868).

On one occasion, Saigo dispatched a functionary to ask Fukuzawa's opinion regarding the establishment of a police system. Additionally, there were numerous incoming students at Keio Gijuku from Satsuma. There were a total of 35 of them in 1873, a figure that accounted for some 15 percent of the incoming class. It appears that recommendations from Saigo lay behind such a large intake.

Even after Saigo left Tokyo himself, he continued to read Fukuzawa's writings. In a letter to Oyama Yasuke (later known as Oyama Iwao, Saigo's cousin) which was dated December 11th, 1874, Saigo wrote, "Thank you very much for sending Fukuzawa's book. As I was leisurely reading it, I received a real shock. For several years a number of people have been writing about maritime defense, but in my opinion no one compares with Fukuzawa." Saigo can be seen here as both thanking Oyama for the book and praising Fukuzawa for his work. Unfortunately, modern researchers have been unable to pinpoint which of Fukuzawa's works Saigo is referring to. One view is that because installments twelve and thirteen of *An Encouragement* did not come out until that December, Saigo's comments must refer to the eleventh installment or earlier. An alternate view is that Saigo is referring to an article that appeared in some other journal. Saigo also seems to have read *An Outline*, because he praised it for its "high intelligence and excellent discussion" and recommended it to those around him.

Why did Saigo read such works, and how did he feel about them? He read *An Encouragement* approximately one year after leaving Tokyo. One wonders what he found of interest in it regarding Japan's foreign policy. He probably read *An Outline* in the latter half of 1875. Perhaps Saigo was deeply interested in the Fukuzawa's arguments regarding independence and freedom from government.

Fukuzawa's attitude toward Saigo was already clear in his essay "The Separation of Powers." The description of a person lacking advanced knowledge but nevertheless possessing a superior moral character could be applied to Saigo.

When the Satsuma Rebellion broke out, Fukuzawa advocated sending a special envoy to hear out the aims of the former vassal who had previously provided such meritorious service to his country. The idea was to then compose a written petition, jointly signed by the samurai of the former Nakatsu domain, and submit it to the Emperor's temporary residence in Kyoto. However, due to transportation issues and other circumstances, there was insufficient time to implement this plan. Fukuzawa did, however, call for a temporary cessation of hostilities, the opening of provisional courts of law, the summoning of the Satsuma leaders, and their being dealt with in a fair manner. This petition was submitted to the Emperor on July 24th. By this time, however, Saigo's army was already showing signs of defeat.

Ultimately, Saigo died by his own hand at Shiroyama Castle in September. Immediately following, Fukuzawa wrote his well-known *Meiji junen teichu koron* [Opinion of 1877]. The first major argument of this work was that the spirit of resistance was vital. In other words, it was all too easy for government to drift and become autocratic. Thus, the people must resist such developments. Since the Meiji Restoration, however, Fukuzawa argued that the spirit of resistance within society had gradually declined. Although he could not endorse Saigo's resistance by means of military force, Fukuzawa nevertheless viewed the underlying spirit of resistance as something important. The second major argument he espoused was that former rebels should be treated with forbearance. Fukuzawa wrote that, in the past, men such as Otori Keisuke and Enomoto Takeaki had been pardoned and thereafter they had been of service to the government. Indeed, there were many who could be forgiven for their previous offenses against the state. This second argument was later to be linked to the debate over reconciliation between officials and the people *(kanmin chowa ron).*

However, what gives *Teichu koron* its unique flavor is the reverence and affection Fukuzawa displays for Saigo. Fukuzawa praises him for his deep veneration of the Imperial Household, his sense of personal integrity and even his attitude toward political parties. Fukuzawa writes, "Saigo has no superior as a man of character. However small Japan may be, no matter how severe its national laws, how can it not have the leeway to accept a single individual? Japan does not exist for just a day nor will its laws exist forever. There must have been a time when this figure would have been elevated. How sad this is." This passage is one of the most passionate in all of Fukuzawa's writings. When written, Saigo was an insurgent, a rebel, and the newspapers and magazines were all severely critical of him. Fukuzawa's essay made a frontal attack on their position yet, given the social undercurrents at the time, it seemed difficult to publish this piece. Indeed, it remained unpublished for some 20 years.

Chapter 10

"Discourse on the National Assembly" and the Political Crisis of 1881

Interior of the Mita Enzetsukan, the first such auditorium in Japan, built in 1875. (Courtesy of Keio University Library Archives)

Keio Gijuku's Operational Crisis

Let us now turn to the situation at Keio Gijuku during this period. Student enrollments at the school had risen from 100 students in 1868 (Keio 4=Meiji 1) to some 377 students in 1871. However, student numbers then declined to 240 by 1873. Thereafter, enrollments slightly rebounded to 273 students by 1875, but they fell away again to a mere 105 students in 1877. This level of enrollment was on a par with the numbers recorded a decade before.

In all likelihood, the decline in student numbers might have been because fewer entrants were being drawn from the samurai class. At the outset, almost the entire student body came from either the aristocratic or samurai ranks, and many were supported by their home domains. Following the abolition of the domains, however, such largesse dried up and the number of samurai enrollees fell. By contrast, the number of students from a commoner background continued to increase during this period. By 1880, their number outstripped those of a samurai origin. Moreover, the overall size of the student body again began to climb.

Tuition gradually rose, keeping pace with price inflation. Initially, the school charged each student 2 *bu* (50 sen) for instruction. In due course, this figure rose to a high of 2 yen and 25 sen. However, in 1879 tuition was revised downward to 1 yen 75 sen because the higher figure was a considerable financial burden for students to shoulder. It is said that Tanakadate Aikitsu (later a geophysicist and professor at the University of Tokyo) was unable to bear the financial burden of studying at Keio. Thus, he transferred to the University of Tokyo, where the tuition was 50 sen.

By contrast, Keio teachers received low wages. Even if they carried out administrative duties in addition to teaching, they only received between 50 and 60 yen a month. If they were employed outside the school, it was commonplace to receive two or three times as much. That alone indicates how strongly attached the instructors were to Keio.

Nevertheless, between 1877 and 1878, the school's financial situation became critical. Fukuzawa considered taking the plunge and retrenching the teaching staff in order to cope. However, there was major opposition to the idea. Thus, salaries were reduced across the board. For example, some staff saw their base salaries of 42 yen (amounting to 55 yen per year when other benefits were added) unceremoniously chopped to just 13 yen per year.

At around the same time as the Satsuma Rebellion (1877), Fukuzawa came up with several bold proposals to secure funding. One of these was to borrow ¥200,000 for ten years without interest, and then use the interest that could be earned through investments for the operation of the school. A second was to sell the school's land, buildings and books for ¥200,000—yielding ownership of the school to another party—and then have Fukuzawa donate the ¥200,000 to the school and become the school's caretaker. A third proposal was to have someone buy just the land for ¥200,000, and then have the school use the proceeds to move to another location.

The grounds for the figure of ¥200,000 were as follows: at that time, the government issued bonds to replace the stipends that had traditionally been given to the nobility and the samurai. These yielded 7 percent interest per annum. Thus, if the school had ¥200,000 to invest in the bonds, in one year it could earn ¥14,000 in interest. At the time, the calculation was that, even with some inflation, the school would be able to operate for ten years. Fukuzawa made a serious attempt at this venture, taking an active part in trying to obtain funds, especially from the Tokugawa family. However, he was ultimately unsuccessful. These events took place in 1878.

Concurrent to these attempts, in hoping that he could borrow capital from the government, Fukuzawa consulted with his close friend Okuma Shigenobu. Okuma was personally well disposed to the idea, but the government as a whole was not. Fukuzawa was seen as belonging to the people's rights faction, and because government expenditures were rising, it was difficult to provide any further subsidies. He was told that it would be impossible for a school to obtain funding, but it might be possible for a business enterprise to do so. Thus, Fukuzawa submitted a petition requesting a loan of capital to use in a business exporting tea. He also proposed that if ¥250,000 (the figure was raised) at no interest was not possible, perhaps ¥400,000 at low interest might be an alternative. However, all his efforts came to naught. He poured out his heart to Inoue Kaoru, who opposed his various petitions, saying that the government was giving ¥15,000 every year to the Mitsubishi merchant marine school and allowing a shoemaker (Isekatsu) to borrow ¥50,000 to make shoes, so why wouldn't the government loan money to a school?

In the end, the results of his petitions fell short of expectations. Within the government there were some who thought Fukuzawa a nuisance, and it was proposed that he should be bought off with an official honor and told to shut up. Indignant at such suggestions, in June 1879 Fukuzawa withdrew all of his petitions. Under the circumstances, he resolved to close the school. Learning of this decision, people connected to Keio sprang into action. They created a means of sustaining the school and began a fund-raising campaign. With these initiatives, the school was finally able to continue operating.

Some readers may find it hard to imagine that Fukuzawa would even think of turning to the government for help. That he did so shows just how difficult it was to maintain financial independence within education. Further, what also merits attention is that after these events, the more time passed in the years following, Fukuzawa maintained a certain distance from the government. It may come as a surprise to some readers that he had at one point even considered closing down Keio Gijuku completely. During this period, Fukuzawa was not in severe financial straits himself, so he might well have invested some of his private funds into running the school. However, for him that idea may have seemed to contradict the sustaining of independence. An independent spirit began with economic independence, and it was essential that both students and teachers made efforts to help themselves. Fukuzawa strongly supported the school management in terms of financial resources, but if the school began to take that for granted, there might have been no value in teaching the spirit of independence to the student body. It is typical of Fukuzawa to show that beyond a certain point he would discontinue the school rather than break with principles.

Introducing Public Speaking

Fukuzawa's reputation spread around the country following the publication of *An Encouragement of Learning* and his activities extended beyond the walls of Keio Gijuku. To begin with, however, the activities of Keio Gijuku itself expanded beyond the campus.

In June 1874, the *Mita Enzetsukai* (the Mita Speech Society) was inaugurated. As we have seen, Fukuzawa had a strong interest in public speaking. In May 1875 the Enzetsu-kan (Speech Hall) was opened to provide a location and efforts were begun to promote the giving of speeches.

Constructed next to that building in November 1876 was the *Banraisha*, a small building with two rooms, a larger 20-mat room and a small 8-mat room, which was designed for free gatherings and friendly conversation. The building was intended to serve as a type of clubhouse for social gatherings. It is said that Fukuzawa frequently joined in informal conversations with visitors there.

His lectures at Keio Gijuku seem to have halted in about 1874. That was the year he became engrossed in study in preparation for writing *An Outline*, so he probably did not have time to spare for lecturing.

However, he did resume again in October 1878. Three times a month, Fukuzawa delivered lectures to both students and the general public, charging the latter an admission fee of one yen per month. His first lectures were on *An Outline* but the topics expanded in many different directions, and once he got started he could go on for two or three hours at a stretch. It was said that Fukuzawa looked like a brigand sitting cross-legged and smoking a thick Japanese tobacco pipe while he lectured. The number of attendees at these lectures, however, gradually decreased and within a year or two the events ended.

Outside the school, Fukuzawa's activities expanded to include participation in the Meiji Six Society. The society was formed in February 1873, the 6th year of Meiji, to bring together famous intellectuals. The person who suggested this forum was Mori Arinori. Fukuzawa was nominated to serve as the society's first president, but he firmly declined the honor, and Mori served in his place. In addition to Mori and Fukuzawa, ten other members, all scholars of Western Studies, joined the proceedings, with the membership rolls including such luminaries as Tsuda Mamichi, Nishi Amane, Nakamura Masanao, Kato Hiroyuki and Mitsukuri Rinsho.

The *Meirokusha* held regular meetings and, through the publication of its magazine, had a major social impact. They carried on spirited debates and there were a large number of published rebuttals regarding Fukuzawa's discussion of "the duty of scholars" in *An Encouragement*. There were also some who opposed Fukuzawa's endorsement of the art of public speaking on the grounds that the Japanese language did not lend itself to such a pursuit. On one occasion Fukuzawa stood and told the gathering that he wanted to speak. He then gave his opinion on the current topic of sending a military expeditionary force to Taiwan. Following his comments, he asked the assembled members whether or not they understood and agreed or disagreed with his view. Everyone agreed that they had understood. He then added, "What I have just said to you is, in effect, a public speech, and those who say that such speeches cannot be delivered in Japanese are clearly mistaken." The group laughed and conceded that Fukuzawa had made his point.

Mori sent the fourth installment of *An Encouragement* to Okubo Toshimichi, strongly recommending that he read it, saying, "This is one of the best works of recent years....Several passages are somewhat disquieting, but overall it is quite appealing....I believe it is a volume that all interested persons should read, for its logical development and for the ideals that it presents." Mori from time-to-time stood in opposition to Fukuzawa, but this recommendation shows that the leading scholar of the day possessed a generous broad-mindedness. It also reveals that the distance between politics and scholarship was not that great.

At the end of 1878, the Minister of Education, Tanaka Fujimaro, invited seven people, Fukuzawa, Nishi Amane, Kato Hiroyuki, Kanda Takahira, Tsuda Mamichi, Nakamura Masanao and Mitsukuri Shuhei, to serve as a deliberating body for advanced learning and education. He listened to their counsel regarding the establishment of the Tokyo Academy. The first meeting of this group was on January 15th, 1879, and Fukuzawa was selected to serve as the first chair. The organization that resulted from these discussions later evolved to become the Imperial Academy and today is known as the Japan Academy.

Almost all of these men were also members of the *Meirokusha*. Fukuzawa participated quite earnestly in this forum but withdrew in December 1880. His departure seems to have been related to a change in the atmosphere of the Ministry of Education. Even so, Fukuzawa definitely was not indifferent to the idea of associating with serious academics.

However, Fukuzawa no longer had the spare time to participate in such activities. In the first prefectural assembly elections held in Japan at the end of 1878, which came about due to decisions made at the Osaka Conference of 1875, Fukuzawa was selected as the top candidate to run from Shiba-ku. He received some 200 votes, the highest of any candidate in Tokyo. The second most popular candidate was Fukuchi Gen'ichiro. This suggests that the knowledge possessed by candidates at the time was both respected and valued.

It was widely anticipated that Fukuzawa would turn down the opportunity to serve in the assembly, but surprisingly enough, he accepted the post. Judging from the fact that he advocated decentralization and held serious views regarding local self-government, perhaps his decision was only natural. In January 1879, he was elected vice-chair of the prefectural assembly, but he declined. For approximately a year, he served as an assemblyman, but he showed no active involvement and resigned in 1880. Later in life he was elected several times, but he declined on each occasion.

Kojunsha, a social and political club, was founded in January 1880, and it followed in the footsteps of the *Banraisha* built on the Keio Gijuku campus in 1876. However, the atmosphere of the *Kojunsha* Club was organized more formally. Its first preparation meeting was held on August 4th, 1879. Its purpose was to create a forum where graduates of Keio Gijuku could mingle with the spirit of gentlemen and thereby help contribute to improving the manners of society at large. As we have already seen, Fukuzawa stressed the importance of social interaction and the nurturing of knowledge and virtue.

A large number of people were interested in joining this club, and by the inauguration ceremony on January 25th, 1880, there were some 1,767 members on the books, of which 596 attended the ceremony. Of the members residing in Tokyo, some 93 percent attended on that day. Of the total membership, 24 members including Fukuzawa were selected as permanent members and, of those, half were not graduates of Keio Gijuku.

The Yokohama Specie Bank was established in February 1880. It was later renamed the Bank of Tokyo and today it is incorporated into the Mitsubishi Tokyo UFJ Bank. Prior to World War II, it was the only bank in

Japan that specialized in foreign exchange. Fukuzawa had for some time lamented the fact that profits from foreign trade were monopolized by merchants from foreign countries, and he thought a major bank should be established to protect the profits of Japanese foreign trade merchants. Fukuzawa advocated the establishment of such a bank to Okuma Shigenobu, who agreed and brought it to realization. The bank's president Nakamura Michita and the vice-president Koizumi Nobukichi both had Fukuzawa's recommendation. Koizumi was Fukuzawa's earliest follower, and while Nakamura had not been a disciple, he and Fukuzawa were quite close.

In addition, Fukuzawa was somehow involved in a large number of other enterprises, including what later became Keio University Press, Maruya Shosha (founded by Hayashi Yuteki, and now known as Maruzen, a trading company dealing mainly with foreign books), and other trading companies where Horikoshi Kakujiro and Morimura Ichizaemon were employed, Nippon Railway (Japan's first railway company which Fukuzawa encouraged Iwakura Tomomi to establish), and Meiji Life (a life insurer). Fukuzawa was either directly or indirectly involved in the establishment of many new businesses.

"Discourse on the National Assembly" (1879) and the Movement to Establish a National Assembly

From the autumn of 1877 when the Satsuma Rebellion ended, Fukuzawa's vigor was so astonishing that it seemed as if he were actually putting into practice what he had written in his *Encouragement of Learning*. During the years 1877-1880, when the operations of Keio Gijuku were in a critical state, Fukuzawa's interests seemed to expand beyond the school itself.

Between July and August 1879, Fukuzawa wrote a series of articles titled "Discourse on the National Assembly" *(Kokkairon)*. According to his autobiography, following the Satsuma Rebellion, the world of politics settled down and the people began to suffer from boredom for a lack of excitement. Thinking that if he wrote about establishing a national legislature, his ideas might gain some traction in the public domain, he penned one article that he gave to Fujita Mokichi and Minoura Katsundo of the *Yubin Hochi Shimbun*, he then had them reword it so that nobody would discover the true identity of the author. They published the article and subsequent material in a series of special editorials in the *Hochi* and an open discussion of the subject developed in the newspapers of Tokyo. In his autobiography, Fukuzawa writes that his submissions to the *Hochi* promoted a groundswell of interest in a legislature.

Fukuzawa's suggestion that he was the one responsible for starting the movement to establish a national legislature cannot simply be taken at face value. Indeed, let us reexamine the events that led up to what happened.

In 1875, the *Risshisha* founded by Itagaki Taisuke, of the former Tosa domain, called for a national gathering in Osaka to establish the *Aikokusha*. This group became the first political party with a reach throughout Japan. It was comprised of 40 some members. However, because Itagaki shortly thereafter entered government service, the group went into hiatus.

In 1878, following the Satsuma Rebellion, Itagaki embarked on reviving the fortunes of the *Aikokusha* in Osaka and he achieved this in the autumn. The *Aikokusha* held its second meeting in Tokyo in March 1879 and, at its third meeting in November of that year, it laid down the goal of establishing a national legislature. The movement quickly picked up steam over the winter and at its fourth meeting in March 1880, a group led by Kataoka Kenkichi and Kono Hironaka submitted a written petition calling for the establishment of a national legislature. The petition was signed by more than 87,000 people.

In the wake of the Satsuma Rebellion both the Freedom and People's

Rights Movement *(Jiyu minken undo)* and the calls for a national legislature intensified in volume. This was because the people came to realize that even the use of military force by strong Satsuma soldiers could not overcome the government's will. Considering this background, it would be hard to argue that Fukuzawa's national assembly series, which was published in the summer of 1879, some three or four months prior to the *Aikokusha* third meeting in November, did not have a significant impact on the movement to establish a legislature.

Further, as previously mentioned, the establishment of the *Kojunsha* Club occurred in January 1880. It is not surprising that this development was seen in an interesting light, with its membership that included a thousand prominent figures drawn from many different fields. With a membership roll that boasted nationwide representation that was also not limited to people with links to Keio Gijuku, some saw the forming of the club as being paramount to the forming of a Fukuzawa Political Party.

Moreover, within Keio Gijuku itself, public speaking events were being held. At some point, these events transformed into mock sessions for a national legislature. At the first such session on March 6th, 1880, Inukai Tsuyoshi was among the central figures. Following this, sessions began to be held twice monthly. One group of participants assumed the role of government delegates, while another acted as members of the legislature. Meanwhile, elderly participants fulfilled the role of speaker. When Fukuzawa occupied the speaker's chair, he would sometimes interrupt the members and offer his own views on the topics at hand. These outbursts earned him a rather bad reputation. On one occasion, a student adamantly insisted that it was a violation of the rules of procedure for the speaker to offer his views whenever he felt like it. Fukuzawa fired back that the participants were unable to express what they were thinking and that he was just filling in the gaps out of sheer exasperation. In the early days of Keio Gijuku before Fukuzawa was deified, the atmosphere was apparently rather lively.

The Political Crisis of 1881 (Meiji 14)

Toward the end of 1880, Inoue Kaoru contacted Fukuzawa. The government was planning to publish an official gazette, although not the type of publication we think of today. The plan was more in the spirit of an accurate and responsible newspaper, which the government would support. The government was setting about issuing such a newspaper and Fukuzawa was asked to undertake the enterprise.

After giving the matter some serious thought, and realizing the publication of a newspaper was a major undertaking, Fukuzawa asked for information and clarification about how committed the government was. Inoue confided in him that the government had determined that a national legislature would be established, and that being the case, it was felt necessary to have a publication that would lead public opinion in the right direction.

Since Fukuzawa had been unaware that the government was so committed to the idea, he felt delighted and communicated that he would be willing to cooperate. In January 1881, Fukuzawa joined a gathering attended by Inoue Kaoru, Ito Hirobumi and Okuma Shigenobu. They openly discussed subjects such as who would hold administrative power and who would be the next to lead.

At the time, in response to the movement for setting up a national legislature which had being gathering steam since 1879, the government felt the need to table its own proposal. Each member was asked to present his own proposed draft. For a time, however, Okuma Shigenobu, who occupied the most senior position within the Council, did nothing to present his own ideas. However, the Grand Minister of State, Sanjo Sanetomi, finally forced Okuma's hand. Subsequently in March, Okuma submitted his own proposal for a constitution. He asked, however, that Sanjo show it to nobody. It was a rather radical plan calling for elections by the end of

1882, the opening of a national legislature in 1883 and a system of government that featured a cabinet built on parliamentary principles.

Okuma's proposal, however, did not surrender political power to the Freedom and People's Rights Movement. At the time, Okuma was the single most powerful person in government, but across the entire government, the Satsuma and Choshu factions still dominated. Thus, Okuma's status was somewhat unstable. By having Fukuzawa join him in supporting the proposed constitution, perhaps Okuma thought he could strengthen his own position. Even if there were slight differences of opinion between himself and Ito, with a few fait accompli like gaining Sanjo's consent, he thought he might win over Ito and his followers.

Taken aback when he learned of Okuma's plans, Sanjo consulted Ito and the other members of the Council of State. Discovering that Okuma had tried to outmaneuver him, Ito flew into a rage. Through the intercession of Sanjo, the relationship between Ito and Okuma was partially restored, but there is no doubt that there remained a stubborn undercurrent of hard feelings between both men.

Just as the wrinkles in the relationship between Okuma and Ito were being ironed out, in July another issue arose. This was the major scandal over the proposed sale of assets belonging to the Hokkaido Colonization Office. Since 1871, the Colonization Office under the leadership of Kuroda Kiyotaka, a powerful figure from Satsuma, had invested close to ¥15,000,000 of government money in the development of the northern island. When that policy came to an end in 1881, the assets created were to be sold off to the private sector. *Kansai Boeki Shokai*, a consortium of businessmen headed by former officials mainly from Satsuma with Godai Tomoatsu as president, won the bid to take over these assets. The value at that time was said to have been ¥30,000,000, but Kuroda allowed the consortium to make a purchase in thirty annual installments, free from interest, of ¥380,000, for a grand total of ¥11,400,000. Kuroda claimed to have a rationale for his actions. There were several sectors that were still unprofitable among the assets. Furthermore, it was thought desirable that everything be sold as a block, rather than being disposed of piecemeal. Whatever the motivations, however, on the surface, the sale clearly seemed to unfairly benefit the consortium, which in turn benefited the former domain of Satsuma. The newspapers had a field day. Among them, it was the publications with connections to Fukuzawa that exercised major influence. The interests who had lost out to *Kansai Boeki Shokai* in acquiring the assets originally were Okuma Shigenobu and the Mitsubishi consortium, with whom Okuma enjoyed close ties.

Seen in the light of these relationships, it is not so curious that conservative factions within the government, especially Satsuma, might have thought that Fukuzawa and Okuma were colluding to take over the administration. Even after Saigo Takamori's departure from the government, and the failure of the Satsuma Rebellion, the faction still possessed considerable latent strength within the ranks of the police and army.

Thus, Ito and Inoue were confronted with the option of either forming an alliance with Satsuma or continuing to negotiate with Okuma. If they joined Okuma, it would make enemies of those in the Satsuma faction who wielded real power. Moreover, they would place themselves in a subservient position to Okuma. On the other hand, if Ito and Inoue joined forces with Satsuma, they would be forced to slow down the pace at which civilization and enlightenment were being brought to Japan. However, they realized that civilization and enlightenment were inevitable developments, irrespective of the pace at which they occurred. Furthermore, because the Satsuma faction was incapable of assuming leadership so as to achieve such aims, only Ito and Inoue were truly capable. It is my opinion that Inoue and particularly Ito decided to throw Okuma to the wolves in order to resolve these matters.

On October 11th, 1881, at a meeting of the Council of State which was attended by the Emperor, it was decided that Okuma Shigenobu would be relieved of his post. The sale of the assets of the Hokkaido Colonization Office would also be cancelled, and the establishment of the national legislature was set to occur in 1890. These decisions were announced to the public the following day. These tumultuous events became known as the Political Crisis of 1881. In opposition to Okuma's dismissal, numerous government officials resigned their posts. Their number included such luminaries as Yano Fumio, Ozaki Yukio, Inukai Tsuyoshi, Nakamigawa Hikojiro and Ono Azusa. The nucleus of this group was comprised of people with links to Fukuzawa. Thus, in much the same way as Okuma was effectively cut off from the center of power through dismissal, so were Fukuzawa and his followers.

From Fukuzawa's perspective, however, these developments were baffling. He had believed that Ito, Inoue and Okuma had formed a united front. On October 14th, 1881, Fukuzawa sent a long diatribe to Ito and Inoue demanding an explanation for what had taken place. He wanted to know how what had happened had come to pass. Inoue responded that he would explain at some future time, however, he never did. Ito didn't even respond.

Jiji shogen (Current Affairs)

The year 1881 brought some other dramatic changes for Fukuzawa. That was the year he authored a long work entitled *Jiji shogen* [Current Affairs], which was described as a lengthy critique of the trend of the times.[40] In it, Fukuzawa discussed what type of government could be expected once the national legislature was established. In other words, he discussed the formal changes that would necessarily result from establishing a national assembly.

The first section of this work was entitled *Naian gaikyo no koto*, and its focus was two-fold. Firstly, it discussed what Japan needed to achieve in order to avoid unnecessary internal conflict *(naian)*. Secondly, it discussed preparing Japan for competition with the outside world *(gaikyo)*. Even though the nations of the West at the time continued to advance, Fukuzawa argued they had not progressed to a point of being beyond Japan's reach. Indeed, he suggested that Japan eagerly pursue the West with *naian gaikyo* ("stability within and competition without") as its motto.

Fukuzawa also distinguished between power and the business of government. He asserted that, what the Freedom and People's Rights Movement was aiming to achieve was a reform of government organization rather than a reform of the business of government. Fukuzawa thought that, irrespective of who held the reins of power, there would not be much difference in terms of the actual business of government.

Fukuzawa's ardent desire for the establishment of a national legislature came as a consequence of his dissatisfaction with Satsuma, Choshu and Tosa monopolizing all important government posts. So as to eliminate the cause of this discontent and maintain public order, Fukuzawa wrote there was no other option than to open a national legislature and completely change the government organization.

Fukuzawa did nevertheless acknowledge the value of what Satsuma-Choshu had done up until that point. People from those domains were the ones who had taken great risks in order to achieve significant gains. When one looked at the bureaucracy, there were many men from Satsuma and Choshu in the top positions to be sure, and just prior to and after the Meiji Restoration there were many who had lost their lives in taking care of problems affecting the existence of the country. That men from these domains now occupied positions of power was only natural.

However, what brought about the Restoration was not the great deeds of extraordinarily heroic figures. Rather, the ultimate stimulus for change was the trends of the times. Furthermore, to claim authority once matters had settled just because of certain great achievements was impermissible. Those who would attempt to retain the reins of power under such conditions constituted "a faction."

Fukuzawa also pointed to the emergence of a post-Restoration generation. A new generation was assuming power and only those people who were 33 or 34 years old or more knew what things had been like previously. The younger generation was unaware of the major achievements brought about by the Restoration movement. Fukuzawa wrote, "In the minds of the older generation, like the author,...the events of the Meiji Restoration 13 years ago are as fresh in memory as the events of yesterday. The same is probably even truer for those who participated in the government." This passage suggests that Fukuzawa may have been beginning to feel his age.

The new generation that did not know the past state of affairs might well have felt discontented with the appropriation of power by the Satsuma and Choshu. The current government, Fukuzawa continued, had carried out a truly major reform that was both bold and determined. It had involved the abolition of the old feudal domains and the establishment of the new prefectures. There had been legal reform and enhancement of the military. Culture had been bolstered while industry was promoted. Fukuzawa felt it would be odd for these intrepid statesmen to now hesitate over an issue such as the establishment of a national legislature. Even with the opening of such a deliberative body, it would be impossible to exclude all those currently in power and still hope to maintain the business of the government.

While expressing these views, Fukuzawa wholeheartedly criticized those advocates of people's rights who sought to capture the reins of government for their own agendas. He also scorned those who pressed for a complete change in the institutions of state. That is, he argued that the government should make concessions and incorporate members of the Freedom and People's Rights Movement; however, such advocates should nevertheless accede to a continuation of the manner in which the institutions of state were administered.

Fukuzawa felt that reform was called for by the trends that dominated at that time and he saw such measures as being indispensable for domestic tranquility. Since reform had to be provided in any way possible, he contended, it should be undertaken in one fell swoop. The reader should note that Fukuzawa was not making a case for a reduction of power. Indeed, in order to establish the foundations of the state, he held that political power should be strengthened. He hoped for a government that would be rigorous while not ruling with an iron fist. In this he saw something similar to the United States, an administration that possessed dignity but which lacked the harshness of despotism.

What then did Fukuzawa consider to be the political affairs or policy topics that should be continued?

Firstly, he prioritized military affairs. He pointed out that in contrast to the 400,000 samurai who had previously received stipends the 70,000 conscripts who existed at that time were a far lighter burden on the national economy. The purpose of this military was to ensure the stability of East Asia. "It is our responsibility to protect East Asia and we must be prepared to carry this out." In this, Fukuzawa used a metaphor to explain his thoughts: "Even though one's own house may be constructed from stone, there is danger posed by fire spreading from a neighbor's house which is made of wood and catches on fire." This meant that in regard to Japan's neighbors, Japan should protect them with military power, lead them toward civilization, and provide them with an example, so that all might rapidly join the ranks of modern, civilized states. Further, if it should become necessary, there should be no hesitation in using military force against any power that might attempt to impede Japan's progress in this process. I will return to this point later, but it is important here to recognize that the very first thing Fukuzawa stressed with respect to political affairs was an enhancing of Japan's military strength.

To achieve this, Fukuzawa asserted, aggressive financial policy was essential. In his view, Japan was affluent. Admittedly, following the Restoration many people lost their jobs. The palanquin bearers, for example, lost their jobs to the rickshaw pullers, but he doubted that anyone would stand up and call for a return to the old days just because of that. The power of progress was irreversible. Fukuzawa recognized that public finances were strained, but nevertheless the public had the capacity to pay taxes. It was the public that would understand the necessity of government and would help carry it forward. While repeatedly emphasizing "independence of the individual for independence of the country," Fukuzawa stressed the need to educate the Japanese nation to see their own individual destinies as tied to that of the state.

The arguments of *Jiji shogen* correspond precisely with the principles of the reforms that Fukuzawa hoped to implement in alliance with Okuma, Ito and Inoue. Because the previously-held thoughts of Fukuzawa began to evolve with the publishing of *Jiji shogen*, he was criticized in some quarters. Some saw this transformation as resulting from the closer ties he had developed with government.

However, within the context of putting his principle of "the individual's independence and the independence of the country" into realistic practice, I believe that such a transformation for Fukuzawa was inevitable. I shall address his theory of "Pan-Asianism" in more detail later; however, it seems to me that to a considerable extent *Jiji shogen* represents the logical consequences of Fukuzawa's thinking up until that time.

Of course, his scheme to ally with Okuma, Ito and Inoue was an important starting point for Fukuzawa and his rationale. Moreover, he never backed away from any of the opinions he expressed in *Jiji shogen*. From this point onward, no longer able to partner with those inside the government, Fukuzawa, while continuing to emphasize even more vehemently the importance of being independent from the government, nevertheless put forth even stronger arguments than the government did with respect to the building of "a rich country and a strong military" *(fukoku kyohei).*

Chapter 11

Home and Daily Life

Photo of Mr. and Mrs. Fukuzawa taken in 1900.
(Courtesy of Keio University Fukuzawa Memorial Center)

The Foundation of Morality Is the Husband-and-Wife Relationship

Due to the setback he experienced in the Political Crisis of 1881, Fukuzawa distanced himself from the government. In this behavior he was so successful that he established a public persona of somebody who was able to impartially advise society via his written and spoken words. He had of course maintained an independent stance in his discourse prior to 1881, but one detects a certain tentativeness in his earlier actions. For example, his behavior at that time did not exclude him from sometimes making requests of the government. He also actually considered closing Keio Gijuku at one point. Following his brush with the government and the 1881 crisis, however, such indecisiveness disappeared. Even in the field of public discourse, Fukuzawa seems to have finally hit full stride.

At the time, Fukuzawa was 46 years old and had finally reached full maturity. At this point, I would like to comment on him as a husband and father.

Fukuzawa attached great importance to an equality of opportunity. He believed that if an individual were allowed to manifest his abilities freely, social progress would be born from the resulting competition. In contrast to this, he viewed the family as a realm of affection. Thus, the competition of the outside world formed a counterpoint to the intimacy of the family. In his emphasizing of competitiveness, Fukuzawa was unique. What is more, in attaching great importance to affection within the home, he was even more unusual. This uniqueness can be understood when set against the backdrop of the dominant view of the family in his day, with its strong underpinnings of authoritarianism and its main current of the Confucian notion of male superiority and female inferiority *(danson johi)*.

The key to Fukuzawa's view of the family is the relationship between husband and wife. In *Nakatsu ryubetsu no sho* which was published in

1870, Fukuzawa wrote, "The foundation of morality lies in the relationship between husband and wife. From this springs the relationship between parent and child and between older sibling and younger sibling."[41] He judged the relationship between husband and wife to be the basis of all others. "Heaven created Man, and from the beginning it was meant that one man and one woman would be together. Having lasted several billion years, there can be no change in this equation of one man, one woman. Whether a man or woman, each is an individual and there is no reason to discriminate against either." Fukuzawa clearly asserts equal rights for men and women and that monogamy is the only matrimonial relationship.

As we have discussed, Fukuzawa married in 1861. Looking back on his marriage sometime later, he is recalled as saying, "neither before nor after my marriage did I have relations with another woman" *(Fukuzawa sensei aitoroku)*. Kin, his wife, was treated with courtesy by Fukuzawa who always referred to her politely as Kin-*san*. He also extended his use of the honorific –san when addressing his own children, as he did when interacting with students and visitors alike.

The couple's first child was a son they named Ichitaro (born 1863), who was followed by a younger brother called Sutejiro in 1865. The boys were then followed by a succession of five daughters: Sato (1868), Fusa (1870), Toshi (1873), Taki (1876) and Mitsu (1879). After all these girls there was the final addition of two more sons, Sanpachi (1881) and Daishiro (1883). Thus, there were four sons and five daughters in total in the Fukuzawa household. All the children survived to adulthood, a rather rare occurrence at the time given childhood mortality rates. Fukuzawa was 48 years old when his youngest child was born. In addition to the children, the family also took in Fukuzawa's mother Ojun in 1870. She was to pass away in 1874. Fukuzawa's nephew Nakamigawa Hikojiro was also a frequent lodger, thus the household seemed to be rather crowded.

The Fukuzawa family often went on excursions together. This tradition evolved in the wake of Fukuzawa himself contracting typhus in 1870. After being critically ill for some time, he began to show signs of recovery in the early autumn. Subsequently, as his strength returned, the entire family set off for a restorative cure at the hot springs in Atami where they stayed for almost a month. This was the first extended excursion for the family. In 1873, the family stayed at Tonozawa in Hakone, while in 1876 Fukuzawa took his two eldest sons on an odyssey through the Kansai region. It should be stated that the frequency of these trips was rather unusual in that day.

Guidelines for the Education of Children

Fukuzawa's views on education placed primary importance on the physical health of children. He believed that parents should give their offspring nourishment, guide them towards a kind but vigorous adulthood, refrain from coercion when relating to them and never resort to physical punishment.

In 1871, Fukuzawa started writing "Daily Lessons" *(Hibi no oshie)* for his sons Ichitaro and Sutejiro. These lessons were intended to teach the fundamentals of reading and writing as well as the basics of morality. The boys were then eight and six years old, which by modern standards might be considered somewhat slow. However, Fukuzawa's own introduction to literacy had occurred even later. The first of these "Daily Lessons" is set out below:

The Rules

1. You must not lie.
2. You must not take things that are not yours.
3. You must not accept presents without your parents' permission.
4. You must not be obstinate.
5. Quarreling between brothers is strictly prohibited.

6. Gossiping about people is strictly prohibited.
7. You must not covet things that belong to others.[42]

On November 26th of the same year, Fukuzawa wrote the following passage for his boys. The fact that he took time from his busy schedule to put pen to paper highlights both his deep affection and his concerns regarding the boys' education.

> In reading a book, if you forget its first part it is like drawing water into a bucket which has no bottom. There will only be the hard work of drawing the water, and the water will not remain in the bucket. Therefore, if you do not go over what you have read and memorize it, both of you will have wasted your labor in reading and will have learned nothing.[43]

In 1878, Fukuzawa sent the two boys to the *Tokyo Daigaku Yobimon* (the Preparatory School of the Imperial University of Tokyo), which later became the *Dai-ichi Koto Gakko* (the First Higher School). Meanwhile, Keio Gijuku had just established a curriculum for boys in their seventh year of schooling, so this decision to send his sons elsewhere seems somewhat unusual on the part of Fukuzawa. Perhaps he thought that, the Imperial University of Tokyo, with the support of the government behind it, had the most to offer the boys, or perhaps he was worried that they would be spoiled if they attended Keio Gijuku.

However, once the boys had settled in the *Yobimon* dormitory, both began to suffer stomach trouble so Fukuzawa brought them home for treatment. Once they had apparently recuperated, they returned to the dormitory. However, the stomach issues arose again. Thus, Fukuzawa withdrew them from the *Yobimon*. They were subsequently enrolled in the general studies course at Keio Gijuku.

In 1883 Fukuzawa sent his two sons to the United States to study. To be able to send his children overseas for their education had been his heartfelt desire for a long time. Previously, in 1871, a wealthy merchant in Yokohama had asked Fukuzawa's help in opening a school of Western Studies. In exchange, the merchant offered to cover Fukuzawa's children's expenses if they went abroad to study in the future. Fukuzawa had vacillated considerably before ultimately declining the offer. To be sure, he wanted to send his children overseas for their education, but he simply could not come to the decision to depend upon the financial resources and goodwill of somebody else. Fortunately, however, subsequently he was able to send his sons overseas using his own financial means.

At the time of their departure, Ichitaro was 19 while Sutejiro was 17 years old. Both boys were able to read English competently. Furthermore, they enjoyed conversational fluency in the language due to a succession of American and British tutors over the years. Their father sent them off with strict orders to write home regularly, even if all they wrote was that they had nothing to report. Fukuzawa himself would write over 300 letters to the boys during their sojourn abroad.

Prior to the boy's departure, Fukuzawa wrote the following set of directions for the travelers. Firstly, whatever might happen in Japan during their absence, the boys should not return unless specifically instructed to do so by their parents. Even if they heard that their parents were on their death beds, the boys should not become upset and seek to return home. Secondly, health was to be the first and foremost consideration for the boys, and whether they took three years or five years to complete their studies was of no consequence. Regarding their careers after graduation, since Ichitaro had chosen agriculture, he should not forget the importance of its practical application and he should direct his efforts toward achieving his goal. Sutejiro was encouraged to pursue physics, but ultimately the decision of what to study was up to him. Fukuzawa also wrote a poem with sets of seven characters per line which translates roughly as:

Words to send two off to the West

Ichitaro and Sutejiro, go forth and endeavor,
Each of you, spread your wings and fly high in the sky,
As simple words of farewell upon your journey to the West,
Forget neither your own country nor your own self

Fukuzawa apparently liked this last line so much, he frequently quoted this when preparing his own students who were going overseas to study. It is quite typical of Fukuzawa to say that studying in the West was only important if it was in the name of independence for Japan, and that one should not forget his own country or forget who one was.

Of the two boys, Ichitaro went to Cornell University to study agriculture but changed courses midway and returned to Japan without graduating in 1888. Upon returning to Tokyo he began to teach British and American literature at Keio Gijuku, while working at *Jiji Shimposha* where he negotiated with overseas newspapers and news agencies. Later, after Fukuzawa and Obata Tokujiro had both passed away, he became the president *(shato)* of Keio Gijuku. Meanwhile, Sutejiro studied rail and civil engineering at MIT and after graduating returned to Japan with his brother. He took employment at *Sanyo Tetsudo* (the Sanyo Railway Company) and worked as an engineer under the guidance of Nakamigawa Hikojiro. In later life he was to become the president of *Jiji Shimposha*.

Incidentally, during his time in the United States, Ichitaro had thought seriously about getting married to an American girl. When he consulted his father, Fukuzawa said that it would be all right, as long as he could earn a living to support himself. When Ichitaro asked once again, Fukuzawa stated his opposition, his rationale being that it would be hard to really earn enough to satisfy a foreign woman and if Ichitaro did not have confidence that he could achieve that, he should give up the idea.

As to the education of Fukuzawa's daughters, it basically took place in the home, or at the *Yochisha* (an elementary school built inside Keio Gijuku).

Fukuzawa had at one time enrolled the three oldest girls in the *Kyoritsu Jogakko*, a mission-founded school in Yokohama. However, it seems that he missed having his daughters around so he quickly brought them back home. Other sources say it was actually his wife who made the decision.

From the above snippets, we can tell just how much Fukuzawa loved his family. Moreover, there is another episode that illustrates this inclination even more strongly.

Fukuzawa's third daughter, Toshi, developed an ovarian cyst. In an article entitled, *Dobyo Aiawaremu* (literally "Companions in Misery"), published in the *Jiji Shimpo* on March 25th, 1891, Fukuzawa related the story as follows.

> Once we found out about the situation, we agonized over how to tell our daughter about it. Whenever we were around her, we tried to smile and act as we normally would, taking sightseeing excursions and spending happy days together. However, when my wife and I sat facing each other alone in our room, the topic would come up constantly, we would then fall silent and end up in tears. On the day we finally decided to have her undergo a surgery, after we saw her off to the operating room, we felt like we were hardly alive. In the eyes of her mother and father, as the nurse helped our adorable 17-year-old child toward the surgery, she seemed to us like a flower or a pearl…We felt as if there was nothing inside to hold us up.

Luckily, news came that the operation was a success. "All of the tension that had built up was released and it was as if we were looking at a dream." And after that, "just as when our daughter had been born, the family's joy was hard to express in speech or writing. All we could do was be grateful for the kindness shown to us by so many people." "The parent's worries before the surgery may have shortened their lives by three years, but the success brought happiness that could make life three hundred years longer."

This passage was written by Fukuzawa to pay homage to Western medicine, and he revealed how his heart was about to break with worry prior to the surgery, but how filled with joy he was once the surgery was successful. The passage displays no regret whatsoever about showing the deep affection he felt at the time. It is well known that his motto, as he offered it in his autobiography, was to not show on the surface normal human emotions but rather to remain impassive. But the real Fukuzawa was actually rather intense both in the feelings he had and the way in which he expressed them.

A Hearty Eater and Heavy Drinker

I would like to at least briefly touch on Fukuzawa's health and diet. We have records from Fukuzawa's application for life insurance with the Meiji Life Insurance Company at the age of 48 years old. According to this application, Fukuzawa weighed some 70.2 kg and stood 173.5 cm tall. Compared to the national average height of 158.7 cm at that time, Fukuzawa possessed a rather outstanding physique. In most contemporary photos, he is shown towering above his peers. Even his recorded lung capacity was huge at some 5159 cubic centimeters, compared with the national average of 3041.

Fukuzawa was a hearty eater and a heavy drinker. One might say he drank like a fish and ate like a horse. Upon entering middle age, however, he began to exercise a degree of moderation in consuming both food and drink. The impetus for modifying his lifestyle was the bout of typhus suffered in 1870.

As already mentioned, Fukuzawa had consumed alcohol from childhood. With the exception of the year of abstinence in Nagasaki, he proved to be very fond of drink. He had tried abstaining during his years at Ogata's *Tekijuku* and took up smoking instead. But he failed to give up alcohol and instead ended up with a smoking habit to boot. Both of these weaknesses continued until the illness at the end of his life.

He began to seriously cut down on his drinking in 1870 when he came down with typhus. From then onward, he began to reduce his intake, first by eliminating his morning tipple, then by giving up drinking during the day. The only exception to this rule was when entertaining guests. Eventually he completely quit all daytime consumption of alcohol, and even reduced what he drank with his evening meal. It took him roughly three years to settle into this routine, after approximately ten years of considerable consumption. He also became more attentive to the quality of liquor he drank. Only genuine saké brewed in Nada would do (a district of Kobe known for its long history of brewing), and Fukuzawa even claimed that he could distinguish between the different Nada brands. In his later years, he also became accustomed to drinking beer. Although early on he had been a heavy drinker, no matter how much he consumed, his face did not show it nor were there changes in his behavior or speech. His conversation simply became a bit more animated.

A hearty eater early on in life, Fukuzawa's eating habits too began to diminish during his thirties. Not extravagant by nature, and because he always had a drink when he ate, he ate slowly and always chewed his food well. He also ate nothing between meals. In later life, Fukuzawa ate so slowly that whomever he was with would end up eating his portion as well. By the time he was ready to eat a second serving, often everything had already been consumed. This seemed to have caused problems for those he shared his table with.

In 1895, Fukuzawa attended an alumni gathering in Shizuoka Prefecture. He was 60 years old and he actually took the time to write a note outlining his food preferences to the person arranging his accommodation. According to this correspondence, Fukuzawa wanted to have *miso* soup using *Sanshu miso* for his breakfast, and it was to be served without either fish or dried bonito flakes. Instead, he wanted just a few spring onions or some tofu added to the soup. He also expressed his gratitude in advance if prior to breakfast some milk with black tea or coffee in it and toast with butter could be made available. For lunch he wanted to have two side dishes with fish, meat and vegetables. For dinner, he hoped to receive a slightly large portion of fish and a little top-quality saké.

Polishing Rice, *Iaido* and Walking

Fukuzawa kept extremely early hours (he was early to bed and early to rise). He woke each morning at 4:00 a.m. and went to bed at around 10:00 p.m. With many visitors to talk to during the day, his early morning hours served as a valuable time for writing.

Fukuzawa was completely indifferent when it came to clothes. His dress usually consisted of a casual kimono with a *haori* of the same pinstripe pattern (a short coat worn over a kimono). When he went out for a walk, he wore close-fitting trousers with the hem of his kimono tucked up, and this hardly made for a refined appearance. Generally, he wore clothes in the Japanese style. This was a curious decision. At a time when an adopting of the Western-style of dress was being promoted along with an associated rhetoric of "civilization and enlightenment," there was Fukuzawa, at the extreme right-wing of the Westernizers, choosing to dress himself in traditional Japanese garb.

Fukuzawa undertook his writings in a very small room. He said such surroundings enabled him to feel a certain calm and composure. He had no interest in issues of décor or decoration. Typical of the sort of person who likes to display his shortcomings, he declared that the best decorations were fakes.

When he wrote his manuscripts, he used a brush and ink. He always chose a short inkstone and felt that the ideal method for inking the brush was to hold it horizontal to the surface of the ink, but since that was impossible, he explained, he selected a short inkstone. For everyday clothing he wore cotton kimono, but once he grew older, he realized that because the sleeve of a silk kimono slipped smoothly with less friction, it made writing easier.

As a boy, Fukuzawa had been accomplished at various simple tasks and even as an adult he worked diligently at all kinds of minor chores. When it came to hulling rice for consumption, he carried out the entire process, from the initial husking through to cleaning up afterwards. If he ran out of paper while writing, he would not call out to have the maid bring him more but would quickly get up and go for it himself.

The exercises he enjoyed matched his physical strength. He was particularly good at polishing and preparing rice, and the martial art of drawing the sword, called *Iaido*. Because the lower-echelon samurai within a domain during the Edo period received their rice stipend in the form of rice still in its husks, rice hulling had been part of Fukuzawa's routine chores since childhood. Even after moving to Edo, he occasionally polished rice, and went so far as to build a rice-hulling shed after relocating to Mita. Summer or winter, he would put on a single-layer yukata and polish a handmill full of rice, which would be either consumed by the family or given to close friends.

Fukuzawa had also begun training in *Iaido* when he was a boy. Believing that he ought to become accomplished in at least one martial art, he took instruction in *Iaido* from a sword master named Nakamura. When anti-foreign sentiment had been widespread, he was ready to sell off his sword because of the danger involved. However, once things settled down, he took out his sword again and resumed practicing. In a letter to a friend back in Nakatsu in 1890 Fukuzawa wrote, "To my good fortune, things are going well, and even now I get exercise polishing rice and practicing the sword skills that I learned under Nakamura Shobei-sensei. Recently I believe that I have become a bit more skillful than before. But I regret that there is no instructor of the Tatsumi Shinryu school of *Iaido* here to correct the places where I am making mistakes."

From notes that he left, we get a glimpse of just how much Fukuzawa practiced.

November 17th, 1893: 1,000 sword draws in total
9:15-12:00: 640 sword draws
2:00-3:30: 360 sword draws
Sword Length: 2 *shaku* 4 *sun* 9 *bu*
Weight: 310 *monme*

October 25th, 1894: 1,200 sword draws in total
9:15-12:00: 680 sword draws
2:00-4:00: 520 sword draws
Sword: same as last year

December 31st, 1895: 1,000 times
8:30-1:00: without intermission
Sword: same as last year

Could it be that Fukuzawa used this list to keep a record of his diminishing physical strength? At any rate, the volume of exercise is certainly impressive.

When he was a child, the Kabuki actor, Onoe Baiko VI, often visited the Fukuzawa home with his adoptive father, Onoe Kikugoro V. As such, since it was the host's custom to practice drawing his sword after dinner, the child witnessed Fukuzawa's training routine. Fukuzawa apparently was very skilled at drawing his weapon in confined spaces. He would balance a chopstick on the hilt, draw quickly and slice the chopstick in half before it hit the ground. When he traveled, because he did not need to hull rice, he took a sword along for practicing *Iaido*. When staying somewhere on one occasion, a maid entered his room unexpectedly after dinner while Fukuzawa was brandishing his sword. She apparently ran off shrieking in fear. The only assessments we have of Fukuzawa's martial prowess come from people close to him. Thus, we cannot truly judge his skill. However, given the training numbers listed in his notes, Fukuzawa must have been quite capable.

In his later years, Fukuzawa's doctor warned him about exercising excessively and advised him to give up either rice-polishing or the sword. When Fukuzawa asked which the doctor would recommend, rice-polishing was suggested because it required more strength. Fukuzawa claimed that the doctor's response came from his ignorance of *Iaido* and the strength it required.

Horse riding was another of Fukuzawa's great enjoyments. After recovering from his bout of typhus in 1870, riding was recommended to him as a possible form of exercise. It quickly developed into a passion. There were riding grounds in Mita, and Fukuzawa started to ride regularly when he went out. In fact, when *Jiji Shimpo* relocated its offices to Nihonbashi 3-chome in 1883, Fukuzawa would saddle a horse and ride to the office. This practice was to continue until Fukuzawa fell off his mount on one occasion and the family made him give it up. After this, the single horse was replaced by a horse-drawn carriage. These events took place around 1884 or 1885, when Fukuzawa was about 50 years old.

It need hardly be pointed out that lower-echelon samurai did not traditionally engage in the skills of horsemanship, so imagining Fukuzawa riding a horse to the offices of his newspaper is somewhat difficult. However, from 1877 onward, Fukuzawa began to reassess some of the traditions of his class. This soul-searching saw some traditional samurai customs reintroduced to the daily lives of the Fukuzawa family.

Going on long rambling walks was another Fukuzawa pastime. January 19th, 1888 was a Sunday, and Fukuzawa and three of his daughters set out for Yokohama. Their plan was to walk the entire distance. However, if they grew tired in the vicinity of Omori or Kawasaki, they would stop their hike and take the train back to Tokyo. As things turned out, they left home at 10:00 in the morning, reached Kanagawa station at 5:30 p.m. and caught the train home from there. Fukuzawa recalled this family adventure in a *Jiji Shimpo* article: "They talked and laughed as they made their way along the Tokaido....Sitting at a tea stall drinking astringent green tea and eating baked sweet potatoes was a new experience for the three girls but they enjoyed all the events of the day. It was impossible to prevent them from inviting their father to take them out somewhere the following Sunday. This is what makes for a happy family life." It is peculiar that he writes about this in the third person, but Fukuzawa must have wanted to recommend the pleasures of walking. He also must have wanted to offer it to others as an inexpensive way of creating a happy family circle.

Toward the end of his life, Fukuzawa walked roughly six kilometers every morning with a young student as his companion. He would usually wear a kimono with the hem tucked up, a pair of close-fitting trousers and a hunting cap. He would also carry a bamboo cane, and, when it was chilly, he would wear a pair of gloves. His sandals were of lightweight paulownia wood that he ordered specially made. In two months, Fukuzawa would wear through five pairs of them. They cost about 35 sen a pair, which was cheap compared to the 2 yen sandals he had previously worn. When the bottoms of these sandals wore down unevenly and made walking difficult, Fukuzawa would even off their soles with a hatchet. Skilled as a boy in such mundane tasks, he remained capable as a man. When walking became part of Fukuzawa's daily routine, students from the dormitory and nearby lodging houses gathered to accompany him. They referred to themselves as the Walking Party. This morning tradition continued until Fukuzawa fell ill.

Chapter 12
The Korean Issue

Photo of Fukuzawa Ichitaro and Sutejiro with students from Korea taken around 1882. (Courtesy of Keio University Fukuzawa Memorial Center)

The Aim of Publishing the *Jiji Shimpo*

The Japanese government underwent a major transformation due to the Political Crisis of 1881. The several years that followed were characterized by the rise and fall of the Freedom and People's Rights Movement, tensions regarding Japan's policies with respect to Korea, and a growing conservativism within the government's policies.

Let us first consider the Freedom and People's Rights Movement. On October 18th, 1881, the Liberal Party *(Jiyuto)* was established. This occurred a week after Okuma Shigenobu had been dismissed from government service. The following month, Itagaki Taisuke became the party's president. Meanwhile, on March 14th, 1882, the former bureaucrats who had supported Okuma and resigned when he was dismissed announced the establishment of the Constitutional Reform Party *(Rikken Kaishinto)*. They did this in conjunction with a number of prominent figures. This development was followed by Okuma being appointed the party's leader on April 16th. In other developments, Fukuchi Gen'ichiro and others formed a third political force called the Constitutional Imperial Rule Party *(Rikken Teiseito)* on March 18th. This group positioned itself in opposition to both the Liberal Party and the Constitutional Reform Party. The next big development occurred on April 6th. While in the middle of a nationwide electioneering tour, Itagaki, the Liberal Party President, was attacked and wounded in Gifu Prefecture by a would-be assassin. Out of this incident came the legend of Itagaki, who when attacked, goaded his would-be nemesis with the memorable line, "Itagaki may die, but liberty never!" This incident was symbolic on two fronts. It highlighted both the upsurge of support for the Freedom and People's Rights Movement as well as the resistance to it.

The *Jiji Shimpo* went to press for the first time on March 1st, 1882. This was after the Liberal Party had been established and just prior to the setting up of the other two parties.

As has been discussed, as a result of an agreement between Okuma, Inoue and Ito, Fukuzawa had planned to establish a national newspaper in 1881. However, the plan had been temporarily derailed by the upheaval of the Political Crisis. Nevertheless, Fukuzawa had long been intrigued by the idea, and he could not give up on it easily. Indeed, because preparations to launch the paper were already underway when the political crisis struck, he made up his mind to keep going regardless of the consequences. Fukuzawa turned to his nephew, Nakamigawa Hikojiro, to be the president of the new paper. Nakamigawa had both studied and taught at Keio Gijuku. He had also studied in the United Kingdom at Fukuzawa's expense, before returning to Japan and entering the Foreign Ministry. His bureaucratic career saw him rise to the rank of bureau chief. However, he was one of the numerous bureaucrats who had resigned in the wake of Okuma's ouster from power. It was soon after this that Fukuzawa approached his nephew regarding the new enterprise.

Until that time, there had been two major types of Japanese newspaper: one was the "big" newspapers whose editorial pages focused on major political and economic issues; the other was the "small" newspapers whose focus might be best described as day-to-day news and social developments. It is important to note that each of the "big" newspapers was allied with a political party and reflected their views in the individual newspaper's editorial stance. Thus, Fukuzawa took great delight in the idea of publishing an alternative whose perspective was independent of any political group and free of political bias.

In his autobiography Fukuzawa writes that the Political Crisis of 1881 was bringing about bitter rivalry, which included:

> ...a quarrel within itself. It was logical to expect similar reactions in subsequent economic and industrial rivalry. The greatest need in such a

time is an instrument of nonpartisan, unbiased opinion. But it is easy to make satisfying theories about nonpartisan opinion and not so easy to realize it in practice, for the usual man, conscious of his own personal interests, cannot lightly throw off his partisanship. As I looked about the country, I decided to myself that there were not many besides myself who were independent in living, and who had worthwhile ideas in their heads, and who could yet be really free from political and business interests. With this reasoning, I set myself to the task of establishing a newspaper which became the Jiji Shimpo.[44]

Fukuzawa wrote in a letter to Motoyama Hikoichi of the *Osaka Shimpo* that the *Jiji Shimpo* would commence publication on the 1st of March. He also indicated that he had written a sort of editorial as a rehearsal for the upcoming publication. "I've gradually gotten used to it and can do it with ease. I chuckle to myself because compared with writing a book it is much less hard work and I can do it without racking my brain." To Fukuzawa, it was not a difficult task to quickly assess various world issues and write his opinions in clear and precise prose. He could be called a natural-born newspaper reporter, or perhaps more appropriately, a born opinion leader.

In the masthead of the first edition of the *Jiji Shimpo*, Fukuzawa clearly stated his motivations for publishing the newspaper. His assertions tied in closely to the educational ethos of Keio Gijuku. By the time of the newspaper's birth, there were some 3,500 Keio graduates throughout Japan. These were individuals who had been exposed to lectures based on English and American texts, and they had both proactively adopted modern civilization and worked to develop it even further after their graduation. They had studied in an atmosphere of independence and had enjoyed a sense of freedom from restraint. It was this same ethos that Fukuzawa had in mind when he wrote, "the paper will write about recent civilization and discuss every measure to further promote it, without delay in delivering the news and informing the people of that news."[45]

Fukuzawa then further elaborated on his aims:

> It is to be hoped that our scholarship is independent and not to be disparaged as the aping of Westerners. We aspire to carry out our business independently and not under Westerners' control. We aspire to keep an independent legal system that will not be taken lightly. We aspire to maintain the independence of our religions that cannot be trampled on by them. In other words, we place a premium on the independence of our country of Japan. The object of our lives is to sustain the rights of the country *(kokken)* and anyone who shares with us this objective is a companion of the school, and in reverse, anyone who opposes this, either directly or indirectly, must be considered by all of us as an opponent.

In every field of endeavor, Fukuzawa stresses, the aim is to achieve true independence for Japan. The editorial position of the *Jiji Shimpo* was that it was in favor of the opening of a national legislature. The reason for this was that through the establishment of such an institution, the power and influence of the government would be strengthened, as it was a "concentration in one place of the power of all the people of the country." In an editorial, Fukuzawa added that recently political parties had emerged but people had lost sight of the importance of the power of the state *(kokken)*.

From that point on, Fukuzawa noted, political parties would compete with one another, evolve, disappear, and unite, thus changing in many different ways. The *Jiji Shimpo*, however, was not a political party, and it possessed absolutely no political ambitions. "What we take as our doctrine is the spirit which expands the independence of the individual and the independence of the household even further to attain the independence of our country." In other words, in his writings for the newspaper, Fukuzawa emphasized the principle that the independence of the country and the independence of the individual were co-dependent and the objective of the *Jiji Shimpo* was to promote this idea.

Before long, the *Jiji Shimpo* established its reputation as Japan's premier newspaper. Later, in 1910, when a member of Britain's royal family visited Japan, two representatives from the newspaper industry were invited to attend a formal reception to honor the visitor. One of the two was the *Jiji Shimpo* and the other was to be selected from the various other newspapers.[46]

Harmonizing the Officials and the People *(Kanmin chowa ron)*

The upsurge in the fortunes of the Freedom and People's Rights Movement did not last for long. On June 3rd, 1882, the government revised the Public Assembly Ordinance. This revision prohibited political activity by students in particular and seriously curtailed political activities in general. In the following year, the Press Ordinance was revised. The changes that were made gave prefectural governors certain practical administrative powers. These could be used to discipline the press and to enforce control over the newspapers.

In the autumn of 1882, the Liberal Party's Itagaki Taisuke revealed plans to visit the West. This development was problematic because it effectively meant that the head of a major political party was to be absent from the country for an extended period during a critical time. Additionally, however, there were suspicions that the government was actually going to bankroll the Itagaki trip to get him out of the country. In other words, what was going on was part of a larger government plan to strike a blow against the Freedom and People's Rights Movement. However, despite all the rumors, Itagaki ultimately did depart from Japan on November 11th together with Goto Shojiro. These two would be away from the country until June 22nd of the following year. There was criticism within the Liberal Party over this issue, and also criticism from within the Constitutional Reform Party. Meanwhile, the Liberal Party counterattacked the Constitutional Reform Party. (This counterattack became known as the "movement to eradicate the counterfeit political party," and a core criticism that it sought to make was that the Constitutional Reform Party was actually a sham front supported by funds from the Mitsubishi Zaibatsu). The net result of this bickering among the infant political parties was incalculable damage to the Freedom and People's Rights Movement as a whole.

Furthermore, the deflationary policies pursued by Matsukata Masayoshi in the role of Finance Minister continued during this time. One result of the "Matsukata Deflation" was that the price of rice dropped by almost half within two years. This development inflicted a serious blow upon the wealthy farmers who represented the backbone of the Freedom and People's Rights Movement.

Finally, the movement reached a state of paralysis. Its radical elements who wanted quicker change began to radicalize further. This disaffected the rank-and-file membership who began to defect. This development in turn placed the movement in a vicious cycle. In 1884, violent strikes broke out frequently with some of the events subsequently being known to history as the Gunma Incident, the Kabasan Incident, the Chichibu Incident and Nagoya Incident. Then in October, the Liberal Party dissolved, a mere three years after its establishment. The Constitutional Reform Party did not fare much better. In December 1884 Okuma Shigenobu withdrew, and although the party did not fold, its strength waned significantly.

In the midst of all of this, as we have already discussed, Fukuzawa came out with his speeches on independence and freedom. In his arguments he most strongly criticized the Constitutional Imperial Rule Party.

Fukuzawa's initial criticisms were directed at the names of the fledgling parties. The names of the political parties, he commented, were supposed to distinguish one from another and indicate the policies that they wanted to promote. But, to his way of thinking, the names of the Liberal Party, the Constitutional Reform Party and the Conservative Party should in reality indicate how they differ from others in terms of their policies. However, there was no one anywhere who opposed having the Emperor reign over the country. Thus, for the members of a party to pointedly call themselves the "Constitutional Imperial Rule Party" was like some group from the former Kaga domain referring to themselves as the "Maeda Party" (the name of their former lord). It also implied that everyone else was part of the "Non-Maeda Party," which was a completely meaningless assertion.

Fukuzawa was strongly opposed to involving the Imperial Family in politics. If we borrow our present-day wording to express their role, Fukuzawa's position was that the Imperial Family is a symbol of the unity of the Japanese people. His stance was that it was not permissible to employ the Imperial Family within the practice of politics in order to divide the people into factions. However, it should be noted that one part of the reason why Fukuzawa criticised the Constitutional Imperial Rule Party, was because of the party's criticism of Fukuzawa and the long-lasting difficult personal relationship Fukuzawa had with Fukuchi Gen'ichiro. Then again, his stance on the Imperial Family and its role in politics was one that he had long embraced, and he had even referred to the idea of the Imperial Family getting involved in politics as ominous (March 31st and April 1st). Indeed, in May of 1882, he published an article on this very subject entitled, "On the Imperial Household" (*Teishitsuron*).

Of course Fukuzawa's criticism of the Constitutional Imperial Rule Party was also a condemnation of the government as well. Between May 17th and June 17th, 1882, he published a serialized discussion entitled, "Oligarchs of the Clan Clique". In this, he plotted the development of the government following the Meiji Restoration. According to Fukuzawa, it had been supposed that real power in the post-restoration government would fall into the hands of the lords of the stronger domains. However, it had actually fallen into the hands of samurai from the strong domains which created a government in which a small number of elite individuals held actual power. This unexpected development had played a major role in abolishing a government dependent upon lineage. It had also promoted the process of enlightenment. This government of "oligarchs" brought about changes such as allowing commoners to ride on horseback, allowing them to take family names (surnames), and it had also promoted civil rights. However, as the hectic times abated, adverse effects had come to the fore. The discussion of people's rights was now swallowing the elitist government that had followed the restoration. Fukuzawa argued that the government should properly accept capable people from outside its small circle of talent and become less a government run by a limited number of elites and more a government run by the many. Because his criticism of the government was then considered extremist, Fukuzawa's articles earned the *Jiji Shimpo* a limited publication ban from the government censors.

In July, the Imo Military Rebellion *(Jingo jihen)* broke out in Korea and the attention of Fukuzawa and indeed of all Japan was diverted in that direction. I shall discuss the Korean problem in detail later in this work, but here let us note that in terms of domestic politics, these events further strengthened Fukuzawa's ideas as to the necessity of a harmonious collaboration existing between the public and private sectors.

On August 6th, Fukuzawa wrote to Iwakura Tomomi saying that the perfect moment for the "harmonizing of the officials and the people" *(kanmin chowa)* had arrived. The reasons Fukuzawa gave for this belief were as follows: Government power was at a high point, and if people from outside were taken into the administration at this point, such decisions would not be seen as a sign of weakness. Indeed, accepting outsiders into the fold would be seen as engaging such people to play important roles at a time when numerous affairs of state needed to be addressed. If Prince

Arisugawa and Ito Hirobumi, who were then abroad, were to be called home, and if members of the opposition, such as Soejima, Goto, Itagaki, Okuma and other retainers who had rendered meritorious service during the restoration, were involved in the decision-making, the members would be gathered as a government-appointed assembly, which in itself represented a step forward on the road to achieving a publicly-elected legislature. At any rate, if a government comprised of five or as many as seven members were to definitely invite discord, then the same could be said of one with fifty to seventy members. Even two hundred members was perhaps possible and it would attain a degree of popular favor. Fukuzawa asserted that there would be no change in "the fact that the leading lights of the restoration would control the Meiji government." The story that Fukuzawa proposed that these leading members of the opposition should be introduced into the body of Councilors resulted from the visit he paid to Iwakura at the end of June, prior to the Imo Military Rebellion.[47]

The confrontation between the government and the People's Rights Movement that followed the autumn of 1882 was a cause for apprehension in Fukuzawa's eyes. On September 29th and 30th that year, he wrote editorials titled "Extremes" in the *Jiji Shimpo* on what he viewed as the polarization of society. He criticized those political forces that would divide the nation into two camps, one supporting the government officials and one supporting the People's Rights Movement, and then consider one as loyal and the other as disloyal, one as law-abiding and the other as traitors. He described this attitude as "those who make allies where there are no enemies" (November 13th). Regarding the Constitutional Imperial Rule Party and the *Tokyo Nichinichi Shimbun*, who were absorbed in such activities, he described their situation with a metaphor which said that a dog will be well cared for when there are rabbits to hunt, but when the rabbits disappear, it will be eaten.

If the government in a similar way drove the People's Rights Movement into a corner, Fukuzawa worried the latter might eventually turn into a destructive power. Looking at what happened to the Liberal Party after 1883, this proved to be an entirely accurate forecast.

The Anti-Fukuzawa Movement

Behind the government suppression of the People's Rights Movement described above were policies based on a strongly conservative ideology. Within government ranks from the Political Crisis of 1881 onward, there was a faction that viewed Fukuzawa Yukichi as an opponent. After the crisis, this faction gained political power and they worked to establish a means by which to reduce Fukuzawa's influence.

At the center of this group was Inoue Kowashi, who was then Secretary of the Council of State. In a written opinion dated November 7th, 1881 (Meiji 14), he wrote that Fukuzawa's influence was to be feared, and that in order to diminish it, other newspapers should be encouraged to adopt an anti-Fukuzawa stance, middle schools and vocational schools should be reformed, and Chinese and German Studies encouraged.

Clearly, the government until that time had focused its efforts on primary education. Meanwhile in the field of higher education, Keio Gijuku had come to occupy the top rank. Additionally, as fallout from the Political Crisis of 1881, Okuma Shigenobu had left government service and founded *Tokyo Senmon Gakko* in October 1882 (which would later become Waseda University). Thus, the government decided to take measures that would reduce the appeal of Keio Gijuku.

The survival of the study of Chinese Classics, the strengthening of Confucian virtues, the enhancement of German Studies and the bolstering of the University of Tokyo for the training of government officials were all fostered following the Political Crisis of 1881. In dealing a blow to Keio Gijuku, the cancellation of the deferment of conscripted military service had a particularly strong impact. Until this policy change, students enrolled at Keio had been temporarily exempt from conscription. At the end of 1883, under a revision of the Conscription Ordinance, this exemption was nullified. This was a major shock to the students, and of the 588 students then enrolled, more than 100 withdrew from their studies. Fukuzawa naturally protested strongly against this revision, criticizing the government, saying that there was no difference between government colleges and private institutions in serving the state through scholarship.

The pressure that was applied to Keio did not begin with the Political Crisis of 1881. Rather, as early as the movement to establish a national legislature back in 1879, voices within the government began to call for a shift away from education that placed an emphasis on civilization and enlightenment. The first move occurred in August 1879, when the Emperor expressed his wishes regarding education. He ordered his tutor, the Confucian scholar Motoda Nagazane, to strengthen the tenets of Confucian moral education, and the Emperor's desire was reflected in the Education Order of 1879. In the following March, the Vice-Minister of Education, Tanaka Fujimaro, was appointed Minister of Justice. The rumor was that his departure from the Ministry of Education was due to his responsibility in the "Europeanizing" of education.

Following Tanaka's departure from the Ministry of Education, the actual bureaucratic powerbroker within the ministry became Kuki Ryuichi, who had begun his studies at Keio Gijuku in 1871. In 1872, he had entered the Ministry of Education. From that point onward, Kuki was partially responsible for Europeanizing education but somewhere around 1880 he became estranged from his alma mater. Furthermore, although he had been involved in the formation of the *Kojunsha* Club, he never put in an appearance at their activities. In the summer of 1881, he reestablished contact with Fukuzawa, but ties broke off again suddenly with the outbreak of the Political Crisis. Thereafter, Kuki aligned himself with the critics of

Fukuzawa, and within Keio there was some resentment at his change of heart, and he was criticized as a kind of spy.

In 1884 Kuki was assigned to Washington, D.C., as Japan's Minister to the United States, and prior to his departure he called on Fukuzawa. The latter would relate this visit in a letter to Murai Yasukata of the Morimura Gumi in New York.

He wrote that Kuki had begun his studies in the early years of Meiji and though he was not particularly talented in reading, he had a natural cleverness that made him stick out. They were on close terms back then, Fukuzawa said, and even after Kuki entered the bureaucracy, he often came by the Fukuzawa home, where he was treated like a member of the family. But three or four years previously, "he seemed to find an 'interest' in something" and completely stopped coming by the Fukuzawa home. Then he suddenly showed up again, talking about how he wanted to do something for Fukuzawa's sons. Fukuzawa declined the offer, but Kuki was absolutely shameless. He had known the Fukuzawa children since they were young and said he had been asked to "look after" them. Fukuzawa wrote that Kuki annoyed him immensely and that from that time on he could not forgive his former student.

The Korea Problem

Using the *Jiji Shimpo* as his platform, from the summer of 1882 onward, the issue that Fukuzawa dealt with most was Japan's policies toward Korea. In due course, his interest in these developments would lead Fukuzawa to publish his *Datsu-a-ron* [Departure from Asia] in 1885. In time, this interest in Korean developments would also lead to Fukuzawa seeking to glorify the Sino-Japanese War of 1894-95. In the modern world in which we now live, Fukuzawa has been severely criticized for holding such views, and they are perhaps the most difficult elements of his legacy to reconcile when trying to undertake any assessment of his philosophy. How exactly are we to understand the relationship between Fukuzawa and Asia?

When seeking to do so, it is first important to discuss the specifics of the Korea problem. Generally speaking, Japanese-Korean relations during the Edo period were tranquil. Indeed, relations between the two countries were managed through the Tsushima domain. This domain maintained the Soryowakan Guesthouse in the city of Pusan and even conducted trade within Korea. Each time a new shogun came to power in Japan, the Koreans sent major embassies *(tsushinshi)* to Edo to congratulate the new incumbent, and the Japanese received these missions warmly. Each of these imposing missions consisted of several hundred people and they were known for the leisurely pace at which they progressed to and retired from Edo. During their residence in the city, many Japanese scholars visited the lodgings of the Koreans and exchanged poems and prose. At the time, the study of Confucianism was flourishing and Korea was felt to be at its leading edge. Moreover, the Korean entourages also participated in both diplomacy and trade with their Japanese hosts. As such, although Japan is often portrayed as being *sakoku* during the Edo period (literally "a country closed to the outside world"), its seclusion was not total. Indeed, Japan's diplomatic exchanges were limited to Korea, while its trade relations were confined to business conducted with Qing China and the Netherlands.

However, this state of tranquility did not last. In October 1868 when Japan notified the Korean authorities as to the restoration of imperial rule in Japan, the Korean government refused to receive the official documents. The reason given for the refusal was the wording of the pronouncement. The points of contention were *tenno* ("emperor") and *chokugo* ("imperial rescript"). Such wording was rejected because Korea still maintained a relationship of loose dependency with Qing China. The Imperial Court in Korea, in exchange for acknowledging the dominance of the Qing dynasty, received Qing recognition of its subordinate kingship. Moreover, the Qing used the term *kotei* (emperor) while the Koreans used *kokuo* (king) to describe their respective sovereigns. Thus, from the Korean perspective, "emperor" and "imperial" were terms to be applied solely to the Qing dynasty, and to no other country.

In Japan during the Edo period, even though he was more figurehead than actual ruler, the Emperor was nevertheless positioned above the shogun. Consequently, if the Korean king was of equal status to the Japanese shogun, then the emperor of Qing was of equal status to the Japanese emperor. This was the kind of logic that was accepted in Japan.

However, if the Japanese emperor were to be considered to have the same status as the Korean king, that would place Japan under the authority of the Qing dynasty. In order for Japan to assume parity with Qing China, the logic was there were basically only two options available to Japan. One was for Japan to assume a position of superiority to Korea just as Qing China had. The other was for the Kingdom of Korea to take a position independent of China.

During this period, actual power in Korea was held by the king's father, a regent referred to as Taewon-gun [Daeweon-gun], who had assumed a strong anti-foreign stance. In 1866, he attacked and sank an American merchant ship and repelled a French naval squadron. He also took pride in these successes. In June of 1871, however, an American naval squadron arrived in the kingdom seeking redress for the 1866 sinking and it also demanded the opening of the country to trade. Once again, however, the Americans were driven off. Taewon-gun had made every possible effort to equip a gun battery constructed on Kanghwa Island [Ganghwa-do] with the most modern armaments available. But these proved to be no match and they were completely destroyed by the Americans. The intruders, however, withdrew as before. This development was then portrayed as a victory by those who advocated the exclusion of foreigners.

Against this backdrop, it was understandable that Korea would not easily succumb to Japan, thus negotiations between the countries came to an impasse. In Japan some hawks contended that Korea had been discourteous and ought to be punished. Others suggested that the dispatch of an expeditionary force would divert the energies of the anti-government samurai forces. In January 1869, Kido Takayoshi consulted with Omura Masujiro about the various options available. The sending of forces abroad for the sole purpose of eliminating domestic discord was a preposterous idea, but Kido, despite being known as a liberal, considered doing just that. Such was the temper of the times, and the authorities were just extremely anxious about the potential trouble that restless samurai might stir up.

The government, however, decided instead to try to rectify relations with China, and on September 13th, 1871, it signed the Sino-Japanese Amity Treaty. As a result of this agreement the countries achieved parity with each another.

The suspension of trade relations with Korea, however, could not be left unattended. The new government in Japan had abolished its feudal domains and established prefectures in their place, and the diplomacy that had formerly been conducted by the heads of the Tsushima domain was taken over by the new national government. Furthermore, in April 1873, the Japanese government acquired the Soryowakan Guesthouse in Pusan, this made relations with Korea even more complicated. Out of these complications erupted the debate over whether or not to send a punitive military expedition to Korea.

Fukuzawa was opposed to dispatching such an expedition, as he had been in 1874 regarding an expedition to Taiwan. After the Taiwan Expedition came to an end, Okubo Toshimichi successfully concluded negotiations with the Chinese in Peking. At about the time of Okubo's return to Japan, Fukuzawa wrote in the *Meiroku Zasshi* that the ones who actually profited from the war were the foreign merchants, whose benefits far exceeded the indemnities Japan received. Fukuzawa found this to be immensely frustrating. For him, the real parties to be cautious of were the Western merchants. Moreover, he saw the issue at hand as being a business and trade conflict.

In November 1873, Taewon-gun was brought down by Queen Min and the Kingdom of Korea began to move toward opening itself to the outside world. Seeing this as an opportunity, in September 1875, Japan provoked Korea, causing a military confrontation at Kanghwa Island, and it demanded that Korea subsequently take responsibility for the incident. Korea opened the country by signing the Treaty of Kanghwa (also known as the Japan-Korea Treaty of Amity) in February 1876. The strategy adopted by Japan was typical gunboat diplomacy, of the type learned from the great powers of the West.

Fukuzawa wrote in the *Yubin Hochi Shimbun* that "peace or conflict with the various countries of Asia is neither glorious nor disgraceful as far as I am concerned." In saying this, the point he wished to make was that the real issue for Japan was competition with the West, not militarily but in terms of trade and commerce. Picking a quarrel with Korea over some supposed slight was a case of mistaking the relative significance of matters. He insisted that the promotion of Japanese industry and concern being given to domestic issues should take priority.

The Imo Military Rebellion of 1882

The beginning of Fukuzawa's calls for a military buildup appeared in *Jiji shogen* [Current Affairs](1881). As has already been stated, Fukuzawa pointed to the frightening prospect of the advance of the Western powers. Japan must, he claimed, protect the countries of Asia and lead them to civilization and enlightenment, adding that should the situation call for it, even use coercion and threats to force the countries of Asia into action.

These calls for a military buildup coincide almost precisely with the beginning of Fukuzawa's strong attention to developments on the Korean Peninsula. In June 1881, three young men from Korea came to visit him. Of the three, two stayed in Japan and pursued their studies. In a letter Fukuzawa wrote to Koizumi Nobukichi, who was then in London, dated June 17th, he stated:

> At the beginning of this month, several Koreans came to Japan to observe the situation here, and two of them have come to study at our school. I have put them up in my house and am giving them guidance. I can't help but sympathize with them and remember what it was like for me in a similar situation 20 years ago. For these Koreans, it is their first time overseas and by sheer chance, they are the first students from overseas that we have accepted. Through this turn of events, we have regular visitors from Korea now coming to the house. As I listen to them, I cannot help recalling Japan as it was 30 years ago. It is my hope that we will continue our close relationship and that they will be able to further enlighten their country.

In other words, Fukuzawa felt strong empathy with the Korean people who were aiming for modernization, and he made every effort to cooperate with them. This empathy with the Korean reforms was one major reason for the change in Fukuzawa's attitude. Furthermore, Kim Ok-gyun, a prominent leader in the Korean reform movement visited Japan in December 1881 and in June 1882, he called upon Fukuzawa at his home.

On March 11th, 1882, the *Jiji Shimpo* carried an editorial entitled "On relations with Korea" in which Fukuzawa argued that it was Japan that led Korea to opening its doors, just as the United States had opened up Japan years earlier. And just as the U.S. played a leading role in Japan's diplomatic relations, Tokyo should now play a leading role in Korea's relationships with the outside world rather than leaving matters to chance. Not only that, Fukuzawa argued that the Western nations were steadily advancing in Asia and the only centralized force that could stand in opposition to them was Japan. Neighboring China and Korea should move to counter the West, and they should seek to rely on Japan. However, Fukuzawa stated that they were both obstinate and stubborn, and if they were left to their own devices, they would surely fall into the hands of the Westerners. If the Chinese could control China by themselves, and the Koreans of the day could control their country, then there would be no particular problem. On the other hand, if they lost national sovereignty and fell under Western control, that would be a matter of enormous consequence for the region. Thus, in order to protect its own house from catching fire from the house next door, under such circumstances Japan would have to intervene in the affairs of both China and Korea.

Fukuzawa also contended that the Japanese should not only play a role in bringing civilization and enlightenment to Korea. Rather, he argued that Tokyo should also station troops there to protect the safety of Japanese residents of Korea. During Japan's own Bakumatsu period, there had been frequent attacks on foreigners. In response to these incidents, Great Britain and other foreign powers had stationed detachments of troops in Yokohama. On March 31st, 1882, in an incident at Wonsan [Weonsan] Harbor in Korea's north, an outbreak of violence had left one Japanese dead and two severely injured. Fukuzawa wrote about this particular incident in an editorial in the *Jiji Shimpo* on April 25th. He detested the incident as being stupid, piteous and outrageous; however, he argued that not all the fault for it lay on the Korean side. The first steps toward civilization and enlightenment, Fukuzawa commented, were sometimes difficult. But if there had been three Japanese warships in the harbor, 50 Japanese policemen and 20 Japanese army officers, then the incident would not have occurred. Fukuzawa emphasized the importance of making such advance preparations at Wonsan, Pusan, and the other port that was about to be opened at Incheon. In this editorial, one can feel the influence of Fukuzawa's own agonizing experience when trying to deal with the Richardson Affair of 1862.

Shortly after these events, the Imo Military Rebellion (also known as the Imo Incident) broke out on July 23rd in Korea. The roots of this upheaval can be traced as follows: as previously stated, back in 1873, the kinsmen of Queen Min had deposed the faction led by the Taewon-gun. Measures were then taken to modernize the Korean army, and these measures included the establishment of newly-selected special units. At the center of the initiative to establish the new units was a group of Japanese military advisors under the command of a Lieutenant Horimoto. However, matters did not proceed smoothly in that the high-handed nature of Queen Min and her kinsmen differed little from that of the deposed Taewon-gun. Thus, traditional units within the Korean army remained unpaid for a period of ten months. By contrast, the newly-selected special units were provided with favorable treatment and this created friction with the rest of the army. Aware of these developments, Taewon-gun, the deposed regent and father of the king, incited the troops toward violence. They massacred the group of Japanese military advisors, attacked Japanese who were living in the city, and even forced their way into the Japanese Legation. Japan's envoy Hanabusa Yoshimoto was barely able to escape and he managed to reach Incheon. Once there, however, he was once again attacked by a violent mob. He finally managed to get aboard a fishing boat and while it drifted on the open sea, he was picked up by a survey ship of the British navy which eventually delivered him to Nagasaki.

In the final analysis, the whole incident was a counter-revolutionary coup d'etat orchestrated by the Taewon-gun. However, one of its developments was that the Japanese government started heated discussions about what to do in way of response. It was eventually decided to carry out tough negotiations with Korea with the goal of realizing peace and on August

12th Hanabusa returned to Korea, accompanied by Japanese troops. Even under such circumstances, the Taewon-gun proved to be uncompromising in his stance. China, however, decided to act. In an attempt to regain control of the situation as quickly as possible, it boldly abducted the regent and confined him at Tianjin. On August 30th, the Treaty of Chemulp'o was signed between Korea and Japan, with Korea paying an indemnity.

As events transpired, Fukuzawa called for the dispatch to Korea of sufficient military force to deal with the incident. He also wanted those responsible punished and for the government to take a resolute stance in dealing with the situation. The crux of his argument, however, was not for war. Rather he demanded a not excessive indemnity be imposed so that stability could be achieved once more.

It was China that took astounding actions during this period. The Qing dynasty was then dealing with France in the south of its territory and had no desire to concurrently confront Japan. It had implemented bold measures that displayed its firm grip as the suzerain state with power over Korea. The central figure in this was a twenty-three-year-old named Yuan Shikai, who would later become the first president of the Republic of China.

Enhancing Armaments and the *Datsu-a-ron* (Departure from Asia)

Initially Fukuzawa seemed to be satisfied with the Treaty of Chemulp'o. However, over time his interest in Korea deepened even further. In October 1882, Kim Ok-gyun once again arrived in Tokyo as a member of the mission that was sent to apologize to Japan (with Park Yong-hyo as its senior envoy and Kim Man-sik as his junior). This opportunity to visit Japan allowed Kim Ok-gyun to deepen his friendship with Fukuzawa. The number of Korean students studying at Keio Gijuku had increased, and

Fukuzawa was to send Ushiba Takuzo to Korea as an advisor on Korean domestic reform. As words of farewell to his friend, Fukuzawa wrote a two-part editorial entitled, "Ushiba Takuzo goes to Korea", in the *Jiji Shimpo*.

Following the events of the Imo Military Rebellion, Fukuzawa pressed even more strongly for enhancing Japan's armaments. Between December 7th and 12th, 1882, he wrote a serialized editorial entitled, *Toyo no seiryaku hatashite ikansen*. In this series of articles, Fukuzawa discussed the importance of the situation in Korea. Furthermore, he stressed the importance of a rich country and a strong army for Japan. According to Fukuzawa, with regard to Japan's objective of promoting civilization and progress in the three countries of the East, China could be considered as being bold, it even pondered at one time the turning of an independent Korea into a Chinese province whose name was to be Koryo. Fukuzawa also thought that Russian ambitions in the region were a cause for concern, and it was not at all inconceivable that it might dispatch warships off the coast of Wonsan. If that scenario eventuated, then it was hard to believe that the other European nations would remain on the sidelines as simple spectators. Despite such risks, Japan had not strengthened its military to any perceptible degree over the last ten years.

Fukuzawa also reflected upon his own attitudes. Whereas a few years earlier he had contended that the most urgent business for Japan was giving priority to domestic affairs and also promoting industries including mining as well as the building of infrastructure such as port facilities, he now felt ashamed of having made such assertions. Nevertheless, he felt it was still not too late and that all possible effort should be devoted to strengthening Japan's military. To accomplish such a policy would necessitate an increase in taxation, and to get the public to accept such a burden would require closer relations between the government and people. His assertion was that, to achieve such a state of affairs, leaders from outside the government should be brought into the administration.

Fukuzawa's promotion of a strengthening of Japan's military was not merely a narrow interpretation of the issue in that it focused purely on the question of a buildup of armaments. Rather, he had long been an active proponent of the development of railways, and following the Imo Military Rebellion, he focused on their military worth and became even more vocal in expressing his opinions (*Tetsudoron* [On Railroads], September 22nd and 25th, 1882). Furthermore, on April 17th, 1883, he wrote an editorial in the *Jiji Shimpo* about gradually increasing the speed at which the promotion of civilization and enlightenment occurred. He commented that Italy, which could hardly be called a rich nation that possessed a strong military, was laying 200 to 300 miles of railway track per year, while Japan spent one year deliberating the topic and then one year constructing it, the net result being the annual laying of a mere 50 miles of track. Fukuzawa felt that such a slow rate of progress was absurd and he pressed strongly for a speeding up of development.

In Korea, as a result of the abduction of the Taewon-gun, following the Imo Military Rebellion, Queen Min and her clansmen returned to power. However, the government of Queen Min was strongly conservative by nature and it deepened its traditional dependence on the Qing dynasty. Meanwhile, on the recommendation of the Chinese, this dependence led to the German Paul Georg von Möllendorff being appointed to manage the Korean Customs Service. From this financial source, funds were secretly diverted into the coffers of the Imperial Court. The funds, however, were in fact earmarked for use by the Chinese to fund conservative forces within Korean politics (the "Serve the Great Party" also known as the "Conservative Party").

In response to such developments, elite young bureaucrats such as Kim Ok-gyun and Park Yong-hyo thought that real reform was necessary in Korea. Kim was born in 1851 and was 31 years old at the time of the Imo

Military Rebellion. He had only been 23 years old when he passed the intensely competitive civil service examinations at the top of all the applicants in his year. Park was 10 years younger and came from a distinguished family with royal connections. Both men believed it was necessary for Korea to become completely independent from Qing China and they called themselves either the Independence Party or the Enlightenment Party. In short, they were quite close to Japan. It is not accurate to think of the relationship between the Serve the Great Party and the Enlightenment Party as a power struggle by proxy between Japan and China. Rather, the conflict between the Korean political parties involved the issues of whether to carry out a reform of the absolute monarchy and whether to enter into modern international relations. It is perfectly natural that the views of both Kim and Park had been greatly influenced by the ideas espoused by Fukuzawa. Indeed, the one who presented the clearest answer to this conundrum, for Japan and even the world at that time, was none other than Fukuzawa.

The Enlightenment Party eagerly sought the support of Japan, but the Japanese themselves were cautious. However, in August 1884 when China and France clashed in Indo-China and war between the two countries broke out, the Qing dispatched half of the 3,000 troops they had stationed in Korea further to the south. As a result of this development, Japan's attitude changed. Taking advantage of the opportunity, the Enlightenment Party, with support from King Gojong, and with cooperation from the Japanese army, attempted a coup on December 4th. The Enlightenment Party with 100 men, the Japanese with 200 men and 400 troops from the palace guard garrison attempted to strike against 1,500 Chinese troops in what became known as the Kapsin Coup (or the Kapsin Incident).

The Enlightenment Party overthrew the prominent figures of the Serve the Great Party and temporarily set the king up as their leader. The king then sought the protection of the Japanese army. Japan's Minister Takezoe

Shin'ichiro led Japanese troops into the palace and on the 5th, the Enlightenment Party government came into existence. However, on the following day, Chinese troops began a counteroffensive. Park and Kim fled and sought refuge in Japan and Minister Takezoe and others made a narrow escape. The attempted coup was an absolute failure. To what degree Fukuzawa was involved in this attempt is not clear, but one theory holds that he was deeply committed to it, including support with weaponry.

In January 1885, Japan and Korea signed the Kanjo Treaty (the Treaty of Hanseong). Ostensibly, Japan was the aggrieved party who had suffered damage in the wake of the failed coup. Thus, Korea promised to send a mission to offer apologies and pay an indemnity of ¥110,000 for the casualties and damages caused. It also promised to arrest and execute the murderer of Lieutenant Isobayashi, as well as pay ¥20,000 for the construction of a new Japanese Legation (the old one having burnt down). However, because the actual opponents in the incident were Chinese troops, negotiations were also carried out with China, with Ito Hirobumi in April visiting Tianjin to negotiate with Li Hong-zhang and to sign the Tianjin Convention. The outcome of these negotiations was that, within four months, Japan and China would withdraw all troops from Korea. Furthermore, Japan and China would cooperate in dispatching military instructors to train Korean troops; and both sides would notify the other party in writing in the event that troops were to be dispatched to Korea.

The Japanese public was dissatisfied with the Tianjin Convention. However, the government cracked down strictly on any criticism of the convention. Thus, the newspapers and magazines in Japan were not able to criticize it freely. Fukuzawa was unable to seriously attack it, but he did write an essay during this period in which he criticized France's attitude toward China in signing for peace as being weak-kneed. This argument by Fukuzawa was seen as an indirect criticism of the Tianjin Convention as well.

Fukuzawa's famous *Datsu-a-ron* [Departure from Asia] was published on March 16th, 1885 prior to the signing of the Tianjin Convention. In it, he argued that Japan was already leaving a backward Asia in its wake. He also expressed the opinion that China and Korea, two Confucianist states, had neither evolved nor had they displayed any inclination to introduce Western civilization. If such trends were to continue, he prophesized, both might become targets for partitioning by Western countries. By contrast, Japan did not have any leeway that would allow it to wait for its mainland neighbors with respect to the latter taking steps to throw off their backward Confucianist past. Indeed, in speaking specifically about Japan, Fukuzawa clearly stated that "it is better for us to leave the ranks of Asian nations and cast our lot with civilized nations of the West."[48] Having joined the West, Japan should then treat its unenlightened neighbors the same way that the Western powers had been want to treat the nations of Asia. One who associates with the wrong crowd cannot escape gaining a bad reputation, so Japan would have to make up its mind, he said, to leave Asia behind.

The reference to treating Japan's neighbors "the same way that the Western powers had" could possibly be construed to mean the practice of "invasion." Fukuzawa's use of "treatment" in this context, however, simply meant that Japan should deal with the nations of Asia in a manner similar to that employed by the West. Behind this argument lies the fact that Fukuzawa had given up on the cherished scenario he had held since 1881, a scenario which would have seen Japan lead Korea to enlightenment through a process of independence, thus creating a unique and close bilateral relationship. In other words, "Departure from Asia" was a statement of defeat by Fukuzawa, who had previously been enthusiastic about leading Korea to becoming an enlightened and open country. While saying this, there can be no denial that Fukuzawa would later contend that Japan should have a showdown with China; however, it is inappropriate to read

"Departure from Asia" as simply Fukuzawa advocating a policy of hardline diplomacy.

Chapter 13

Establishment of the Cabinet System and Treaty Revision

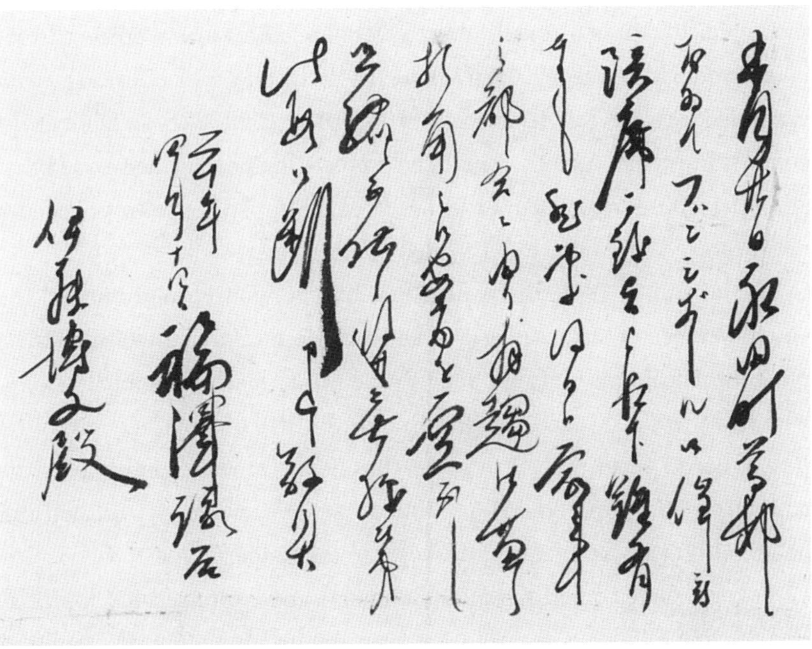

Letter addressed to Ito Hirobumi declining an invitation to a ball.
(Courtesy of Keio University Fukuzawa Memorial Center)

Emergence of Prime Minister Ito Hirobumi

When relations with Korea had somewhat settled by the conclusion of the Tientsin Treaty in April 1885, the focus of politics within Japan started to plot a new course. Steps began to be taken to commence the final stage of establishing a modern state.

Ito Hirobumi, who had traveled to Europe in March 1882 to survey constitutional systems on the Continent, returned home in August 1883. An office for the further investigation of such systems was then created within the Imperial Court and Ito was appointed as its head. He and his colleagues began groundwork in preparation for the establishment of a constitution. For example, the Peerage Act of 1884 created a new peerage that, in addition to drawing on former court nobles and former daimyo, was expanded to allow for a number of newly-ennobled individuals. With the establishment of a constitution, it would be necessary to create a legislature, and within the legislature there would be an upper house. Thus, an expanded peerage was felt necessary in order to fill such a chamber. In contrast European nations, where the pre-existing peerage demanded that an upper house be created, in Japan when an upper house was needed a new peerage system had to be created to fill its seats.

At the end of 1885, the system that had previously underpinned the Grand Council of State was revised and a modern cabinet established in its place. Ito Hirobumi was appointed Prime Minister while Sanjo Sanetomi, who had previously served as the Grand Minister of State, was given the post of Lord Keeper of the Privy Seal, thus he was made responsible for the daily affairs of the Imperial Household. Sanjo's post was newly-created and he was also to act as an aide and advisor to the Emperor.

Fukuzawa welcomed these developments and expressed his appreciation in the following terms: what was important within the political reforms was that Sanjo became Lord Privy Seal and Ito became Prime

Minister. Up until then, the apparatus of government had lacked a clearly-defined locus which meant that each Councilor serving on the Council of State enjoyed equality with his peers. Now, however, Ito had been established as the central political figure. Thus, it was now justified to refer to the apparatus of government as the government of Count Ito. Following the Meiji Restoration, it had been possible to refer to the Okubo administration, due mainly to Okubo Toshimichi's competence. However, the current administration was the Ito government, and in Fukuzawa's view, to have such a political core was a cause for celebration.

Fukuzawa further felt that Ito's position should be officially designated as the most important within government. "No matter how often the old is replaced by the new, it is to be hoped that the Japanese government will always consist of a cabinet system and a prime minister as its responsible agents." Fukuzawa's reception of this central seat of authority was most favorable.

The inauguration of the cabinet system and the swearing in of Ito as Prime Minister was an epoch-making event. The previous Grand Council of State had consisted of the Emperor, under whom served the Grand Minister of State, the Minister of the Left and the Minister of the Right. Beneath these posts were the Councilors of State and under that there were nobles who served as Chief Administrative Secretaries. Because members of the Council of State often simultaneously served in the role of Chief Administrative Secretaries, theoretically the traditional system of administration was a dual or triple-level structure.

There were also other restrictions built into the traditional system of administration. In the first instance, the occupants of the ministerial posts immediately subordinate to the Emperor had to come from one of the top three ranks of the court nobility. Traditionally, however, bureaucratic competence among the court nobility was a rare thing. Thus, a structure with the Emperor at the apex with three ministers immediately below him was a hollow one. The reason why such a system had survived until then was because after the Meiji Restoration the Minister of the Right had been Iwakura Tomomi, a court noble of exceptional ability. When he died in 1883, the Meiji government was left in a very difficult position. There were only two paths open to it. One was to appoint a competent statesman who might be of a more modest status, such as Ito Hirobumi, to a minister's position. The other alternative was to overhaul the government with a new system. Ultimately, it was the latter alternative that was chosen, and the more efficient cabinet system was brought into effect to replace the Grand Council of State.

Compared with the period of the bakufu, the new system represented an enormous innovation. Previously, the shogun had served under the Emperor, and under the shogun was the top echelon of the bakufu. This group was comprised of the shogun's senior councilors *(roju)*. These men were drawn from the Tokugawa's hereditary vassals who themselves were daimyo. It was they who managed the day-to-day business of government. Under the new system, Ito Hirobumi, whose origins lay in the lowest of the samurai's ranks (*ashigaru*), held a position that was much more important and powerful than those previously held by the Tokugawa vassals. Nothing could illustrate more vividly the Meiji Restoration's revolutionary impact than this new method of selecting suitable people of whatever status for the highest positions. Fukuzawa was fully aware of the importance of this reform.

Arguments for Expanding the Navy *(Kaigun kakucho ron)*

More than anything, Fukuzawa appealed to the new cabinet to strengthen Japan's military preparedness, especially that of its navy.

In August 1886, four modern warships belonging to the Qing dynasty's northern squadron (the *Zhenyuan*, the *Dingyuan*, the *Jiyuan* and the

Weiyuan) visited the Port of Nagasaki. At the time, the ships were among the newest and most powerful in the world and they represented the pride of the Qing fleet. However, when granted shore leave, the Chinese sailors landed and proceeded to get drunk and out of control, and when Japanese police officers moved into arrest some of them, approximately 300 Chinese naval personnel attacked. This led to a massive brawl. The result was a major incident with one Chinese officer and three seamen dead as well as one Japanese police sergeant. There were also more than 80 casualties on both sides.

Fukuzawa was outraged by this incident. He insisted that this incident was no mere drunken brawl, the commander of the flotilla should be held responsible, and reparations should be paid. He pushed for the rapid completion of a railway link between Tokyo and Nagasaki.

The editorial in the *Jiji Shimpo* of September 21st, 1886, "What should be done with the Miyako Islands and Yaeyama Islands?" is also very interesting. In it, Fukuzawa wrote that his consistent view was that military preparedness should be expanded, and that once Japan opened relations with foreign nations, it was only natural that Japan needed to be prepared to protect its independence. Reflecting on the strengths and weaknesses of nations, Fukuzawa felt that national strength should not be viewed as feeding an ambition to wage war on other countries nor should it be corrupted in order to take land by force, rather national strength should be seen as essential to a nation's protection of itself through its own power. His criticism was that, at that time, Japan was not even prepared to defend the Okinawan islands. He contended that, at a minimum, a man-of-war should be stationed at Yaeyama or that troops should be stationed there on land. He also argued that telegraph lines be laid between Yaeyama, Miyako and Okinawa through to Kagoshima, and that even in times of peace warships should be placed on patrol. Great Britain at that time had occupied the Komundo [Geomundo] Islands in Korea, and a similar thing could happen in Japan. Fukuzawa argued that other nations should be deprived of the opportunity to take over any of Japan's strategically-important islands.

However, what Fukuzawa was calling for was not just self-defense in its narrowest sense. On January 6th, 1887, in an editorial in the *Jiji Shimpo* entitled, "Korea is Japan's bulwark," he implied that the line of defense protecting Japan was Korea. Thus, if the Korean Peninsula were to fall under the control of Japan's enemies, it would not be in Japan's interest, and the resources required to protect Japan would suddenly multiply. Fukuzawa also argued that Japan would seem to have forgotten Korea since the Kapsin Political Coup, but he warned that Japan should be warned that China was actively involved on the Peninsula, having dispatched Yuan Shikai, laid telegraph lines and attempted to lease the Komundo [Geomundo] Islands.

In actual fact, the Japanese government was making efforts to strengthen its military, especially the navy. Comparing 1886 with 1884, the budgets of other ministries did not increase significantly, but naval procurement rose by ¥1,650,000 while army procurement increased by ¥1,210,000. Additionally, in 1886, the government floated public bonds of ¥5,000,000 for the purpose of naval expansion, and the following year another ¥6,480,000 was floated for the same purpose. However, Germany's budget for 1886 by comparison was 705,880,000 marks, with military expenditures accounting for more than half this total. By contrast, Japan's military outlays of ¥24,050,000 were less than one-third of the total budget of ¥79,930,000 passed in the same year. Fukuzawa insisted that this amount was still insufficient (*Kaibohi no kashi*, April 4th, 1887).

In March 1887, the Imperial Household donated ¥300,000 from its own allocated budget for naval expansion. Fukuzawa welcomed this and compared it with foreign countries. The royal households he listed, with the Japanese yen equivalents of their allocated budgets, were ¥4,880,000 for Austro-Hungary, ¥3,890,000 for Italy, ¥2,570,000 for Great Britain and

¥1,470,000 for Germany, the last two allocations being in addition to the enormous assets that the royal households in question already possessed. Russia did not have a budget allocation for its Imperial Household but the Czar possessed enormous assets from which he gained an annual income of ¥15,700,000. Compared to these entities, the expenses of Japan's Imperial Household were ¥2,500,000 annually and the income derived from other Imperial Household assets was slight. The point that Fukuzawa was trying to make was that the donation from the Imperial Household to the navy was more than one-tenth of its actual annual allocations. He held that government officials should follow suit and donate a percentage of their own salaries, and that the people should do likewise. Realistically, however, given that a recession had continued for several years, such largesse on the part of the rank-and-file would be difficult.

What could be done? An answer was offered in a *Jiji Shimpo* editorial entitled, "The only course of action is expenditure reductions," which was published on April 5th, 1887. Fukuzawa argued that it was first of all necessary to reduce government expenditures. To do this meant reducing the size of the bureaucracy and the duties of each ministry. Special reductions should be made in education, sanitation and public works. The government should do away with interference in and protection of public activities and abandon large-scale construction projects. In sum, he felt that every effort should be made toward the realization of cost-cutting.

Going a step further, Fukuzawa proposed granting court rank to people who made donations. Around that time, rumors had in fact circulated that individuals could receive court rank by simply donating money, and there had been a backlash of criticism. However, Fukuzawa countered that there was nothing intrinsically wrong with the idea. The authorities had real power, and if some questionable person achieved such a position he might be able to cause real harm, but if the status granted to him were a mere formality, like a court rank, then no harm would result. If soldiers and warriors rendered service with their spears, statesmen and diplomats worked for the country, and industrialists increased the national wealth, then they were all performing meritorious service for the country. Fukuzawa commented that perhaps no one in Japan could compare with America's multimillionaire Cornelius Vanderbilt, who although he did not respond in terms of philanthropic work, had every reason to boast that he was serving the state through what he did, and Fukuzawa agreed with his self-assessment. In this passage Fukuzawa demonstrated why he was well known for stressing the independence of the people from the officials and emphasizing the significance of business and industry.

Inoue Kaoru's Treaty Revisions

The political turbulence of 1887 centered on the issue of Japan's attempts to revise the unequal treaties it had previously signed with the Western powers.

The treaty revision issue was one of the most important confronting the Ito Cabinet, and the individual who found himself at the center of the developing storm was Inoue Kaoru. Inoue had served as the Lord of Foreign Affairs since 1879 prior to the establishment of the cabinet system. He then took up the post of Minister of Foreign Affairs in the Ito cabinet when the latter became Prime Minister. In May 1886, the Japanese authorities initiated meetings with the ambassadors of the various foreign countries. This was done as a prelude to conducting full-fledged negotiations for the purpose of revising the unequal treaties. By April 1887, negotiations between the various parties were approaching a consensus.

Inoue's proposed revisions included the opening of the interior to foreign nationals within two years of any amended agreements being concluded. Foreign nationals would also be permitted to conduct trade domestically and take up residence. They would be granted rights of ownership and mining rights as well. A modern legal code would also be established, and approval thereof sought from the various Western nations. Westerners would also be appointed to serve as judges within the structure of the major courts in order to hear legal cases involving their compatriots. Japan was also willing to establish courts with a majority of judges who were Westerners. The specific purpose of these courts would be to hear cases where the defendant was a Westerner.

During this period, the government also enthusiastically held balls and other social functions at the Deer Cry Pavilion *(Rokumeikan)*. These events took place in order to demonstrate to other countries that Japan was Westernizing. A number of prominent Japanese and Westerners attended a costume ball that was held at the Prime Minister's Official Residence on April 20th, 1887. Fukuzawa Yukichi also received an invitation to attend. However, all he could manage was a lukewarm response in turning down the offer. He declined because Ito and he were still at odds over past events. Furthermore, Fukuzawa was not one who enjoyed displays of pomp and extravagance.

As to the holding of such events as part of the cabinet's attempts to revise the unequal treaties, there were voices of opposition heard from within government ranks. The French jurist and government advisor Boissonade de Fontarabie and Tani Kanjo of the conservative faction (then serving as Minister of Agriculture and Commerce) went so far as to submit their protests in writing. The situation deteriorated further in July when Tani resigned and cabinet split on the issue. These developments forced the government to temporarily postpone the efforts it was making to revise the treaties.

The treaty revision issue breathed life into the Freedom and People's Rights Movement. Furthermore, in around 1885, the impact of the "Matsukata Deflation" gradually began to weaken. On October 24th, 1886, remnants of the former Liberal Party led by Hoshi Toru held a gathering of interested parties from throughout the country.

As a curious coincidence, on the very same evening, the *Normanton*, a British merchantman, ran aground and sank off the coast of Kishu (Wakayama Prefecture). This resulted in all 23 Japanese passengers onboard being drowned. By contrast, the ship's 27 English crew members "miraculously" survived by taking to the lifeboats. The incident was a clear case of the lives of Japanese being treated with contempt by foreign nationals. To make matters worse, at the Board of Enquiry held at the British Court of Japan in Yokohama in December of that year, the ship's captain was given an extremely light sentence of just three months imprisonment. This decision enraged public sentiment and led to strong demands for the system of Consular Courts to be abolished. Given the circumstances surrounding these events, it is hardly necessary to explain their impact on the government-sponsored social functions held at the Deer Cry Pavilion.

In May 1887, supporters of the former Liberal Party held their second gathering of interested parties from throughout the country. Hoshi Toru had also been able to procure copies of the protest letters that both Boissonade and Tani had sent to the government. These he had printed and widely distributed. In September, the former party's supporters moved to initiate a movement that had three major objectives: the reform of diplomatic policies, the reduction of land taxes, and freedom of speech and rights of assembly. The popularity of this protest surged in the period from October through December with the former Councilor Goto Shojiro becoming its leader. Tokyo was thrown into an uproar. A movement that rivaled what had happened during 1881-1882 now had begun in earnest.

By way of response, the government had Inoue resign in September, and Ito then moved to assume responsibility for foreign affairs in addition to his other duties. Ito then resigned from the post of Lord of the Imperial Household for which he had also been responsible, and Hijikata Hisamoto, formerly Minister of Agriculture and Commerce, took over as Minister of the Imperial Household. Kuroda Kiyotaka of the former Satsuma domain, who had served as an adviser to the cabinet, was installed as Minister of Agriculture and Commerce. Making a concession to the conservatives, Ito and Inoue, in order to counter charges that they were monopolizing control within the Imperial Household and the government, strengthened their cabinet by introducing Kuroda. Following these events, in December the government suddenly issued a rash of public security measures and banned approximately 570 people from coming within 7.5 miles of the Imperial Palace. Such a response to events bordered on the implementation of martial law.

In February 1888, Okuma Shigenobu was brought into the cabinet as the new Minister of Foreign Affairs. Plans for this to happen had been around since the previous summer, and it was a step designed to undermine the activities of the *Daido Danketsu* (Great Merger Movement). At this point, it should be noted that the Constitutional Reform Party was not a central force within the Great Merger Movement but it did nevertheless play a role. Further, one year later, the government brought Goto Shojiro into the cabinet as Communications Minister.

How did Fukuzawa view the government's reaction to the uproar surrounding the treaty revisions and its response to the emergence of the Great Merger Movement?

Firstly, concerning the treaty revisions issue, there was the matter of whether to immediately allow foreigners to take up residence in the interior of the country, the initiative referred to as the "mixed residence debate." Those who took the position that it was too early to allow mixed residence claimed that if foreigners were allowed into the interior, their influence would be unrestrainable.

In *Zenkoku zakkyo* on April 21st and 22nd, 1886, he presented the following argument. As to the mixed residence debate, there were two models being proposed: either residence of foreigners anywhere throughout the country or residence limited, for example, to the seats of the prefectural governments. Japan is not a mountain of treasures, and even if the interior were opened to foreigners, they would not come in any great numbers. A further argument called for restricting ownership of land by foreigners. Without question, the U.S. restricted the purchase of land to people who had resided there for a specific period of time, and in Britain until a few years prior, purchase of land by foreigners was limited to specific quantity limitations. However, in Japan, Fukuzawa claimed, none of those restrictions would be necessary. Some people said that if foreigners were to make immoderate purchases of land, it would cause some inconvenience for Japan, but if demand was high, prices would rise and foreigners would not be able to make such purchases. In addition, they would pay taxes, so there would be no particular trouble whatsoever. To the contrary, in a country that has land but no capital for making use of it, like Japan, it would be normal to welcome capital from abroad. Frederick the Great and Alexander I did precisely that. It was entirely desirable to have large amounts of land put to use by non-Japanese, Fukuzawa argued. When he was traveling in Europe, he was surprised to learn that foreigners were able to purchase land freely, and his opinion in this particular article reflected that experience.

While Fukuzawa strongly supported the revision of the unequal treaties, the act of revision itself was not his prime goal. His strongest concerns related as to whether or not Japan could shoulder its responsibilities under a framework of equal treaties, and as to whether or not it possessed a sufficiently-independent spirit upon which it could stand when seeking to maintain its international relationships. On September 6th he wrote, "the joy resulting from any revision of these treaties is not to be achieved free of cost," while on the following day he added, "If the treaties are to be revised, then all aspects of our foreign affairs must be addressed." Together with welcoming the progress that had been made in the revising of the unequal treaties, he claimed that the inequalities that existed until then were less the result of malicious intent on the part of foreign countries, and more the result of their parental desire to protect Japan. His primary concern on a personal level was the tendency in Japan to place government officials upon a pedestal above the people *(kanson minpi)* and therefore, he argued, the primary matter of significance in all these issues was establishing the people's independence.

Consequently, on June 24th, 1887, in an editorial in the *Jiji Shimpo* entitled, "No regrets on the suspension of the renegotiating of the treaties for certain reasons," Fukuzawa wrote that the issue of extraterritoriality was a truly regrettable matter and should be corrected at the earliest possible opportunity. He also stated that progress should be made toward allowing "mixed residence" by foreigners in Japan's interior. To achieve this, he suggested, new laws would be necessary. With regulations as they then stood, he wrote, foreigners would be bound to encounter difficulties. However, Fukuzawa wrote that laws in general were developed against the background of local inhabitant's lives and were set against the conventions of their respective countries of origin. Thus, it would not do to simply transplant a raft of statutes from foreign countries. Fukuzawa thought that Japan should not create laws that were not in accordance with the host country's own wishes.

In putting forward these arguments, it is likely that Fukuzawa himself was well aware of the progress that had been made in the negotiations regarding the revision of the treaties. Indeed, in response to the revisions proposed by Inoue, it may have been that Fukuzawa sought a temporary halt of the negotiations through the editorial. However, Fukuzawa's writings were understood by certain people to represent a serious criticism of the government. Thus, the *Jiji Shimpo* was punished with a publication suspension.

However, as Fukuzawa surmised might happen, the process of treaty renegotiation was suspended shortly thereafter and Foreign Minister Inoue Kaoru resigned. In his article entitled, "Suspension of the treaty revision meetings" on August 4th, he expressed agreement with the postponement of the talks. He also called for the legal code to be revised as soon as possible; he was of the opinion that this should occur prior to commencing the treaty-revision process. On September 19th in his editorial entitled, "Reshuffling cabinet members," Fukuzawa wrote that diplomacy was a matter of cabinet policy and Inoue's resignation did not change the overall situation. Furthermore, though Kuroda Kiyotaka was said to have views that differed from those of the Ito Cabinet, however, once he was appointed to that body, its members would find common ground. Also it was good for the Prime Minister to relinquish his additional duties as serving as the Lord of the Imperial Household and concentrate on Cabinet affairs. Fukuzawa was probably attempting to minimize the impact of Inoue's resignation and the suspension of the treaty renegotiations.

In December 1887, when reflecting on the activities of the *Jiji Shimpo* since its founding as a newspaper, Fukuzawa in his editorial again addressed the *kanmin chowa ron* (the debate on the harmonization of the officials and the people). Japan, he argued, did not consist only of its government or only of its people. It instead consisted of both the government and the people working in harmony with one another. Thus, the government ought not to seek to alienate the people; and the people ought not to seek to resent the government. Neither side of the equation should seek to obstruct the other. Officials should not be placed upon a pedestal above the people they served. Fukuzawa felt that it was a regrettable that such harmonious relations had not yet been achieved, but he nevertheless would continue to persuade the government and the people to this effect.

Just as Fukuzawa was espousing these views, there was some good news and bad news that appeared on the political landscape. The less savory development was the promulgation of the Peace Preservation Law on

December 26th, 1887. This statute banned certain activists from residing within 7.5 miles of the Imperial Palace. It also banned them from venturing to within such a "close" proximity. This measure left some people dumbstruck. In responding to this development, Ozaki Yukio, the famous liberal politician, adopted the pen name *Gakudo* as a protest. When written in Japanese, Ozaki's new *nom de plume* literally meant "flabbergasted." Thus, with a single turn of the legal screw, any debate on the harmonization of the officials and the people was smashed to pieces. By contrast, the good news on February 1st, 1888, was that Okuma Shigenobu would join the cabinet. In his February 2nd, 1888, editorial in the *Jiji Shimpo* entitled, "Replacement of the Minister of Foreign Affairs," Fukuzawa gave this development very warm support.

Okuma's Renegotiation of the Treaties and Fukuzawa

Okuma Shigenobu joined the Ito Cabinet in February 1888 and soon began to grapple with negotiating the revision of the unequal treaties. Consequent to this, there were several changes in the composition of the cabinet. In following up these developments, let us now examine the negotiations in detail and what was happening within political circles. Let us also consider Fukuzawa's reactions to what was occurring.

On April 30th, 1888, two months after Okuma joined the cabinet, Ito Hirobumi resigned his post as Prime Minister to become head of the new Privy Council, a supra-cabinet body, and an advisory organ for the Emperor, while Kuroda Kiyotaka succeeded him to the position of premier.

Through his newspaper writings, Fukuzawa's recommendation was that rather than trying to dexterously deal with complex government and administrative affairs, the new cabinet should place a priority on stability and not attempt to do too much. The reason for this attitude was probably that Fukuzawa basically supported the Ito Cabinet. On the other hand, he was somewhat apprehensive about the power of Satsuma. Concurrently, he also had some qualms about the newly-established Privy Council. In his editorial entitled, "The Cabinet and the Privy Council," which appeared in the *Jiji Shimpo* on May 2nd, 1888, Fukuzawa expressed anxiety about the fact that the authority which had to that point been concentrated in the cabinet would, in addition to the national legislature which was about to be founded, suffer gridlock with the emergence of yet another entity in the form of the Privy Council.

In July of that year, Inoue Kaoru, who had been out of the public eye for about a year, returned to the cabinet as the Minister of Agriculture and Commerce. Fukuzawa did not see this development as particularly surprising. He viewed Inoue's return as natural against the backdrop of Satsuma-Choshu domination and hoped it would change the balance slightly in favor of Choshu. In his editorial entitled, "Inoue reenters the Cabinet," from the *Jiji Shimpo* of July 26th, 1888, Fukuzawa wrote that he hoped Inoue would not try too hard to achieve results quickly. Fukuzawa was naturally more hopeful now that Okuma and Inoue were in the cabinet.

However, he still did not consider the renegotiation of the unequal treaties to be the most pressing issue on the political agenda. In the series of editorials that appeared under the heading of "Not venturing to revise the treaties" on September 1st and 3rd, 1888 in the *Jiji Shimpo*, Fukuzawa wrote that the West was said to be astounded by the progress Japan had achieved thus far. However, he qualified this statement by saying such surprise was due to the fact that the West's previous expectations of Japan had been so low. Indeed, although Japan had achieved surprising progress, it was absurd that the treaties previously signed had not been revised. After all, Fukuzawa argued, revising the unequal treaties would not only benefit Japan but would bring many benefits to foreign countries as well. In spite of this, however, he reasoned that the foreign signatories to the present treaties had not shown much interest in the idea of revision. Unpleasant as the revisions issue might be, Fukuzawa argued, doing nothing would just result in more strident calls for the stricter enforcement of the current treaties. In other words, if the provisions of the current treaties were strictly enforced, foreign nationals would be prohibited from setting foot outside their present settlements. Thus, Fukuzawa encouraged the foreign signatories to become engaged in the renegotiation process so that such strict measures would not be resorted to by Japan.

In March 1889, Goto Shojiro, leader of the Great Merger Movement, joined the cabinet as Minister of Communications, the public was stunned. This development undermined the movement as a whole. Fukuzawa, however, welcomed this initiative in "Goto enters the Cabinet," which appeared in the *Jiji Shimpo* on March 23rd, 1889. While the public may have been surprised, Fukuzawa thought it was an entirely natural development. Indeed, he had long felt it strange that Goto had remained on the outside. Considering those alive who had achieved distinction at the time of the Meiji Restoration such as Kuroda Kiyotaka (700 *koku*) and Yamagata Aritomo (600 *koku*), Goto had received a stipend of 1,000 *koku* of rice. Saigo, Kido, Okubo, Hirosawa Saneomi, and Omura Masujiro were already dead, and of the survivors of the restoration generation, no one who had contributed was more prominent than Goto. While it might have been inappropriate to use past achievements as a standard, Fukuzawa argued that the administration would not work well with such meritorious figures left on the outside given his conceptualization of "the harmonization of the officials and the people." Fukuzawa's view on these developments differed greatly from both the clan cliques and the advocates of people's rights.

The reason the government brought in Goto was that revision of the unequal treaties was once again becoming a major problem. On January 7th, 1889, Minister of Foreign Affairs Okuma Shigenobu presented his proposals for revision to the representatives of Great Britain, Russia, France, Austro-Hungary and Italy and he began the negotiation process. An agreement was reached with the U.S. in February, Germany in June, and Russia in August. Of course, these agreements had to be ratified. Fukuzawa referred to this situation by saying the British were like wealthy merchants, whose great accomplishments had led to opening new markets and who opposed the revisions because they feared that they would lose their predominance, but Fukuzawa thought the Japanese should not be reserved in their negotiating stance, because the British would undoubtedly benefit in the long run.

During this period, in March an inquiry came from Minister to the United States, Mutsu Munemitsu, asking whether the designation of foreigners as judges in judicial proceedings was in violation of the Constitution. The issue arose because in February the Constitution of the Empire of Japan had been promulgated. Okuma responded that it was not a violation.

However, the issue would not go away. In April, *The Times* published the proposed revisions. A Japanese translation of these was then published back in Japan. They appeared in the *Nippon* magazine at the end of May. This development set the cat amongst the pigeons. Toward the end of August, opposition forces in the national legislature held a meeting of people throughout the country to protest. By way of response, so as to support Foreign Minister Okuma, the reformists in late September held their own major assembly which attracted people who supported the treaty revisions.

Fukuzawa became concerned these issues would be abused by factional forces. He was in favor of the revisions themselves. In "Treaty revision, legal code compilation" on July 17th and 18th, and in "Timing of legal code compilation" on July 25th, which all appeared in the *Jiji Shimpo*, Fukuzawa wrote that with regard to the fears of allowing foreigners to purchase land in Japan's interior, while it was true that the Egyptians had been violated by foreign investment, the U.S. to the contrary had developed and benefited from it. The problem was not whether to introduce foreign investment but whether or not the people had the ability to put that capital to beneficial use. He pointed out that the Japanese were different from the Egyptians. Regarding the Okuma Proposal that foreign judges should be appointed only to the Supreme Court and not to lower courts, Fukuzawa contended that it was possible for Japan to endure such a policy for the moment.

However, from around August, little by little Fukuzawa began to consider that the process required to revise the treaties would be a difficult one. Moreover, if anything, the obstacles to be confronted were domestic in origin. In his two-part series entitled, "Difficulties over treaty revision due to behind-the-scenes quarreling," which appeared in the *Jiji Shimpo* on August 9th and 10th, 1889, he commented that, although the issue of the proposed revisions had progressed beyond what it was in 1887, the changes that had been made to the proposals still did not constitute fundamental ones. It was, Fukuzawa wrote, similar to the case of an item that was once selling at ¥100 currently going for ¥50. Furthermore, implying that the revisions were epoch-making would make the people previously involved envious. Indeed, he argued that the progress thus made was simply a result of the changing times, rather than any particular ability being exercised by the authorities. He also cautioned those in power about being the targets of jealousy and also about not claiming that these revisions were solely the result to their own achievements.

As Fukuzawa had anticipated, the revision process soon ran into trouble, Inoue Kaoru was forced to resign and Ito Hirobumi also stepped down as head of the Privy Council. In October, Foreign Minister Okuma Shigenobu was seriously wounded in a terrorist bombing which resulted in the amputation of one of his legs. Despite his injuries, however, the stout-hearted man continued to demonstrate his personal courage.

Nevertheless, in December the Kuroda Cabinet had to resign.

Winding back the clock slightly, in February of 1889, Minister of Education Mori Arinori had been assassinated on the day the Constitution was promulgated, February 11th, 1889. This meant that for Fukuzawa, two of his friends had been the targets of terrorist attack within a single year, one was killed and the other severely wounded. It was a shocking turn of events. Behind these attacks there seemed to be a similar motivation to that which had underpinned the earlier movement that had sought to expel the foreign influence from the country. Such a sentiment had recovered some of its legitimacy in the wake of the Political Crisis of 1881 and the subsequent shift towards more conservative policies on the part of the government.

The Limitations of Political Power

As has been noted, Fukuzawa was fundamentally in favor of the revisions of the treaties but was not unduly enthusiastic about the process itself. He was also somewhat apprehensive about the rousing political fervor that surrounded the revision issue.

In an editorial entitled, "Political maneuverings," that was serialized in the *Jiji Shimpo* from August 15th to 17th, 1887, Fukuzawa argued that generally speaking, every human being would like to achieve "fame and fortune," but what such terms actually entailed depended on each specific society. In Great Britain and the United States, where an emphasis was placed on business, "fame and fortune" lay in the world of commerce. In Germany, where an emphasis was placed on military service, "fame" was to be found among the military men. In Japan, as an outgrowth of the tradition of the samurai who were ardent about politics, "fame and fortune" were said to flow from an involvement in political society. This argument was somewhat reminiscent of his comments in *An Outline of a Theory of Civilization* about placing disproportionate emphasis on authority.

According to Fukuzawa's reasoning, "fame" could easily become the objects of jealousy. He went onto argue that, society is a world of human feelings and is not a world of reason. It is seven parts feeling and three parts rationality. Thus, among statesmen of ancient and modern times, those who have succeeded have not been those who were known for their reasonableness but those known for their wit and intelligence in winning over human emotions.

What does Fukuzawa suggest, in practical terms, to avoid jealousy? First, a statesman should not become involved in any other activity. During the Edo period, he relates, those who were appointed to serve as *metsuke*, or high-level inspectors and censors for the shogunate, avoided contact with even their closest relatives. The only exception to this self-imposed rule was perhaps calling on a parent who had fallen ill. Such social practices were maintained so that the integrity of an official would be above suspicion. Indeed, even a wide circle of friends could condemn a public person to be suspected of some form of impropriety; thus it was important that each individual be ever vigilant. Secondly, Fukuzawa argued that high positions should be created both outside politics and in many centers throughout the country. During the Edo period, the lords of the principle domains were not selected to become *roju* (or senior councilors to the shogun), and there were also powerful temples such as Honganji, Zojoji and Chion'in whose position within the state gave them an authority above that of the feudal lords. These and other measures had been taken in order to avoid allowing authority to be distributed as a flat hierarchy. Thirdly, he argued, those who were statesmen or politicians should be discreet and virtuous in their manner. Emperor Nicholas I of Russia famously had only one pair of shoes to wear in the inner sanctums of his palaces, and when these shoes began to fall apart, he had the Empress mend them. Fukuzawa drew on this episode and used other examples from the Edo period that were familiar to his readership to stress his point about those conditions he considered essential for the stability of authority.

Fukuzawa was not, however, implying that there was anything wrong with the premise of luxury. His comments were limited in scope to the bureaucratic officials. Whatever extravagances the people enjoyed were the products of their own labor, thus, there was no reason at all for them to give them up ("The people's extravagances are to be promoted," September 26th, 1887).

One thing that Fukuzawa thought was as important as the art of politics was that of learning. He put great stock in the importance of independent scholarship. Slightly later, in 1891, a banquet was held to celebrate the publication of Otsuki Fumihiko's *Genkai* [The Sea of Words], the first great dictionary of the Japanese language. The program printed up for the event listed a message of congratulations from Ito Hirobumi first, followed by one from Fukuzawa. When Fukuzawa found out about this, he was displeased that learning and culture were considered secondary to politics, so he asked to have his message left off the program altogether, thus causing a reprinting of the program. While this episode conveys his belief that learning should have equal status with politics, it also shows that he was still displeased with Ito.

Among such ideas of limitations being placed upon political power, Fukuzawa attached importance to a process of decentralization which would lead to administration being devolved to local governments. As one aspect of this reasoning, he advocated a policy which would see the former daimyo actually return to their old feudal domains and take up residence. Previously, when the old domains had been abolished and the new prefectures established in their place, the former feudal lords had relocated from their old territories permanently to Tokyo. Indeed, this development had been an important facet in the transformation of the nation's politics. As commented earlier, Fukuzawa had been greatly in favor of this development; however, over time he had begun to have second thoughts.

Particularly at the local government level, Fukuzawa felt that limitations should be placed upon public administration's involvement in society. In his article, "Prefectural governments should not interfere in the people's pleasures" which appeared in the *Jiji Shimpo* on September 27th, 1887, he argued that self-government by the people represented a fundamental basis of society. He related that, several days earlier he had gone on business to Yokohama and had happened to encounter a great crowd at the festival of Kawasaki Daishi Shrine. It was foolish, Fukuzawa noted, for anyone to criticize such events as being based upon superstitions, as being wasteful uses of both time and energy, or as contributing to instances of robbery or disorderly conduct. He argued that the day of the festival for Daishi stressed the importance of folk customs and it gave believers of such traditions a means by which to satisfy their religious needs. Those who wielded power in the land should not seek to interfere with such practices, as long as things did not break the law. Fukuzawa further commented that the railroads had the right idea about what to do regarding the event. Namely, they cooperated with it.

Elsewhere, Fukuzawa cautioned his own students at Keio Gijuku that they should not simply think the best way to live was to come to Tokyo with the aim of achieving success. Rather, those with the means to do so should return to their local areas and contribute to the enlightening of the provinces ("Lecture on summer holidays at Keio Gijuku," July 31st, 1885). He also warned his young students who had a provincial background against doing anything that might make their parents worry, and he recommended that they frequently write letters home so as to help establish closer relations between Tokyo and the provinces. As we saw earlier, Fukuzawa himself was an ardent correspondent with his own sons when the latter were in the United States.

The Proposal that Japan Be a Mercantile State

As has been stated, in his writings Fukuzawa sought to achieve a society that would be an independent one. Moreover, the role of government within it would be limited. He could also see the necessity of economic strength while recognizing that a strategy would be required to achieve it.

In his essay entitled, *Minjo isshin* [Changing the Sentiments of the People] which was published in 1879, Fukuzawa laid out a broad sketch of how his ideas could be achieved. He described what he imagined to be the four great tools for enlightening the country: steam, telegraphy, printing and the postal service. In doing so, he placed particularly heavy emphasis on the issues of communication and transportation.

Regarding the laying of railways, Fukuzawa was perhaps the most prominent proponent of all. In a series of articles entitled, "On railroads," which appeared in the *Jiji Shimpo* on September 22nd and 25th, 1882, he was to complain that, compared with the major Western powers, Japan was behind in the railway stakes by a considerable margin. He argued that Japan should complete a rail network as rapidly as possible, even if it meant the issuing of foreign bonds to underwrite such projects. In his writings, he also often indicated that the creation of a significant rail network had great military significance as well.

Furthermore, Fukuzawa also contended that an effort be put into the development of a merchant marine. In doing so, he paid considerable attention to the competition that was occurring among companies such as Mitsubishi and Kyodo Transport. Additionally, from around 1886, he began actively lending his weight to promoting projects to lay submarine telegraph cables between Japan and the United States. In other words, Fukuzawa believed that in the sphere of public works, the government should take the lead in financing to ensure that projects quickly commenced.

Consequently, once the construction of a railway network got under way, Fukuzawa was to argue that at a certain point, such assets should pass to the private sector. Against the backcloth of the changing times and technical transformations, he was somebody who gave much thought to the issues of technology. Thus, if he were alive today, Fukuzawa would probably be a strong proponent of the IT revolution.

In his later years, Fukuzawa is said to have enjoyed a close relationship with Goto Shinpei, himself involved in railways and communications. As such, there can be little doubt that Fukuzawa was attracted to the enterprising spirit of Goto and others who conceived large-scale projects.

On the topic of industry, Fukuzawa was one of those who were critical of attaching too much importance to the cultivation of rice. During the Edo period, more than anything else, Japan's economy had been a rice-based one to the extent that, at the beginning of Meiji, rice had been an export money earner. However, in terms of comparative advantage, he felt that rice did not offer much of a future to Japan. Instead, Fukuzawa thought Japan should devote its energies to the development of sericulture to build a comparative advantage in the production of raw silk. Moreover, the nature of the business would ensure the provision of adequate work to the former samurai and their families. As has already been discussed, the lower echelons of the samurai class were already tradesmen in everything but name, and Fukuzawa, a person with lots of personal experience of so-called "side-jobs," understood that the lowly former samurai could handle such work. However, as indicated by his article entitled, "Competition from China in Japan's sericulture industry should not be overlooked," which appeared in the *Jiji Shimpo* on August 5th, 1887, Fukuzawa seemed to be well aware that a comparative advantage in silk production was not something that Japan could rely on forever.

At any rate, Fukuzawa tended to emphasize the significance of trade over everything else. It was an article of faith to him that wealth was derived from commercial activity. Especially for a country like Japan, he was inclined to believe that the economy had to be mercantilist. Moreover, the necessity for Japan to acquire such an economic profile was becoming even more obvious as time passed. Great Britain and the United States dominated world trade, so Fukuzawa felt that Japanese would first need to learn the English language and then learn Chinese. He offered such views in an article entitled, "English and Chinese language," which appeared in the *Jiji Shimpo* on September 16th, 1885.

The topics that Fukuzawa had emphasized through his various writings began to slowly materialize in the public domain. As a consequence, the breadth of the previous socio-economic fissures that had existed between rich and poor began to expand. Fukuzawa's essay, "Wealth and poverty," was published in a serial format between October 24th and 30th, 1884. In it, he wrote that people were not born equal and that people were poor not because they failed to study but because as a consequence of being poor they did not have an opportunities to gain education. This argument was contentious because it represented almost the exact opposite of the views he had expressed in the opening of *An Encouragement of Learning*, where he had argued that people were poor because they had no opportunity to receive an education. That being said, however, it is typical of Fukuzawa to suggest that the socio-economic ills could be rectified by creating millionaires.

Chapter 14

The Early Diet and the Sino-Japanese War

Photo taken around 1891, which served as the main model for the image of Fukuzawa that appears on the current ¥10,000 bill. (Courtesy of Keio University Fukuzawa Memorial Center)

Opposition to Reduction in Land Tax

On July 1st, 1890, the first general election for the Lower House of the Diet (the national legislature) was held. The government maintained the principle of transcendence, which is to say it adopted the position of having nothing to do with the political parties; thus, there was little interference in the process so the election itself was rather clean. Fukuzawa was also pleased with the outcome, writing a piece for the *Jiji Shimpo* entitled, "Results of the election of Diet members," which appeared on July 9th. In it, he stated that, "one cannot help being unexpectedly satisfied with the results of the election," before proceeding to call this exercise in democracy "unreservedly well-done" and "worthy of the praise of Western nations."

The first session of the Diet was held that year on November 25th, and the focal issue was the budget. The cabinet of Yamagata Aritomo made every effort to secure passage of the budget through the support of the people's parties. The Liberal Party and the Reform Party referred to themselves as people's parties while calling the parties that supported the government the bureaucrats' party. These two parties occupied a majority of the legislature's seats. On February 20th of the following year, the government's proposed annual budget of ¥83,075,000 was reduced by the people's parties by some ¥8,500,000 and, with this as a source of revenue, the legislature sought to reduce land taxes. They made their case on the basis of there being an economy in government expenditures and on the storing up of domestic resources.

Due to these reductions in government expenditures, proposals for systematic reforms such as abolishing the Metropolitan Police Agency were included. However, in accordance with Article 67 of the Meiji Constitution, which stated, "Those already fixed expenditures based by the Constitution upon the powers appertaining to the Emperor…shall be neither rejected nor reduced by the Imperial Diet, without the concurrence of the Government," such proposed reforms were taken to be outside the law.

Fukuzawa was strongly in favor of the reduction of government expenditures. However, he opposed reforms that would accompany institutional change because any actual reductions in expenditure realized therein would be small when weighed against the drastic policy changes that would be required to achieve them. The alternative he proposed was that the number of government officials should be reduced by half, and that any excess work the bureaucrats did should simply be eliminated. He found fault with public offices where several functionaries did the work that a single person could do, and where work that could be done in an hour took a full day, thereby causing the public unnecessary trouble.

On the other hand, he opposed the reduction of land taxes. Shortly after the opening of the Diet, in a serialized editorial entitled, "Land tax reduction," that was published in the *Jiji Shimpo* between December 3rd and 5th, 1890, he argued that, even if land taxes were lightened, it would be of no benefit to the poor. Rather, farm rents, or more specifically rents for tenancy, were decided on the basis of supply and demand. After all, Fukuzawa pointed out, even with the special land price revisions in 1889, the landowners had not reduced the rent that they charged their tenants. It was true that in the case of landed farmers such a reduction would lighten their burden, but compared with the past, land taxes were already considerably reduced. Hence, he claimed, reducing taxes on land was meaningless.

How should surplus budget funds be utilized? Fukuzawa's ready answer was that subsidies should be given to shipping enterprises. In "Maritime trading country," a serialized article that appeared in the *Jiji Shimpo* from March 18th through 21st, he asserted that Japan had to make its future through its efforts in international commerce. In order to achieve this, just as the British had done, members of the Japanese middle class and above would need to relocate to a variety of places around the world. Maritime trade remained dominated by foreign countries and British people lived all over the world, and this fact had proved beneficial in the development of Britannia's navigation of the seas. Therefore, Fukuzawa reasoned, the government should subsidize Japanese enterprises to do the same. Foreign countries had previously and were still providing such subsidies to their vessels, and without similar support from their government, Japanese enterprises would not be able to compete with the rest of the world. Fukuzawa was vociferous in his support of establishing navigation regulations and providing subsidies based on the length of voyages. Obviously, commerce rather than agriculture was at the heart of his views.

Ultimately, in the deliberations over the budget during the first session of the Diet, the government was able to get the support of the Tosa faction within the Liberal Party, cut the proposed reductions of ¥8,500,000 down to ¥6,500,000 and then pass the budget.

By the time the Diet went into recess at the end of its first session, Prime Minister Yamagata had had enough and resigned his post on May 6th. He was replaced by Matsukata Masayoshi. However, Fukuzawa was somewhat disappointed by this development. Not only did he view Matsukata as being inferior to Ito Hirobumi and his cohorts, he also held a negative opinion of the man's deflationary policies.

Within this low appraisal of Matsukata, however, there was also an element of criticism directed at Ito for not stepping forward. In his *Jiji Shimpo* editorial of June 7th, 1891, entitled, "Our young abdicated leader," Fukuzawa commented that for Ito, the most prominent of the nation's leaders, to not take center stage was like being an adopted son entering a family with a youthful retired head of household. It was hard for the adopted son to do anything at all. Fukuzawa's view was that if Ito was going to evade a position of responsibility, he should retire from politics completely or he should step forward and assume a responsible post.

On May 11th, just after the Matsukata Cabinet was formed, the Russian

Crown Prince, Nicholas Alexandrovitch (later Tsar Nicholas II), who was then visiting Japan, was wounded by a member of his police escort, Tsuda Sanzo. The assassination attempt took place in Otsu and came to be known as the Otsu Incident. It generated huge shock waves throughout the entire country. Fearing a heavy Russian response, some elements within the government put pressure on the courts so that they would deal severely with Tsuda. Under the Criminal Code at the time, the severest punishment for "attempted assassination" was life imprisonment. However, when the law was applied to a case of attempted assassination of a member of the Imperial Family, the courts could hand down the death penalty. Ultimately, however, the Supreme Court managed to overcome the attempts at untoward pressure being exerted by certain members of the former domain-dominated government and instead it sentenced Tsuda to life imprisonment. This case was seen as a splendid step forward for the independence of the judiciary in Japan. (In actual fact, however, this decision was somewhat problematic. For more details see Kusunoki Seiichiro, *Kojima Iken.*)

The Otsu Incident also stunned Fukuzawa, who wrote in the *Jiji Shimpo* on May 14th an editorial that sympathized with the shock the Russian Tsar and Tsarina must have felt about the injury to their son. This was a typical response from the family-conscious man. Fukuzawa also proposed two initiatives in his editorial. The first was to dispatch the Japanese Crown Prince to visit the Russian Court. The second was to assemble the nation's elder statesmen to discuss how to handle the situation. As they had done in the days of the bakufu during times of emergency, he thought that all the former members of the Council of State (fourteen members including Itagaki and Okuma) should be brought together for consultation. This suggestion sprang from Fukuzawa's views on the harmonization of the public and private spheres *(kanmin chowa ron).* As a historical note, the course of action actually adopted by Japan was that the Emperor visited the convalescing Russian Crown Prince. His Imperial Majesty did this because his greater affinity had a much more powerful impact than that of the fledgling government.

Concerning the government's actions in responding to this crisis, Fukuzawa was generally appreciative. It was only natural for the government to seek severe punishment for Tsuda, yet at the same time, it was gratifying that the courts ultimately handed down a decision based solidly on the law of the land. Speaking highly of the government, the court system and the Emperor, Fukuzawa wrote, "Together with the people I celebrate auspicious events with the Imperial Family and at the same time celebrate the independence of our system of laws and courts."

On the occasion of this visit by the Russian Crown Prince, there were various rumors circulating as to the trip's true purpose. Some people passed stories that the Russians were looking Japan over with a view to subjugation in the future. There was even a rumor that the person guiding the imperial entourage was none other than Saigo Takamori. According to this interpretation of events, Saigo had miraculously escaped from Shiroyama at the end of the failed Satsuma Rebellion, then gone to Russia, before returning to Japan to guide the Crown Prince around. In a tongue-in-cheek piece published in the *Jiji Shimpo* on April 10th, 1892, entitled, "No reason to fear Saigo's return," Fukuzawa wrote that if Saigo actually were alive and were to return to Tokyo, he would no doubt be astonished by what he would see. Saigo was an unselfish, unaffected, simple and unsophisticated person, who lived in a hovel that cost only ¥3 a month, ate baked sweet potatoes, drank inexpensive liquor and enthusiastically discussed the literary and military arts. The group to whom Saigo used to serve humble sweet potatoes had since become peers, their wives were now noble ladies, their boys had become young masters, and their daughters had become princesses. They lived in magnificent houses and daily enjoyed themselves at the Deer Cry Pavilion or the Imperial Hotel.

Alarmed at such sights, Saigo would undoubtedly escape from Japan on the earliest possible ship. Needless to say, Fukuzawa was admonishing the leading figures in government for their extravagances.

The second session of the Imperial Diet was called in November of 1891. Once again, the people's parties of the opposition called for reducing government expenditures and recovering domestic strength. By contrast, the government benches aimed at expanding the nation's navy. In reacting to these developments, Fukuzawa felt that the government's budget was rather half-hearted and that it provided few positive projects. He expressed these views in his *Jiji Shimpo* editorial of December 15th entitled, "Contradiction between being passive and being passive." To be sure, the balance on hand of ¥6,450,000 from the 1890 financial year and the reductions of ¥450,000 through government reform yielded a total of ¥6,900,000, but the only new enterprise proposed by the government was a steelworks. Fukuzawa's vision was to reduce government expenditures further and more aggressively undertake one new enterprise after another while appealing to all of the nation's citizens when doing so.

Consequently, the people's parties opposed the government's plan to expand the naval forces and the government dissolved the Diet. Fukuzawa supported the move by the government in a series of two articles ("The House of Representatives finally comes to a close" and "Dissolving the Diet session and what direction the government will take," December 26th and 29th).

However, the confrontations between the government and the people's parties of the opposition arose from emotive issues. Their cause came from the practice of imposing officials over the people and then laying a disproportionate emphasis on authority. Above all, wrote Fukuzawa, this state of affairs should be corrected. The government should abandon its transcendent attitude, and by wholehearted efforts endeavor to obtain the majority. If the structure of government could not obtain a majority in the Diet, he cautioned, it should be prepared to repeatedly dissolve the legislature. Fukuzawa's stance leaned neither toward the government nor toward the opposition people's parties. Rather, he consistently aimed at the issue of policy. Moreover, he believed that those who held power ought to resolutely carry through with their convictions.

The nation's second general election held on February 15th, 1892, resulted from this dissolution of the Diet. The campaign that surrounded the election would prove to be the most violent in Japanese political history. Twenty-five people were killed and another 388 wounded. However, Fukuzawa was not overly critical of events.

Following the election, as had been anticipated, the people's parties obtained a majority and in the third session of the Diet, the Matsukata Cabinet agonized over how to deal with the legislature. Another issue was criticism from within the government around Ito Hirobumi who favored taking a more flexible approach toward political parties. Matsukata resigned and Ito Hirobumi formed a cabinet composed entirely of the most powerful statesmen of the day.

Disillusionment with Ito

Based on his opinions up until that time, Fukuzawa welcomed the cabinet that was formed and in his *Jiji Shimpo* editorials, "Forming a new cabinet" (August 9th) and "The new cabinet's measures" (August 10th), he introduced the cabinet lineup and commented on each member. He wrote that the appointment of Inoue Kaoru to the position of Home Minister was somewhat unexpected, but that his selection was nevertheless well made for such a position of importance. Regarding the new Minister of Foreign Affairs, he commented that Mutsu Munemitsu had both skill and experience and expressed strong hopes that "if he dedicates his life to the task before him, our foreign affairs will before long undergo a complete transformation." He also welcomed the selection of Oyama Iwao as Minister of the Army and Nire Kagenori as Minister of the Navy as both being well qualified. He also added that the inclusion of two leaders with experience as Prime Minister, Yamagata and Kuroda, added weight to the cabinet. Fukuzawa wondered whether this cabinet would continue to take a hard line toward the people's parties or adopt a softer attitude. He also expressed the hope that the cabinet would go beyond the debate over hard and soft policies toward the opposition parties.

Despite his personally welcoming the advent of the new cabinet, however, Fukuzawa did not believe that the rank-and-file of the Diet would warmly welcome the development. Indeed, he felt the opposite was more likely. He commented that the formation of the Ito Cabinet was certainly a major event, but he also anticipated that the people's parties would ever more vigorously oppose it. Thus, he proposed that the cabinet show some flexibility in its dealings and appear in the Diet more often in order to explain the details of its policies. It would be necessary for those in authority to fend off the intemperate counter-arguments of the people's parties' legislators like a willow bending in a storm while employing all possible compliments and charm. Moreover, if necessary, they might even resort to bribery on occasion. Fukuzawa also proposed that Itagaki and Okuma, outstanding statesmen of the Meiji transition who were certainly no less prominent than Ito, Kuroda and Yamagata, should be brought into the fray. However, whatever political tactics they resorted to, the new cabinet absolutely should not carry out a reassessment of land values or reduce land taxes. ("Proposal for the new Cabinet for dealing with the Diet," August 12th, "Hopes for caution by the new Cabinet," August 13th, and "Hopes for harmony within the Cabinet structure," August 18th).

Despite his expectations, however, the policies of the Ito Cabinet were not what Fukuzawa had hoped for. He was particularly disappointed with the proposals for the reform of assessment of paddy and field lands to reduce land taxes. His assessment was that the land tax had already been reduced due to the rise of the price of rice. Another reduction was not necessary. Was the government weak or strong? In 1876, land taxes were reduced from 3 percent to 2.5 percent and in 1889 a special reform was implemented that resulted in tax reduction of more than ¥3,000,000. These reforms caused no small disappointment to local people of means and knowledge of the situation. At any rate, Fukuzawa wrote, "land tax is the foundation upon which the country stands, and whatever ideas an enlightened government may have, it should not weaken that foundation." During the Edo period, when a castle was handed over to the shogunate, first the castle was vacated, second the weapons were surrendered, and third, the annual land-tax registers were turned over. Therefore, reducing the land taxes was equivalent to surrender. Fukuzawa called the submission of the reform proposal a major misstep on the part of the Meiji government ("What is the government's opinion regarding the proposed revision of land valuation?" January 13th, 1893).

Moreover, within the navy's plan to expand armaments, the budget proposal for constructing iron-clads and cruisers were both rejected. In comparison with the army, the navy's organization was not yet effective. There was some truth to the criticism that the navy could not be left as it was, but if one refused expansion, then nothing would ever be done. The only alternative was to take the bold course of issuing an emergency Imperial Edict and obtain *ex post facto* approval. However, if one did this, the subsequent legislature would refuse approval, the result being that the government would have to resign itself to repeatedly dissolving the Diet. Fukuzawa grew more vehement ("How resolute the government must be in response to rejection of the budget for warships," January 12th).

As a result of the confrontation between the cabinet and the political parties, for five days beginning January 17th, 1893, the legislature adjourned and the House of Representatives on January 23rd submitted to the

Emperor a motion of censure against the government. The House of Representatives adjourned again from February 7th for 15 days. Finally, on February 10th, the Emperor issued an edict calling for the government and the legislature to find a compromise, with the government reducing annual government expenditures and the legislature approving the reduced budget. The Emperor overcame the crisis by disbursing ¥300,000 annually from the allowance for the private expenses of the Imperial Family.

No detailed account of his response to these events remains, but one can assume Fukuzawa was opposed to this measure. Just prior to it, when the petition to censure the government was submitted, he was opposed to that action, because it was undesirable to bring the Emperor into government affairs.

However, he did feel that the elder statesmen were growing old. In "I will cooperate with the young" (March 16th, 1893), Fukuzawa wrote that in general, men in their prime often consider things in straightforward ways, are taken in, miscalculate and are liable to make mistakes, yet out of this, much progress can take place. In contrast, the older generation gives minute consideration to everything, meticulously pondering every possibility, and there is little worry that they will make mistakes. But because the latter group is so focused on defense, they show little spirit in attempting progress. Cooperation between the older and younger generations is desirable, he wrote, but ultimately he was willing to turn things over to the next generation.

At the beginning of the Meiji period, figures such as Eto Shimpei, Maehara Issei and Saigo Takamori may have employed methods to achieve their aims that seemed unreasonable. However, they threw themselves into the fight in accordance with their principles, while their opponents among the government authorities did the same. Some of these figures won while others lost; however, Japanese society itself continued to progress. In contrast to this, Fukuzawa saw the political circumstances of his own day as merely seeking to achieve amicable solutions. With no word of complaint, Yamagata Aritomo departed the post of Minister of Justice. Saigo Tsugumichi, who had once been criticized by Ito as a member of the Matsukata Cabinet and had resigned his ministerial position as a result, was now back in Ito's favor as a member of his cabinet. Each of the players concerned in these dramas ought to be asserting their principles; however, due to private circumstances, they would not express their ideas in public. Thus, the group of elder statesmen who had once been a rowdy bunch had mellowed with age.

The Korean Problem and National Unity

Having grown dissatisfied with the way things were going in the early Diet, Fukuzawa began to see developments overseas as a key to achieving a breakthrough.

In an essay entitled, "Requiring a significant wise decision," which appeared in the *Jiji Shimpo* on the July 19th and 20th, 1892, Fukuzawa ruminated that the people's parties were one of the most dreadful entities that the Meiji government faced. The Satsuma Rebellion and other insurgencies could be suppressed by military force. The people's parties, however, held a legitimate place within the legislative branch of government, and depending on the circumstances, they might even form a cabinet that would be responsible to the Diet. However, although there were numerous figures within the people's parties, many were lacking in experience. The Meiji government, after more than 20 years of law and order, was on the verge of crisis. Referring to Kido Takayoshi's proposal for sending a military expedition to Korea in the early years of Meiji, he had suggested that the unity of domestic politics might be achieved by diverting attention to overseas issues. The target of such adventurism could be the seas to the south, but Korea seemed to represent a better option. The method that underpinned such an expedition should not be one of a meaningless war that would expend enormous sums of money. Rather, by means of active diplomacy, it had to touch the hearts of the ordinary people while alleviating the serious situation in Korea and protect Japanese interests. However, any such action would have to weigh both the advantages and disadvantages for Japan.

Fukuzawa wrote that Imperial Russia had ambitions in Korea but, more than anything, the problem was Korea's relationship with Qing China. Whether Korea was to belong to China or become independent was the point of contention. However, terms such as "belonging to" or "being independent" were at best exercises in semantics, and of much greater importance was the actual situation on the ground. For the sake of Korean independence, it was necessary to fundamentally reorganize internal affairs, and then establish enterprises in Korea that dealt with issues of military preparedness, public finance, a postal service, telegraphic communications, steamships and railways. Japan should not sit idly back and simply abandon Korea to its fate; rather it should support the Koreans via these various advances.

Previously, Fukuzawa had emphasized the unity of the whole country in dealing with external issues. However, this time his ideas possessed a more hazardous undercurrent in that he was promoting certain external issues as a means by which to unify domestic public opinion.

During this period, a certain incident occurred that would have a long-term impact on Fukuzawa. This was the exile of Kim Ok-gyun as a result of the Kapsin Political Coup of 1884.

In the wake of the failed coup attempt, the Korean government repeatedly demanded that Japan hand over Kim. However, this demand met with refusal. Despite this, however, Japan's attitude toward Kim was largely cool. In November 1885, it was then revealed that Oi Kentaro and others had plotted to assist Kim by procuring explosives for use in an invasion of Korea (the Osaka Incident). This forced the government's hand and it had to crack down. The following year, Kim was sent to the remote Ogasawara Islands because he was seen as an impediment to Japan's relations with China. Once there, he fell ill, and he was relocated to Hokkaido. Finally in 1890 he was allowed to return to Tokyo and take up residence.

Apparently up until that point, the Japanese government had provided Kim with minimal living expenses. However, when he returned to Tokyo, the government cut this allowance. Thus, Kim was left dependent on funds provided by sympathizers. Fukuzawa was one of the leading figures of this group. Kim and the young people who followed him would gather together to share information about what was taking place in Korea. They also felt it was necessary to gather funds, essentially war funds, which could be used at some future date. Obviously, such funds represented a considerable sum of money.

A complicating factor was that, among those Koreans who claimed to be disciples of Kim, there were evidently a number of spies sent from Seoul. One of these was an individual called Hong Jong-u, who proved competent enough to entice Kim to China. Once there, he tricked his quarry into visiting Shanghai and then successfully assassinated him. Kim Ok-gyun departed Japan in early March of 1894, while Fukuzawa was away. Thus, Fukuzawa did not hear about the demise of his friend until the 28th. Li Hongzhang [Li Hung-chang], the general and diplomat of late Qing China, heard about the assassination while in Tianjin and sent a celebratory telegram to the Korean government. He had an official from the Korean government stationed in Tianjin go to Shanghai to secure Kim's body and his assassin. The government then put Kim's decapitated and dismembered body on public display in Seoul. Hong Jong-u was hailed as a hero and awarded an official position.

Fukuzawa grieved over Kim's death as if Kim had been a member of his own family. He had a memorial tablet set up at home complete with a posthumous Buddhist name inscribed. At 5:00 p.m. on April 24th, Fukuzawa held a quiet memorial service for Kim. Miyake Hyozo (the secretary of Goto Shojiro who had been close to Kim) and Kai Gunji (who had been taken care of by Kim in Seoul and who had been enraged by the placing of Kim's head on public display but had nevertheless managed to retrieve a few clippings of hair) both attended the ceremony along with Wada Enjiro, a youth long in Kim's service. It was just these close associates who gathered unobtrusively in the exile's memory.

On May 20th, a more impressive memorial service was held for Kim at the Asakusa Higashi Honganji Temple. The mourning party assembled at an office at Yurakucho, went to Asakusa, and proceeded from there to Aoyama Cemetery. Attendees at the service included Konoe Atsumaro, Tani Tateki, Ozaki Yukio, Inukai Tsuyoshi, Oi Kentaro, and Inoue Kakugoro. Roughly 1,000 people attended the event. Grief at the death of Kim and anger over the brutal, contemptible acts carried out by Korea and China increased to new levels. It was this that generated the emotions that led to the Sino-Japanese War two months later.

The Sino-Japanese War

What triggered war between Japan and China was the Tonghak Rebellion of 1894. "Tonghak" ("Eastern Learning") was a name codified in opposition to Western Learning and was a popular Korean religious cult that combined elements of Confucianism, Daoism and Buddhism. It was opposed to Christianity. The Seoul government attempted to suppress the cult, but at the end of 1893 a major rebellion broke out when the peasantry allied with it against the government's forces. Unable to quell the uprising, Korea called upon China to intercede militarily.

In a series of articles in the *Jiji Shimpo*, Fukuzawa argued that, if the situation was such that China was required to intercede, Japan should also do so immediately ("Regarding the Tonghak Rebellion" May 30th, 1894;

"Immediately deploy troops," June 5th; "Hoping for an expeditious embarking rather than a cautious plan," June 6th).

Learning that Seoul had called for aid from China, the Japanese government on June 2nd immediately decided to dispatch troops. As specified in the Treaty of Tianjin of 1885, in which Japan and China agreed to notify one another of any intention to dispatch troops to the Korean Peninsula, on June 6th, China notified Japan that it was sending troops to protect its dependency. Japan protested that Korea was not China's dependency and on June 7th announced that it was sending in its own troops to protect its legation in Korea.

Japan moved resolutely under the leadership of Foreign Minister Mutsu Munemitsu to destroy the Chinese forces in Korea. Tokyo proposed a cooperative effort for putting down the Tonghak Rebellion as well as cooperation in a reform of Korea's internal affairs. When China rejected these proposals, Japan unilaterally demanded reforms of the Korean government, and on July 20th pressed for annulment of Korea's tribunal relationship with China. When these moves were rejected, on the 23rd, Japanese forces occupied the Korean Royal Palace and moved to disarm Korean troops.

In this manner, Japan adopted the stance that it had only acted out of necessity because its legitimate diplomatic demands had been rejected and had taken the military initiative. Due to an earlier lack of military strength during the periods of the Imo Military Rebellion and the Kapsin Political Coup, Japan had been defeated by Chinese forces. However, it had seized the initiative on this occasion, and when China belatedly attempted to dispatch significant military forces in an escalation of the conflict, the navies of the two countries clashed on July 25th in the Battle of P'ungdo. Following this, fighting continued on land, and war was formally declared on August 1st.

Fukuzawa went all out to cooperate in the prosecution of the war. It was his general rule not to donate to ordinary public causes, but on this occasion, a movement to contribute to military expenditures developed and a national service organization (the *Hokokukai*) was formed. However, just as this was getting under way, the government announced that it would issue government bonds for military expenditures, and the members of the movement flowed in that direction. Fukuzawa was not pleased with the situation and began handling donations through the *Jiji Shimpo*, giving ¥10,000 himself. In today's money, that would easily exceed ¥100,000,000. Of those who contributed through until the end of the Sino-Japanese War, the largest donors were Mori Motonori (¥15,000), Fukuzawa, Ii Naonori, Sakai Tadanao and Yoshida Saburoemon (¥10,000 each).

Fukuzawa was neither a member of the peerage nor a person of great wealth. He had a significant income to be sure, but he also had to cover significant expenses. In *Kosho*, it was stated that he "consulted with his whole family and they agreed to cut back on everything possible," and therefore he was able to contribute a total of ¥10,000.

Fukuzawa enthusiastically supported the Sino-Japanese War as a war of civilization against the uncivilized. He took a hard line saying that even during a suspension of hostilities, one should not rest from one's labors. However, in March 1895, when China's General Li Hongzhang was targeted by a Japanese sniper, he strongly protested the tactic. Further, regarding the Triple Intervention of 1895, he thought that there was no alternative but to make concessions ("Wait for another day," May 7th, 1895). Indeed, he did not hold a hard line to the point of being reckless.

Nevertheless, his attitude during the war was definitely enthusiastic. Indeed, some of the essays and *Mangen* that appeared under his name at this time—but whose authorship is now disputed—are blatantly discriminatory in the terms they used to reference Koreans and Chinese. To put it bluntly, certain prose definitely raised some eyebrows.

From this perspective, one might even be justified as viewing Fukuzawa as the philosophical parent of the government policies of expansionism on the continent. Thus, prior to World War II, he was much appreciated, whereas after the war, he was seen in a more critical light.

However, I believe such interpretations are faulty.

Firstly, Fukuzawa conceived of the Sino-Japanese War as a war of enlightenment against the forces of barbarism. He welcomed it, because at that time the Qing Dynasty was an ethnic minority rule by the Manchu. The Chinese had been forced into accepting the culture of the Manchu, such as pigtails and bound feet. It was evident that Qing China, as it existed, would be unable to defend itself against the advance of the West. Under the influence of the Qing by extension, Korea would not merely lose its independence but would also fail to make any progress. Thus, it was not easy to reject the idea that this was indeed a conflict between civilization and the uncivilized.

Secondly, Fukuzawa was seriously thinking about the independence of Korea. In his *Jiji Shimpo* editorial entitled, "Korean independence" (September 29th, 1894), he asserted that Korea should be free to decide whether to take Japan as its teacher or some Western country as its guide. Whether Korea looked to Great Britain, France, Germany or Russia—all civilized nations of the West—there would be no problem as long as the choice it did not work to the disadvantage or have a negative impact on the honor of Japan. "Regarding the annexation of territory or making Korea a protectorate, even if the occasion should present itself, Japan should not take advantage of it." Fukuzawa clearly rejected the notion of annexing Korea or turning it into some form of protectorate.

Thirdly, Fukuzawa continued to oppose letting the Japanese governmental bureaucracy expand. Administering a colony, whatever economic benefits might accrue, would give rise to an undesirable expansion of government bureaucracies and the merchants that would live off of it like parasites. Japan's eventual administration of Korea and later of Manchuria

—as we now look back on the mid-20th century—brought in the wake of the bureaucratic posts it created, the economic safeguards it required and the political power it generated, a paralysis of government on the mainland of Japan. It was this that Fukuzawa was so averse to. It is utterly inconceivable that Fukuzawa would have set aside this consistent view and endorsed colonization.

Fourthly, Fukuzawa believed that the future of Japan was to develop as a mercantilist state. I do not believe that he had any thought of Japan's future as a continental state. There is very little discussion in his writings about the resources of China or Korea. He had absolutely nothing to do with the ideas of those who looked to the continent as a means of attaining security and affluence through territorial expansion.

One further consideration is that with recent developments in research on Fukuzawa, it has become fairly clear which of the editorials in *Jiji Shimpo* can be legitimately attributed to Fukuzawa and which cannot. Of the leading articles in the newspaper, there were a variety ranging between articles that he actually wrote himself and articles written by others which he simply amended. However, there is a growing recognition of the fact that, of the articles taking a hard-line stance, many were written by other people without input from Fukuzawa (Ida Shinya, "Fukuzawa Yukichi *Jiji Shimpo* ronsetsu no sainintei [Reconfirming the editorials by Fukuzawa Yukichi in *Jiji Shimpo*]", *Shiso*, September 1998).

Chapter 15

Last Years and Death

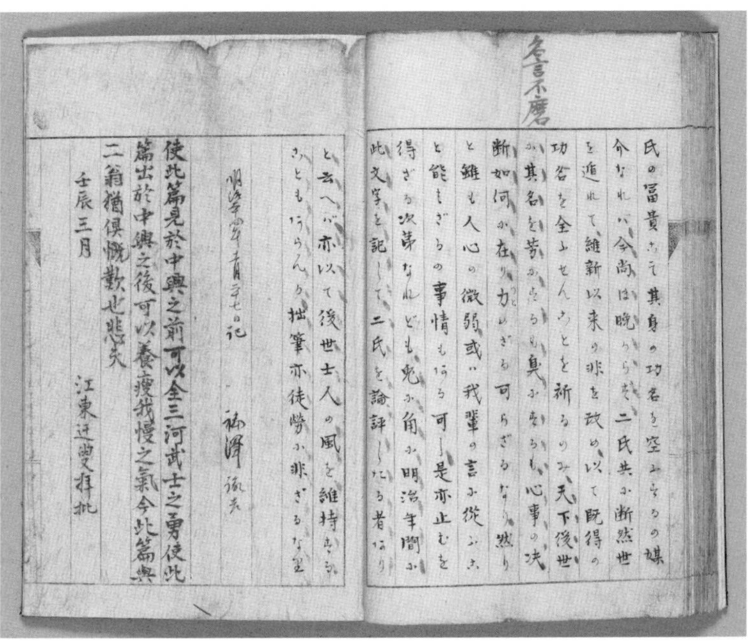

名言不磨

氏の冨貴をえて其身の功名を空ふするの媒介なれば今尚は晩からず二氏共に断然世を遁れて維新以来の非を改め以て既得の功名を全ふせんことを祈るのみ天下後世に其名を芳ふするも臭ふするも心事の決断如何に在り力めざる可らざるなり然りと雖も人心の微弱或は我輩の言に従ふと能はざるの事情もある可し是亦止むを得ざるの次第なれども兎に角に明治年間に此文字を記して二氏を論評したる者なりと云へば亦以て後世士人の風を維持する

拙筆亦徒労に非ざるなり

福澤諭吉

使此篇見於中興之前可以全三河武士之勇使此篇出於中興之後可以養瘦我慢之氣今此篇與二翁猶俱慨歎也悲夫

壬辰三月

江東迂叟拜批

This handwritten copy of Fukuzawa's *Yasegaman no setsu* has notes written in by Kurimoto Joun, from about 1891. (Courtesy of Keio University Fukuzawa Memorial Center)

Fukuzawa and Religion

Fukuzawa turned 60 in 1894. However, the celebration of his reaching such an auspicious age was postponed one year due to the outbreak of the Sino-Japanese War. For Fukuzawa, the conflict represented the peak of his life, with the grip of old age finally sneaking up on him.

There are few people who can live their final years as fully as Fukuzawa did from his 60th birthday until his death in 1901.

Beginning on March 1st, 1896, at a pace of two or three times a week, Fukuzawa published a series entitled the "One Hundred Discourses" *(Fukuo hyakuwa)* in *Jiji Shimpo*. These serialized articles continued until July 4th, 1897, and were shortly thereafter published as a single volume. The "One Hundred Discourses" is a rather peculiar work, differing markedly from his previous writings. Contrasting with the active, pragmatic Fukuzawa of an earlier age, in this work he places relatively more importance on issues of religion, and also ponders philosophy. There is also the Buddhist sense of the world's mutability which hangs over all. As an advocate of enlightenment, even when he had previously touched on the benefits of religion, Fukuzawa had rarely taken up its inherent elements, perhaps leaving the reader with a feeling that something was lacking. Toward the end of his life, however, a change in his outlook occurred.

The "One Hundred Discourses" opens with a discussion of the immensity of the universe. In the seventh installment of the series entitled, "Peace of mind," Fukuzawa wrote that within the universe, the earth was like a poppy seed cast in a great ocean, and on it human beings were like bits of dust, larvae and maggots. How strange and pathetic it was within this state, he argued, to become absorbed in wealth and poverty or the vicissitudes of fortune. Yet given that one was born in this world, even a maggot had to have a suitable degree of determination.

> While one knows that human life is intrinsically capricious, one takes each whimsical situation as if it were not so. One works as if it were a serious matter, evading poverty and suffering, seeking wealth and comfort, avoiding causing trouble for one's companions and seeking ease for oneself, considering 50 or 70 years to be a long life, serving one's parents, maintaining harmonious relations as husband and wife, planning for children and grandchildren, working outside the home for the interests of the public, determining to make not a single blunder in a lifetime—consider this the role of a maggot. Yet this is not the maggot's duty; it is only the human being that can boast of this, out of all the souls in creation.

In other words, it is the special character of human beings that condemns them to work earnestly, while nevertheless recognizing that this is a world filled with whim and mischief.

Fukuzawa, who until then had run at full speed through life, reflected on the past and on the meaning of his own passage in the "One Hundred Discourses."

The following poem expresses the intent of his observations thoroughly.

> "Title: Old Fukuzawa's One Hundred Discourses First Page"
>
> One side is the truth, one side is false
> Human beings in all matters are obscure beings upon it
> However verbose I become, do not laugh
> I am still inside the hundred whims

Following the "One Hundred Discourses," Fukuzawa penned the "More Discourses" *(Fukuo hyakuyowa)*. This series was serialized immediately after its predecessor in the *Jiji Shimpo* from September 1897 to January 1898. It appeared again, after a brief hiatus, in January and February 1900. In this series, Fukuzawa returned to his scholarly roots and discussed issues of independence and civilization.

At any rate, Fukuzawa had begun to make a final settlement of accounts regarding his own corpus of work. The year he did this was 1898. He had the *Jiji Shimpo* publish his important works in a five-volume *Collected Works of Fukuzawa (Fukuzawa zenshu)*. The foreword *(shogen)* was written prior to December 1897, but as Fukuzawa himself wrote in it the origin and intent of his works, this chapter is of significance. The publication of this *Collected Works* is important as a summarization of his own literary production and the foreword is especially important.

However, the *Collected Works* did not sell well. Two thousand copies of each of the five volumes were printed and bound, totaling 10,000 copies, but of these only 6,000 were sold. Thus it seemed that the "Fukuzawa period" was drawing to a close.

Immediately after this publishing setback, however, Fukuzawa delivered his autobiography, his all-time bestseller. He finished the manuscript in May of 1898 and began serializing it on July 1st in the *Jiji Shimpo*. It was subsequently published as a single volume in June 1899. I have repeatedly mentioned the value of this work. Not only is it the greatest biographical masterpiece by a Japanese person, but it is one of the world's best and a lasting memoir that depicts the springtime of life. Yet, as I have also mentioned, it barely touches on Fukuzawa's service as a retainer of the shogunate. What is perhaps more surprising is that of the 15 chapters in total, 14 are devoted to his youth. In content, not only time span, it is a book about youth. Indeed, in the last chapter, he wrote very simply in passing about his later years following the upheavals of 1881. In other words, Fukuzawa made a final settlement of accounts in his *Collected Works* and his *Autobiography*, but both were paeans to the first half of his life.

Immediately after completing the manuscript for his autobiography, in May 1898, a garden party was held at the villa in Tokyo's Hiroo District, and Ito Hirobumi attended. It was the first time Ito and Fukuzawa had met following their parting of the ways as a result of the Political Crisis of 1881. Over the years, there had been several unsuccessful attempts to bring together the leading statesman and the leading academic of the time, but this final reunion was actually realized through Ito attending the gathering. It is said that the two men conversed pleasantly as if nothing untoward had ever passed between them.

At the end of the *Autobiography*, Fukuzawa expressed his early hopes. First was that he would be able to elevate the virtue of men and women throughout the country. Second was that the promotion of religions would be established (he did not care whether it was Buddhism or Christianity), and used to soothe the nation's feelings. Third was that a large amount of money could be provided to inculcate true scientific principles in top-level academic research. We will look at the first aspiration in a moment. The second was not realized, so we will pass over it, but let us consider the third here.

Fukuzawa's attitude was that education at the primary level should be carried out by the state, while secondary education should be private. As somebody deeply-versed in traditional liberalism, Fukuzawa naturally sought to limit the role of government. Because national universities charged low tuition, they were able to attract students, and private universities were therefore unable to charge high tuition when competing. His criticism and dissatisfaction resulted from the consequence that private schools were therefore unable to improve in quality. It was his opinion that if both types of school were able to compete on an equal basis and double their tuition fees, the standards of the private schools would improve considerably.

On the other hand, he asserted that research at the highest levels should be supported by funds from the government. At a *Mita Enzetsukai* meeting in November 1893, Fukuzawa commented that academics by nature liked to do research, so even if one gave them no assistance, they would pursue their interests nevertheless. But if you gave five or ten of the finest academics freedom to do research without having to attend to any other duties, they would be able to achieve truly great results. This he said was his own dream.

An example of Fukuzawa's dream was the establishment of the Kitasato Institute. Although Kitasato Shibasaburo had achieved renown in Germany before returning to Japan in 1892, the academic reception that welcomed him home was at best indifferent. Hoping to allow Kitasato to make full use of his abilities as a researcher, Fukuzawa helped him establish the Institute for Infectious Diseases. However, rather unexpectedly their plans brought about opposition from people living in the neighborhood of the facility. This research facility became a national institution and later, when the government's policy changed, it reverted to private status. Nevertheless, Fukuzawa's original invitation to Kitasato had truly been made in earnest and was entirely appropriate as one aspect of his dream of sponsoring research.

Such free-thinking facilities that are driven by no specific research purpose are few and far between in the modern world. If greatly pressed, one might offer Princeton's Institute for Advanced Study as a contemporary example of Fukuzawa's dream. (For more on this idea, please refer to Saito Makoto: "'The use of non-useful studies' in American history," in *Amerika to wa nanika* [What is America?])

"Self-Respect and Independence of Mind" Permeate Wisdom and Virtue

Following the completion of his autobiography, Fukuzawa wrote his

Reproof of "The Essential Learning for Women" (Onna Daigaku hyoron) and *New Essential Learning for Women (Shin Onna Daigaku)*. These volumes ran to 20 and 23 chapters, respectively. "The foundation of morality is the husband and wife relationship," Fukuzawa wrote, and both books are enthusiastic discourses on the elevation of the dignity of the institution of marriage. During the sweltering heat of summer in 1898, he wrote at a pace of one to three chapters per day, finishing both volumes within a month. He became so enthralled in his writing that he "even worked at night for the first time in years."

However, several days after completing the manuscripts, on September 26th, 1898, Fukuzawa suffered a stroke. At one point, he was diagnosed as being in a critical condition, and the Emperor, Empress and Crown Prince had an Imperial gift of wine and sweets sent to him as an expression of their concern for his condition. However, from around the middle of October he began to recover, and by December he was almost completely returned to good health. There is something incredible about the fact that while his entertaining autobiography was being serialized in the *Jiji Shimpo*, Fukuzawa himself was hovering between life and death or subsequently spending most of his days undergoing rehabilitation. During one low point he could not remember his wife's name, and while he was somehow able to write the character for "east," he could not recall the character for "west." Another ironical coincidence was that the cabinet of that period, headed by Okuma Shigenobu, was the one he had the most confidence in of all that had been formed thus far. Sources close to the Okuma Cabinet advocated raising Fukuzawa to the peerage. However, Fukuzawa's eldest son Ichitaro, after consulting with the elder members of Keio Gijuku, declined the offer.

Shortly after his recovery, Fukuzawa turned 64 years old. In anticipation of this day, some of his older students held a get together at the *Koyokan* in Shiba. While he was not completely recovered, the alumni nevertheless held an assembly to celebrate a time in the future when their teacher would fully return to good health. At the gathering, Obata Tokujiro commented that their feeling upon seeing how much Fukuzawa had already recovered was like "a person who was freezing finding fire, a naked person procuring clothes, a merchant receiving a new customer, a child finding its mother, a landing having a boat to offer as a means of crossing, a sick person finding a doctor, and darkness gaining light." Everyone gathered at the event deeply shared the feelings expressed in this speech.

In May 1899, Fukuzawa was well enough to call on the Minister of the Imperial Household to express his formal gratitude for the inquiry after his health that had been made by the Imperial Family. In November, another garden party was held and among the 600 to 700 attending were Prime Minister Yamagata Aritomo, Minister of Finance Matsukata Masayoshi, Navy Minister Yamamoto Gonbei, Minister of Justice Kiyoura Keigo, Minister of Communications Yoshikawa Akimasa and Minister of the Imperial Household Tanaka Mitsuaki. Okuma Shigenobu, Iwasaki Yanosuke, Mitsui Takahiro, Mitsui Hachiroemon, Hayashi Tadasu and Morimura Ichizaemon were also in attendance. The importance placed on social intercourse is clearly self-evident through the guest list.

Following his serious illness, Fukuzawa was unable to write much at all. The last work he attempted was the *Moral Code (Shushin yoryo)*. Fukuzawa dictated its content to a scribe. It argued that the old form of morality had lost its potency and that a new form of morality had not yet appeared. The turbulence of recent times, Fukuzawa reasoned, were related to this turn of events, and thinking that standards of moral teachings appropriate for the times should be promoted, he had those around him put together a draft. It was this draft that eventually became the *Moral Code*.

The fundamental undercurrent of this work was the concept of "self-respect and independence of mind" *(dokuritsu jison)*. Obata Tokujiro was to gain wide approval of his opinion that it was this expression that most fully and accurately portrayed Fukuzawa's words and deeds. In actual fact, Fukuzawa himself had not to that point used the four-character phrase *dokuritsu jison* frequently to express his ideas, but Obata, who knew Fukuzawa as well as anyone, chose them in his place.

In addition to the preface, the *Moral Code* consists of 29 principles, of which 17 actually highlight the four-character phrase. The first principle states:

> It is the universal duty of Man to raise his personal dignity and to develop his wisdom and virtue to their utmost capacity, never to be contented with the degree of development already attained, but ever to press forward to higher attainments. We urge it, therefore, as a duty upon all those who would hold the same convictions as ourselves to endeavor in all things to discharge their full duty as men, laying to heart the principles of self-respect and independence of mind as the leading tenets of moral life.[49]

The subject in this instance is clearly the emphasis that is placed upon self-respect and independence of mind.

The second principle states:

> Whosoever perfectly realizes the principle of Independence, both of Mind and Body, and, paying due respect to his own person, preserves his dignity unblemished—him we call a man of self-respect and independence of mind.[50]

The third principle goes on:

> The true source of independence of life is to eat one's bread in the sweat

> of one's brow. A man of self-respect and independence of mind should be a self-helping and self-supporting man.[51]

From the outset, Fukuzawa stresses the principle of self-respect and independence of mind in relations between men and women, in the education of children and in continuing to educate oneself even after attaining adulthood.

The twelfth principle states:

> The ideal person of self-respect and independence of mind deems it incumbent on himself to go on learning even to his old age, and never to allow either the development of the Intellect or the Cultivation of the Moral Character to slacken or cease.[52]

This same principle applies to the configuration of society. The thirteenth principle states:

> Society having both individuals and families as its units, it should be borne in mind that the foundation of a healthy society is to be found in self-respect and independence of mind of the family as well as of the individuals.[53]

The fourteenth principle states:

> The only way in which social life can continue is for each Individual to keep unimpaired his or her own self-respect and independence of mind as well as that of others. This may be done by respecting the rights and happiness of others at the same time that we seek our own happiness and protect our own rights.[54]

The sixteenth principle states:

> Every man should be faithful in the discharge of the duties of his vocation. He, who, regardless of the importance of the trusts committed to him, neglects his responsibilities, is unworthy to be called a man of self-respect and independence of mind.[55]

The seventeenth principle states:

> Treat others with trustfulness. If you trust others, they will trust you in return. It is this mutual confidence alone that can enable self-respect and independence of mind to be realized in ourselves or in others.[56]

The same principle applies to the state. The twenty-fourth principle states:

> The Japanese people, whether male or female, should never forget their supreme duty to maintain their national self-respect and independence of mind, against all foes, and at the sacrifice of even life and property.[57]

On the other hand, the twenty-sixth principle states:

> The number of countries in the world is by no means small, and they differ from us in religion, language, color and customs. Yet the people of those countries are all our brothers. In our intercourse with them there should be no partiality, and no attempt at swaggering or boastfulness. Such conduct only leads us to despise people from other countries and is wholly at variance with the Principle of self-respect and independence of mind.[58]

Previously in *An Outline of a Theory of Civilization*, Fukuzawa espoused the advancement of wisdom and virtue. That volume was nevertheless aimed more toward gaining wisdom than achieving virtue. However, it was only natural that once a degree of wisdom had been achieved, the objective should shift to ethics. Even in his autobiography he suggested that he wanted to lead the Japanese people toward a higher sense of refinement. And it was "Self-Respect and Independence of Mind" that maintained wisdom and virtue. In the *Moral Code*, the assertions of *An Encouragement of Learning, An Outline of a Theory of Civilization* and numerous other works which had been laid down in their day as means for advancing civilization and enlightenment, appeared once again in the form of a personal ethical code. Wisdom and virtue, for Fukuzawa, sprang from the same roots.

Yasegaman no setsu: the Spirit of Dogged Endurance

On December 31st, 1900, Keio Gijuku held a gathering to send off the past century and welcome the new one. For that occasion, Fukuzawa wrote "Welcoming the new century of self-respect and independence of mind." Apparently it was to form a pair with another piece entitled, "Farewell to the old century of…" but he was unable to find the right phrase to finish the title, thus he never completed the companion piece.

From January 1st through 3rd, Fukuzawa's *Yasegaman no setsu* was serialized in the *Jiji Shimpo* and it created a major stir. In this work, he used the expression *yasegaman* (or "dogged endurance") to refer to the willpower or steadfastness of the samurai. In the serialization, Fukuzawa argued that during the Edo period it was due to this obstinate and determined streak that smaller domains were able to stand up to their larger competitors, retain their independence and that without such a resolute spirit, independence would have been endangered. The targets of Fukuzawa's critique were Katsu Kaishu and Enomoto Takeaki. In his view, Katsu Kaishu's actions in simply handing over Edo Castle, without any resistance, was the antithesis of the spirit of "fighting to the bitter end," the ultimate expression of a samurai's dogged endurance. Although approving of the act in that it resulted in the saving of numerous lives that might have been lost if a last-ditch resistance to the hand-over had occurred, Fukuzawa could not approve of the high status and position that Katsu later accepted within the Meiji government. By contrast, while lauding Enomoto for his decision to fight to the end at the Goryokaku Fort at Hakodate, Fukuzawa nevertheless criticized him, not for surrendering the fort, but for pandering to achieve high office and promotions later in life. How could Enomoto face those who followed him and sacrificed everything in the cold north of Hokkaido?

The essay that was later published as *Yasegaman no setsu* was originally written back in 1891. At the time, Fukuzawa had sent a handwritten copy to both Katsu and Enomoto, asking them to confirm the details. Katsu replied, "I take responsibility for my actions, but praise or blame is the task of others. I neither make claims nor bother myself with such matters."[59] Katsu then added that he had no reservations regarding what Fukuzawa showed to other people. By contrast, Enomoto wrote that he had received the manuscript and would respond at a time when he was less busy, but he never did.

From that point onward, the text was passed around as a handwritten manuscript. One person who read it was a former retainer of the shogun named Kurimoto Joun. By that time, the elderly Kurimoto suffered from poor eyesight, but being nevertheless interested by what he heard from Fukuzawa as to the key points of his argument, the old man carefully read the text. He even wrote comments here and there throughout the manuscript. In the section that addressed Katsu's actions, he scribbled, "The writing flows so effortlessly and the power of the writing brush leaves no room for Katsu and the others to escape. How thoroughly gratifying that is." Then Kurimoto reached the following passage:

> Even foreigners at the time said: 'In general everything that has life will attempt to resist by any means if that life is threatened. Even squirming insects when about to be crushed by a heavy hammer, will gird themselves and assume a position of defiance. How is it that the 270-year-old powerful government of the bakufu, when confronted by the forces of two or three strong domains, showed no signs of resistance and instead only begged for peace? Surely, through the world in ancient and modern times there [is] nothing that can compare with this.[60]

Kurimoto wrote, "When I read this last section, it left me with inconsolable grief." Indeed, he was unable to prevent himself from crying out from contrasting emotions of chagrin and delight.

There was major public reaction to the publication of this essay. Tokutomi Soho argued that in the face of the ambitions of the world powers Japan had been in dire straits at that time and that the actions of Katsu and the others were unavoidable. Fukuzawa, however, knew the state of diplomatic relations at the time and believed that the real apprehension in Japan was not about the powerful nations resorting to military intervention but that the greater concern was with ambitions regarding trade. He had those close to him offer counterarguments.

When *Yasegaman no setsu* was published, Fukuzawa was arranging to have *Meiji junen teichu koron* [Opinion of 1877] see light of day. This latter essay vindicating Saigo Takamori had been locked away and left untouched since it was written. Fukuzawa had not attempted to publish it earlier due to the restrictions that were in place on freedom of speech. But times had changed and he felt that there would be no problem this long after the actual events had occurred. Published as an 8-part series in the *Jiji Shimpo* from February 1st to 10th, 1901, this essay also created a public sensation.

However, Fukuzawa never knew this. A week before the series was to begin, on January 25th, 1901 (Meiji 34), he suffered a second stroke and died on February 3rd.

The House of Representatives passed a resolution expressing the country's sorrow at Fukuzawa's passing. His funeral was modest but solemn; the family firmly declined floral wreaths and other expressions of condolence. The only flowers accepted were those from Okuma Shigenobu, which Okuma had grown and cut himself, offering them with tears in memory of Fukuzawa.

Upon his death, a number of works dealing with Fukuzawa's life and works were published. Among them, in my opinion, that written by Tokutomi Soho, who had almost no personal connection with Fukuzawa and who frequently opposed his views, was right on target in his appraisal.

Tokutomi wrote, "Anyone who lived during the Meiji period and had any connection with it, young or old, is indebted to Fukuzawa." He went on to state that to many people Fukuzawa was a leader, and to a significant number he was a stimulus. In terms of strength and effectiveness exerted on the daily life and the intellectual thought of Meiji Japan, Fukuzawa was virtually without parallel.

While acknowledging Fukuzawa's role as a demolisher, Tokutomi also recognized his major role as a builder and founder. In advocating the importance of money, "he enthusiastically sought wealth, but simultaneously supported the enjoyment of what it made possible." Fukuzawa advocated respect for commerce and industry, curbing the haughtiness of the bureaucrats and rousing the public, avoiding empty talk and adopting practical learning. He supported reforms that would make the structure of society both democratic and practical. All in all, Tokutomi held that Fukuzawa was an outstanding figure among scholars.

Tokutomi especially admired Fukuzawa for using straightforward language that anyone could easily understand and for taking praiseworthy action. Fukuzawa's family life was unsullied, he was tough and manly, he had a patriotic spirit, and he consistently refused to be second-rate. Fukuzawa was "not a worldly philosopher who cunningly taunted and ridiculed" but rather was "a lively child who possessed the essential nature of the true samurai." In his later years, he composed the *Moral Code* in order to inspire the public. Through all of these acts, Fukuzawa remained vigorous and powerful until his death. Tokutomi wrote that if one were to inquire what Fukuzawa's influence would be a century later, rather than mentioning Fukuzawa's collected works one would instead point to his personal character and his conduct as an individual.

Tokutomi's pointing to Fukuzawa's character and conduct rather than to his writings was due to the fact that Tokutomi was critical of several aspects of Fukuzawa's scholarship. From his cozy vantage point of 1901, Tokutomi was probably dissatisfied with works such as *An Encouragement of Learning* and *An Outline of a Theory of Civilization*, yet these same works were unprecedented and remained unparalleled in that they opened up new ground. Fukuzawa himself wrote that morality could not be conveyed by any other means than by showing one's beliefs through one's own actions. Where *An Encouragement of Learning* and *An Outline of a Theory of Civilization* broke new ground was by showing what Fukuzawa himself actually put into practice, and it is this fact that has exerted an enormous impact on subsequent generations. In that sense, Fukuzawa Yukichi is the greatest spiritual leader of modern Japan.

Notes

1 Kenneth E. Boulding, *Primer on Social Dynamics* (New York: Free Press, 1971).

2 See Albert Craig, *Civilization and Enlightenment: The Early Thought of Fukuzawa Yukichi* (Cambridge, MA and London: Harvard University Press, 2009). This superb study is valuable not only in terms of Japan and America. However, its subject matter is limited to Fukuzawa's early period and may be somewhat too specialized for the general reader.

3 *The Autobiography of Fukuzawa Yukichi,* revised translation by Eiichi Kiyooka (New York and London: Madison Books, 1992).

4 Kanae Iida, *Fukuzawa Yukichi* (Tokyo: Chuokoronsha, 1984).

5 One *koku* was a volume of unpolished rice that theoretically could sustain one person for one year. The actual volume varied from approximately 130 to 180 liters.

6 English translation by Carmen Blacker, *Monumenta Nipponica* 9, No. 1/2 (1953): 304-29.

7 *The Autobiography*, 40-41.

8 Ibid., 83.

9 Mikiaki Ishikawa, *Fukuzawa Yukichi den* (Tokyo: Iwanami Shoten, 1935).

10 *The Autobiography*, 91.

11 Ibid., 96.

12 Ibid., 98.

13 Akira Haruna, *Nippon Otokichi hyoryuki* (Tokyo: Shobunsha, 1979).

14 *The Autobiography*, 134-5.

15 Ibid., 129-30.

16 Toru Haga, *Taikun no shisetsu* (Tokyo: Chuokoronsha, 1968).

17 *The Autobiography*, 143.

18 Ibid., 157.

19 Hiroaki Matsuzawa, *Kindai nihon no keisei to seiyo keiken* (Tokyo: Iwanami Shoten, 1993).

20 *Fukuzawa Yukichi on Education: Selected Works*, trans. and ed. Eiichi Kiyooka (Tokyo: University of Tokyo Press, 1985), 15-16.

21 Ibid., 18.

22 *The Autobiography*, 210-1.

23 *Fukuzawa on Education*, 21-22.

24 *The Autobiography*, 208.

25 Ibid., 209.

26 Yukichi Fukuzawa, *An Encouragement of Learning*, trans. David A. Dilworth (Tokyo: Keio University Press, 2012), 3.

27 Ibid.

28 Ibid., 5.

29 Ibid., 6.

30 Ibid., 20.

31 Ibid., 24.

32 Ibid.

33 Ibid., 41.

34 Ibid.

35 Ibid., 62.

36 Yukichi Fukuzawa, *An Outline of a Theory of Civilization*, trans. David A. Dilworth and G. Cameron Hurst III (Tokyo: Keio University Press, 2008), 7.

37 Ibid., 176. Translation slightly revised.

38 Carmen Blacker, *The Japanese Enlightenment: A Study of the Writings of Fukuzawa Yukichi* (Cambridge: Cambridge University Press, 1964), 128.

39 Fukuzawa, *An Outline*, 253.

40 Blacker, *Japanese Enlightenment*, 11.

41 Ibid., 78.

42 *Fukuzawa on Education*, 48.

43 Ibid.

44 *The Autobiography*, 322.

45 Norio Tamaki, *Yukichi Fukuzawa, 1835-1901: The Spirit of Enterprise in Modern Japan* (New York: Palgrave, 2001), 236.

46 Masanori Ito, *Shimbun gojunenshi* (Tokyo: Masu Shobo, 1943), 24.

47 Keio Gijuku, ed., *Fukuzawa Yukichi shokanshu, Vol. 3* (Tokyo: Iwanami Shoten, 2001).

48 Helen M. Hopper, *Yukichi Fukuzawa: From Samurai to Capitalist* (New York: Pearson, 2005), 122.

49 *Fukuzawa on Education*, 270. Translation slightly amended for consistency with earlier translations in this work.

50 Ibid., 270.

51 Ibid.

52 Ibid., 271-2.

53 Ibid., 272.

54 Ibid.

55 Ibid.

56 Ibid.

57 Ibid., 273. Translation slightly amended.

58 Ibid. Translation slightly revised.

59 Yukichi Fukuzawa, "*Yasegaman no setsu:* On Fighting to the Bitter End," trans. M. William Steele, *Asian Cultural Studies* 11 (2002): 151.

60 Ibid., 144.

Bibliography

Works in English

The Autobiography of Fukuzawa Yukichi. Translated by Eiichi Kiyooka. New York & London: Madison Books, 1992.

Benesch, Oleg. *Inventing the Way of the Samurai: Nationalism, Internationalism and Bushido in Modern Japan.* Oxford: Oxford University Press, 2014.

Blacker, Carmen. *The Japanese Enlightenment: A Study of the Writings of Fukuzawa Yukichi.* Cambridge: Cambridge University Press, 1964.

Craig, Albert M. *Civilization and Enlightenment: The Early Thought of Fukuzawa Yukichi.* Cambridge, MA & London: Harvard University Press, 2009.

Fukuzawa, Yukichi. *An Encouragement of Learning.* Translated by David A. Dilworth. Tokyo: Keio University Press, 2012.

Fukuzawa, Yukichi. *An Outline of a Theory of Civilization.* Revised. Translated by David A. Dilworth and G. Cameron Hurst III. Tokyo: Keio University Press, 2008.

Fukuzawa, Yukichi. "Conditions in an Old Feudal Clan." Translated by Carmen Blacker. *Monumenta Nipponica* 9, No. 1/2 (1953): 304-29.

Fukuzawa Yukichi on Education: Selected Works. Translated and edited by Eiichi Kiyooka. Tokyo: University of Tokyo Press, 1985.

Fukuzawa, Yukichi. "*Yasegaman no setsu:* On Fighting to the Bitter End." Translated by M. William Steele. *Asian Cultural Studies* 11 (2002): 139-52.

Hane, Mikiso. "Early Meiji Liberalism: An Assessment." *Monumenta Nipponica* 24, No. 4 (1969): 353-71.

Hopper, Helen M. *Yukichi Fukuzawa: From Samurai to Capitalist.* New York: Pearson, 2005.

Jansen, Marius B. *The Making of Modern Japan.* Cambridge, MA & London: Harvard University Press, 2000.

Karlin, Jason G. *Gender and Nation in Meiji Japan: Modernity, Loss, and the Doing of History.* Honolulu: University of Hawai'i Press, 2014.

Nishikawa, Shunsaku. "Fukuzawa Yukichi (1835-1901)." *Prospects: The Quarterly Review of Comparative Education* XXIII, No. 2-4 (1993): 493-506.

Tamaki, Norio. *Yukichi Fukuzawa, 1835-1901: The Spirit of Enterprise in Modern Japan.* New York: Palgrave, 2001.

Fukuzawa Yukichi's works in Japanese

Keio Gijuku, ed. *Fukuzawa Yukichi zenshu* [The collected works of Fukuzawa Yukichi]. 21 vols. and a supplementary vol. Tokyo: Iwanami Shoten, 1969-1971.

Keio Gijuku, ed. *Fukuzawa Yukichi shokanshu* [The collected letters of Fukuzawa Yukichi]. 9 vols. Tokyo: Iwanami Shoten, 2001-2002.

Hayashi, Nozomu, ed. *Onna Daigaku hyoron; Shin Onna Daigaku* [Reproof of "The Essential Learning for Women"; New Essential Learning for Women]. Tokyo: Kodansha, 2001.

Meiji Junen Teichu koron; Yasegaman no setsu [Commentary on the national problems of

1877; Spirit of manly defiance]. Tokyo: Kodansha, 1985.

Nakamura, Toshiko, ed. *Fukuzawa Yukichi kazoku-ronshu* [Fukuzawa Yukichi on the family: Selected works]. Tokyo: Iwanami Shoten, 1999.

Tomita, Masafumi, and Shunichi Tsuchihashi, eds. *Fukuzawa Yukichi senshu* [The selected works of Fukuzawa Yukichi]. 14 vols. Tokyo: Iwanami Shoten, 1980-1981.

Works on Fukuzawa Yukichi in Japanese

Banno, Junji. *Kindai nihon kokka no koso, 1871-1936* [The concept of the state in modern Japan, 1871-1936]. Tokyo: Iwanami Shoten, 1996.

Doi, Ryozo. *Kanrin Maru umi o wataru* [Kanrin Maru crosses the ocean]. Tokyo: Chuokoronsha, 1998.

Haga, Toru. *Taikun no shisetsu* [Embassy of the shogun]. Tokyo: Chuokoronsha, 1968.

Hirai, Kazuhiro. *Fukuzawa Yukichi no komyunikeshon* [Fukuzawa Yukichi's communication]. Tokyo: Seiji Shobo, 1996.

Hirayama, Yo. *Fukuzawa Yukichi no shinjitsu* [The truth about Fukuzawa Yukichi]. Tokyo: Bungeishunju, 2004.

Hirayama, Yo. *Fukuzawa Yukichi.* Kyoto: Minerva Shobo, 2008.

Hirota, Masaki. *Fukuzawa Yukichi kenkyu* [Studies of Fukuzawa Yukichi]. Tokyo: University of Tokyo Press, 1976.

Ida, Shinya. *Rekishi to tekusuto: Saikaku kara Yukichi made* [History and text: From Saikaku to Yukichi]. Tokyo: Kobosha, 2001.

Iida, Kanae. *Fukuzawa Yukichi to bakumatsu ishin no gunzo. Iida Kanae chosakushu, dai-go-kan* [Fukuzawa Yukichi and the figures of the bakumatsu and restoration period. Vol. 5 of the collected works of Iida Kanae]. Tokyo: Ochanomizu Shobo, 2001.

Iida, Kanae. *Fukuzawa Yukichi: Kokumin kokkaron no soshisha* [Fukuzawa Yukichi: Originator of the nation-state theory]. Tokyo: Chuokoronsha, 1984.

Imanaga, Seiji. *Fukuzawa Yukichi no shiso keisei* [Formation of Fukuzawa Yukichi's thought]. Tokyo: Keiso Shobo, 1979.

Ishikawa, Mikiaki. *Fukuzawa Yukichi den* [A biography of Fukuzawa Yukichi]. 4 vols. Tokyo: Iwanami Shoten, 1935.

Ito, Masao, ed. *Meijijin no mita Fukuzawa Yukichi: Shiryo shusei* [Fukuzawa Yukichi through the eyes of Meiji-era people: A collection of documents]. Tokyo: Keio Tsushin, 1970.

Maruyama, Masao. *Fukuzawa Yukichi no tetsugaku, hoka roppen* [The philosophy of Fukuzawa Yukichi and other six essays]. Edited by Hiroaki Matsuzawa. Tokyo: Iwanami Shoten, 2001.

Maruyama, Masao. *Bunmeiron no Gairyaku o yomu* [Reading 'An Outline of a Theory of Civilization']. 3 vols. Tokyo: Iwanami Shoten, 1986.

Matsuzawa, Hiroaki. *Kindai nihon no keisei to seiyo keiken* [The shaping of modern Japan and the experience of the West]. Tokyo: Iwanami Shoten, 1993.

Miyanaga, Takashi. *Bunkyu ninen no yoroppa hokoku* [The reports on Europe of 1862]. Tokyo: Shinchosha, 1989.

Nagao, Masanori. *Fukuzawa-ya Yukichi no kenkyu* [A study of Fukuzawaya Yukichi]. Kyoto: Shibunkaku Shuppan, 1988.

Nakajima, Mineo. *Bakushin Fukuzawa Yukichi* [Bakufu loyalist Fukuzawa Yukichi]. Tokyo: TBS-Britannica, 1991.

Nakamura, Toshiko. *Fukuzawa Yukichi, bunmei to shakai koso* [Fukuzawa Yukichi: Civilization and social design]. Tokyo: Sobun Sha, 2000.

Nakazaki, Masao. *Fukuzawa Yukichi to shashin-ya no musume* [Fukuzawa Yukichi and the photographer's daughter]. Osaka: Osaka University Press, 1996.

Nishibe, Susumu. *Fukuzawa Yukichi: Sono bushido to aikokushin* [Fukuzawa Yukichi: His bushido and patriotism]. Tokyo: Bungeishunju, 1999.

Nishikawa, Shunsaku, and Kin'ichi Matsuzaki, eds. *Fukuzawa Yukichi ron no hyakunen* [One hundred years of essays on Fukuzawa Yukichi]. Tokyo: Keio University Press, 1999.

Nishikawa, Shunsaku, and Naoko Nishizawa, eds. *Fudangi no Fukuzawa Yukichi* [Fukuzawa Yukichi in his everyday clothes]. Tokyo: Keio University Press, 1998.

Nishikawa, Shunsaku. *Fukuzawa Yukichi no yokogao* [A profile of Fukuzawa Yukichi]. Tokyo: Keio University Press, 1998.

Numata, Jiro, and Hiroaki Matsuzawa, eds. *Nihon shiso taikei: Seiyo kenbunshu* [A systematic collection on Japanese thought: Observations on the West]. Tokyo: Iwanami Shoten, 1974.

Sakamoto, Takao. *Atarashii Fukuzawa Yukichi* [The new Fukuzawa Yukichi]. Tokyo: Kodansha, 1997.

Sakamoto, Takao. *Shijo, dotoku, chitsujo* [Market, morals, order]. Tokyo: Sobun Sha, 1993.

Shirai, Takako. *Fukuzawa Yukichi to senkyoshitachi: Shirarezaru meijiki no nichi-ei kankei* [Fukuzawa Yukichi and British missionaries: The untold history of Anglo-Japanese relations]. Tokyo: Mirai Sha, 1999.

Tanaka, Odo. *Fukuzawa Yukichi*, Tokyo: Misuzu Shobo, 1987.

Tomita, Masafumi. *Kosho Fukuzawa Yukichi* [Study of Fukuzawa Yukichi]. 2 vols. Tokyo: Iwanami Shoten, 1992.

Toyama, Shigeki. *Fukuzawa Yukichi: Shiso to seiji no kanren* [Fukuzawa Yukichi: Relation between thought and politics]. Tokyo: University of Tokyo Press, 1970.

Toyama, Shigeki. *Meiji no shiso to nashonarizumu. Toyama Shigeki chosakushu, dai-go-kan* [Meiji-era thought and nationalism. Vol.5 of the collected works of Toyama Shigeki]. Tokyo: Iwanami Shoten, 1992.

Uchiyama, Hideo, ed. *150-nenme no Fukuzawa Yukichi: Kyozo kara jitsuzo e* [The 150-year Fukuzawa Yukichi: Virtual image to real image]. Tokyo: Yuhikaku, 1985.

Yamaguchi, Kazuo. *Fukuzawa Yukichi no amerika taiken* [Fukuzawa Yukichi's experiences in America]. Tokyo: Fukuzawa Yukichi Kyokai, 1986.

Yamaguchi, Kazuo. *Fukuzawa Yukichi no ao kenbun* [Fukuzawa Yukichi's observations on Asia and Europe]. Tokyo: Fukuzawa Yukichi Kyokai, 1992.

Yamaguchi, Kazuo. *Fukuzawa Yukichi no saiko junreki* [Fukuzawa Yukichi's Western voyage]. Tokyo: Fukuzawa Yukichi Kyokai, 1980.

Fukuzawa Chronology

Western calendar	Age of Fukuzawa	Events in the life of Fukuzawa	His publications and events at home and abroad
1835	0	**January 10** Fukuzawa Yukichi was born in the domainal residence of Nakatsu domain in Osaka.	
1836	1	**July** His father Hyakusuke dies in Osaka.	
		November His brother Sannosuke succeeds as head of the family.	
1838	3		Ogata Koan opens his *Tekijuku* academy in Osaka
1853	18		**July** Commodore Perry's fleet arrives at Uraga
1854	19	**February** At the suggestion of his brother Sannosuke, Yukichi goes to Nagasaki to study Dutch Learning.	**March** U.S.-Japan Peace and Amity Treaty is signed
1855	20	**March** Fukuzawa leaves Nagasaki, sails from Shimonoseki, arrives at his brother's residence in Osaka.	
		April 25 Enters Ogata Koan's *Tekijuku*, commuting from his brother's residence.	
			August *Kaigun Denshujo* [Naval Training Center] established in Nagasaki
1856	21	**April-May** Suffers typhus, receives care from Ogata Koan.	Yoshida Shoin opens the *Shoka Sonjuku* academy
		June-July Brother completes term of service and suffers rheumatism. Brothers both return to Nakatsu.	
		September 2 Yukichi returns to Osaka and *Tekijuku* studies.	
		October 1 Sannosuke dies, Yukichi returns to Nakatsu and succeeds as head of the family.	
		November Yukichi returns to *Tekijuku* as a live-in student.	
1857	22	Becomes head teacher of *Tekijuku*.	
1858	23	**November** Under orders from the domain, Fukuzawa goes to Edo, after visiting his mother in Nakatsu, and opens a school of Dutch Learning at Tsukiji Teppozu in a secondary residence of Nakatsu domain. This is the origin of Keio Gijuku.	**May** Ii Naosuke is appointed chancellor
			July U.S.-Japan Amity and Commerce Treaty is signed, Tokugawa Iemochi succeeds as shogun
			August Ansei Purge begins

1859	24	**July** Visits Yokohama which has been opened to foreign trade, discovers Dutch is useless, decides to switch to studies through English.	
1860	25	**February 10** Appointed as attendant to Kimura Settsu-no-kami and boards *Kanrin Maru*, departing Uraga.	**March** Sakuradamongai Incident—Chancellor Ii Naosuke is assassinated
		March 18 Arrives in San Francisco, after a rough 37-day voyage. Purchases Webster dictionary. Sails via Hawaii back to Japan.	
		December Given a bakufu position as official translator for the minister of foreign affairs. Relocates to Shiba Shinsenza.	
1861	26	Marries Okin, daughter of Nakatsu samurai family.	
1862	27	**January 19** Appointed official translator to bakufu mission to Europe.	
		January 21 Boards ship.	
		January 22 Sails from Shinagawa.	
		January 28 Visits Yamamoto Monojiro residence in Nagasaki en route.	
		January 30 Mission departs Nagasaki. Sails via Hong Kong, Singapore, Ceylon, Suez, Cairo, Alexandria, Malta to Marseilles. Visits France, Great Britain, the Netherlands, Prussia, Russia, Portugal and returns to Shinagawa.	**February** Sakashitamongai Incident **September** Richardson Incident *(Namamugi Jiken)*
1863	28	**Spring** Abandons studies of Dutch and begins serious operation of English Studies at the academy.	**June 25** Choshu domain repulses foreign ships
		July 25 Ogata Koan dies. At wake Fukuzawa is stunned by Omura Masujiro's ardent endorsement for expulsion of foreigners.	**August** British bombardment of Kagoshima **September 30** Attempted coup at Kyoto
		November 22 First son Ichitaro is born.	
1864	29	**January 15** Delivers copy of *Diary of the West* to Kimura.	
		April Returns to Nakatsu, meeting mother for first time in six years. Stays two months.	
		June Hand-written copy of *Conditions in the West* are passed around, but not published.	
		July 29 Returns to Edo with Obata Tokujiro and other youth.	**August** Kinmon Incident **August** First military expedition against Choshu
		October Becomes official translator for bakufu.	**September** Four Western nation bombardment of Choshu batteries at Shimonoseki

1865	30	**October** Second son Sutejiro born.	**November** Imperial sanction for second expedition against Choshu
1866	31	**October** Submission of petition regarding the expedition against Choshu. **Autumn** Sells swords.	**First installment of *Conditions in the West*** is published **July** Second expedition against Choshu begins **August** Death of shogun Tokugawa Iemochi
1867	32	**February 27** Visits U.S. a second time as a member of a government mission to San Francisco, New York, Washington. **July 28** Returns to Japan bringing home a large number of English textbooks for his school and Sendai domain. Complaint filed by Ono Tomogoro for this. Relieved of duty in November.	**January** Tokugawa Yoshinobu becomes shogun **November 9** Return of political power to the Emperor by the Tokugawa shogunate
1868 (Meiji 1)	33	**January 19** Purchases Arima residence in Shinsenza for 355 *ryo* and takes possession. **February** Fukuzawa moves to new residence in Shinsenza. **April** New school building completed, school named "Keio Gijuku" after the year of its founding. **May 2** First daughter (third child) Sato is born. **July 4** During the Battle at Ueno, Fukuzawa lectures on Wayland's economics text. **July 27** Submits resignation from his post and declines subsequent offers of office from the new government. **November** Submits petition to new government regarding pirated editions of his books.	**January 3** Restoration of imperial rule **January** Battle of Toba-Fushimi; Publication of ***Conditions in the West,* Outside Volume** **July 4** Battle of the *Shogitai* at Ueno
1869	34		**July** Return of the domainal registers to the Meiji Emperor
1870	35	**July** Second daughter (fourth child) Fusa is born. **October 8** Falls ill with typhus and takes family to Atami Hot Spring to convalesce. **November 14** Visits Iwakura Tomomi, asks for use of Shimabara domain residence; around this time he is asked by the Tokyo government to research the Western system of police. **December** Leaves for Nakatsu to bring his mother to live with him in Tokyo.	**December** Publishes ***Conditions in the West,* Second Pamphlet** and writes ***Nakatsu ryubetsu no sho***, which is not published

1871	36	**February** Moves to Mita with several students.	
		May 5 Major relocation from Shinsenza to Mita.	
		May 30 Lecture hall construction completed; formal classes begin.	**August** Abolition of the domains and establishment of the prefectures
		November Writes *Hibi no oshie* for sons Ichitaro and Sutejiro.	**December** Departure of the Iwakura Mission, which returns in September, 1873
1872	37	**May 7** Sails from Yokohama, staying in the Kansai region, visiting Kyoto, Osaka and other areas.	**March** Publishes ***An Encouragement of Learning*, first pamphlet**
		June Visits Nakatsu, observes city school, visit former daimyo family, returns to Tokyo.	
		June Takes ownership of the land in Mita that had been loaned by the government.	
1873	38	**March** Stays in Hakone.	
		Spring-summer Holds gatherings at his home, begins practice of public speaking and debate.	
		August Third daughter (fifth child) Toshi is born.	
		September 4 Meets Kido Takayoshi for the first time.	**October** Political disturbance over Korea. Saigo Takamori and others quit government
		End of the year At instigation of Mori Arinori, the *Meirokusha* is formed. Fukuzawa is nominated to serve as first president, but he declines.	**November** Publishes **second pamphlet of *An Encouragement of Learning***
			December Publishes **third pamphlet of *An Encouragement of Learning***
1874	39	Decides to write *An Outline of a Theory of Civilization.*	**January** Petition calling for elected national assembly
		Through installments of *An Encouragement of Learning*, he causes commotion regarding various topics.	**February** Saga Rebellion
		May 8 Mother Ojun dies.	**January** Publishes ***An Encouragement of Learning*** (pamphlets 4 and 5), followed by pamphlets in February (6), March (7), April (8), May (9), June (10), July (11), December (12, 13)
		June 27 *Mita Enzetsukai* formally founded. Fukuzawa ceases lectures at Gijuku.	**May** Military expedition against Taiwan
1875	40	**May 1** Opening ceremony for Mita Enzetsu-kan.	**March** Publishes ***An Encouragement of Learning*** (pamphlet 14)
		June 13 Fukuzawa meets with Okubo Toshimichi.	**August** Publishes ***An Outline of a Theory of Civilization***
			September Kanghwa Island Incident

1876	41	**March** Fourth daughter (sixth child) Taki is born.	**April** Publishes ***Gakusha anshin ron*** **[A Scholar's Division of Labour]**
		May From end of month, Fukuzawa, Ichitaro and Sutejiro travel together through Osaka-Kyoto area.	**July** Publishes ***An Encouragement of Learning*** (pamphlet 15), August (16), November (17)
		November Construction of *Banraisha* in Mita near Enzetsukan.	
1877	42	**July 24** Drafts petition regarding treatment of Saigo Takamori.	**February-September** Satsuma Rebellion
			May Completes ***Kyuhanjo*** **[Conditions in an Old Feudal Clan]** but does not publish it
			October Completes ***Teichu koron*** **[Opinion of 1877]** but does not publish it
			November Publishes ***Bunkenron*** **[Separation of Powers]**
1878	43	**April 10** Meets with Okubo Ichio to discuss borrowing funds for support of Keio Gijuku. Later visits Katsu Kaishu for same discussion.	**May 14** Okubo Toshimichi is assassinated
			January Publishes ***Fukuzawa bunshu*** **[Fukuzawa's Essays]**, part one
		November Calls on Okuma Shigenobu and other government officials regarding funding.	**May** Publishes ***Tsukaron*** **[A Theory of Currency]**
		December Invited by Tanaka Fujimaro to join in establishment of Tokyo Gakushi Kaiin. Fukuzawa is elected to Tokyo Metropolitan Assembly from Shiba Ward.	**September** Publishes ***Tsuzoku minken ron*** **[A Theory on People's Rights]**, ***Tsuzoku kokken ron*** **[A Theory on Nation's Rights]**
1879	44	**January 15** First assembly of Tokyo Gakushi Kaiin.	
		January 16 Nominated to serve as Vice-Chairman of the Tokyo Metropolitan Assembly.	
		January 21 Declines post at assembly meeting.	
		March Fifth daughter (seventh child) Mitsu is born.	**March** Publishes ***Tsuzoku kokken ron*** **[A Theory on Nation's Rights]**, part two
		June Fukuzawa suspends efforts to gain financial support for Keio Gijuku.	**August** Publishes ***Fukuzawa bunshu*** **[Fukuzawa's Essays]**, part two; ***Minjo isshin*** **[Changing the Sentiments of the People]**, ***Kokkairon***
		July-August Publishes *Kokkairon* [Discourse on the National Assembly] under two pseudonyms.	
1880	45	**January 25** Japan's first social club *Kojunsha* is formally established.	
		February 5 Publication of *Kojun zasshi.*	**February 28** Yokohama Specie Bank established
		November Proposal for support of Keio Gijuku by members of the school.	
		December Meets Inoue Kaoru and Ito Hirobumi at Okuma Shigenobu residence and is asked to publish a government newspaper.	

1881	46	**January** Meets with Inoue and accepts proposal to publish newspaper.	
		April 25 Publishes proposal on future constitution in *Kojun zasshi*.	
		July Third son (eighth child) Sanpachi is born.	
		August Announcement of the privatization of Hokkaido Colonization Office properties.	**September** Publishes ***Jiji shogen*** **[Current Affairs]**
		October Political Crisis of 1881 occurs. Fukuzawa is seen as belonging to the Okuma faction and the plan for the proposed newspaper is one-sidedly cancelled.	**October** Political Crisis of 1881
1882	47	**March 1** Keio Gijuku Shuppansha publishes first edition of *Jiji Shimpo* newspaper.	**May** Publishes ***Jiji taisei ron*** **[Current Tendencies],** ***Teishitsuron*** **[On the Imperial Household]**
		June *Jiji Shimpo* publishes his series of articles on former clan cliques within the government.	**July 23** Imo Military Rebellion in Korea
			November Publishes ***Heiron*** **[Military]**
1883	48	**June 12** Ichitaro and Sutejiro leave to study in America.	**February** Publishes ***Gakumon no dokuritsu*** **[Independence of Learning]**
		July 24 Fourth son (ninth child) Daishiro is born.	**April** Commences ***Keio Gijuku kiji***
		December Conscription ordinance is revised, and exemptions for students at Keio Gijuku is eliminated, affecting enrolled students at the school.	**July** Publication of *Kanpo* [Government Gazette]
1884	49		**January** Publishes ***Zenkoku chohei ron*** **[A Theory of Universal Conscription]**
		December After failure of revolt in Korea, Kim Ok-gyun and Park Yong-hyo took refuge in Hiroo.	
			December 4 Kapsin Political Coup
1885	50	**March 16** Publishes *Datsu-a-ron* [Departure from Asia] in *Jiji Shimpo*.	
		April-May Family of 20 spend time together in Hakone.	
			December First Ito Hirobumi Cabinet formed
1886	51	**March 10** As trial for a nation-wide investigative tour of people's lives, leaves Shinagawa by way of the Tokaido for Kansai returning on April 4.	**August** Chinese seamen riot in Nagasaki
			October *Normanton* Incident
1887	52	**February** Adopted son Momosuke departs for study in America.	
		March Sees first theater performance at Shintomiza.	
		April Refuses invitation to costume ball to be held at home of Ito Hirobumi.	

		August-September Travels with family to Hakone and Kamakura to recuperate. From this year on the event becomes annual each summer.	
1888	53	**January** In relation to the arrest of Inoue Kakugoro, the Fukuzawa home is searched, and on March 15 he appears as a witness in court. **November 4** Ichitaro and Sutejiro return from studies in America.	**April** Kuroda Kiyotaka Cabinet formed
1889	54		**February** Constitution of the Empire of Japan established **December** First Yamagata Aritomo Cabinet formed
1890	55	**January** Establishment of Keio Gijuku University, with departments of literature, finance and law.	**July** First election of House of Representatives **November** First meeting of the House of Representatives
1891	56		**May** First Matsukata Masayoshi Cabinet formed **May** Otsu Incident **November** Completes ***Yasegaman no setsu*** **[Dogged Endurance]** but does not publish it
1892	57	**April 25** Family travels to west Japan and returns on May 16. **October 4** Announces research results of Kitasato Shibasaburo. To support Kitasato's research, on December 1, the Institute of Infectious Disease is established in Shiba Koen.	**February** Second election for House of Representatives **June** Publishes ***Kokkai no zento*** **[Future of the Diet],** ***Kokkai nankyoku no yurai*** **[Causes of Difficulties of the Diet],** ***Chian shogen*** **[Public Peace],** ***Chisoron*** **[Land Tax]** **August** Second Ito Hirobumi Cabinet formed
1893	58	**November 11** Publishes editorial *Jinsei no rakuji* in *Jiji Shimpo*.	**May** Publishes ***Jitsugyoron*** **[A Theory of Genuine Businessmen]** **December** Submission of petition regarding the current treaties to the Diet. House of Representatives is dismissed
1894	59	**August** Donates ¥10,000 on the occasion of the Sino-Japanese War.	**March 28** Kim Ok-gyun is assassinated in Shanghai **July 16** Anglo-Japanese treaty of commerce is signed

			July 25 Battle of P'ungdo, Korea
			August 1 Sino-Japanese War declaration
1895	60	**May** Keio Gijuku accepts over a hundred students from Korea.	**March 24** Attempt on life of Li Hongzhang
		August Treaty signed regarding acceptance of Korean students.	**April 17** Peace treaty between ends Sino-Japanese War
		December 12 Fukuzawa celebrates his 60th birthday a year after the delay by the Sino-Japanese War.	**October 8** Assassination of Queen Min
1896	61	**April 21-29** Family travels to Ise Shrine.	**March 1** Publication of ***Fukuo hyakuwa* [One Hundred Discourses]** commences in serialized form
		September Seeks special exemption from conscription for students in the university and lower division.	**September** Second Matsukata Masayoshi Cabinet formed
		November 6-11 Family travels to north-central Japan.	
1897	62	**August** Commencement of collection of donations for Keio Gijuku Endowment.	**July** Publishes single-volume ***Fukuo hyakuwa* [One Hundred Discourses]**
		November 2-19 Travels with family to Kyoto, Osaka and San'yo districts, on what would become his last travels.	**December** Publishes ***Fukuzawa zenshu shogen* [Preface to The Collected Works]**
1898	63		**January** Third Ito Hirobumi Cabinet formed
		May 11 Completes *Fukuo jiden* [Autobiography of Fukuzawa Yukichi]. On the 16th Ito Hirobumi attends a garden party that Fukuzawa held at his villa in Hiroo.	**January-May** Five volumes of ***Fukuzawa zenshu* [Collected Works of Fukuzawa]** published
		September 26 Fukuzawa suffers a stroke.	**June** First Okuma Shigenobu Cabinet formed
		December Almost fully recovered.	**July 1** Fukuzawa's ***Autobiography*** begins serialization
			November Second Yamagata Aritomo Cabinet formed
1899	64		**June** Publishes ***Fukuo jiden* [Autobiography of Fukuzawa Yukichi]**
		November 11 Holds garden party at Hiroo for those who called on him during his illness.	**November** Publishes ***Onna Daigaku hyoron* [Reproof of "The Essential Learning for Women"]** and ***Shin Onna Daigaku* [New Essential Learning for Women]**
1900	65	**February 11** With help of long-term students and teachers, completes *Shushin yoryo* [Moral Code] and on the 24th presents it at the *Mita Enzetsukai*.	

		May 9 Receives ¥50,000 from the Imperial Household for his contributions through writing, translation and education. Immediately donates that to the Keio Gijuku Endowment.	
		December 31 Attends ceremony sending out the old century and welcoming the new as the century of "self-respect and independence of mind."	**October** Fourth Ito Hirobumi Cabinet formed
1901	66	**January 25** Fukuzawa suffers a second stroke.	
		February 3 Dies at 10:50 p.m. at his home in Mita. Funeral held at Azabusan Zenpukuji on the 8th. Posthumous Buddhist name is Daikan'in Dokuritsu Jison koji.	
			April Publication of ***Fukuo hyakuyowa*** **[More Discourses]**
			May Publication of ***Meiji junen teichu koron*** **[Opinion of 1877]** and ***Yasegaman no setsu*** **[Dogged Endurance]**

About the Author

Kitaoka Shinichi

Kitaoka Shinichi was born in 1948 and studied at The University of Tokyo (B.A. 1971, Ph.D. 1976). He taught at Rikkyo University (1976-97) and his alma mater (1997-2004, 2006-12), while serving as Ambassador to the United Nations (2004-2006). Then he became a professor at the National Graduate Institute for Policy Studies (GRIPS, 2012-15), President of the International University of Japan (IUJ, 2012-15), and Chairman of the Board of Nara Prefectural University (2015-). He is currently President of the Japan International Cooperation Agency (JICA). He is Emeritus Professor of The University of Tokyo.

Kitaoka served on many councils and advisory boards for Prime Ministers and Foreign Ministers, including Chair of the Japanese Scholars of the Japan-China Joint Historical Research Commission (2006-2009), Acting Chair of the Advisory Panel on Restructuring the Legal Basis of National Security (2013-14), Chair of the Advisory Panel on Japan's National Defense and Security (2013), and Acting Chair of the Advisory Board for Looking Back on the 20th Century and Providing a Vision for the 21st Century (2015). He has also been serving as Executive Director of Research at the Institute for International Policy Studies under former Prime Minister Nakasone Yasuhiro.

He has published many books and received many awards including the Yoshida Shigeru Award (1996), the Suntory Award for Liberal Arts (1997), the Yomiuri's Opinion Leader of the Year (1992), the Yoshino Sakuzo Award (1995), and the Imperial Medal with Purple Ribbon (2011). He is a regular contributor to many newspapers and magazines.

（英文版）独立自尊—福沢諭吉の挑戦

Self-Respect and Independence of Mind: The Challenge of Fukuzawa Yukichi

2017年3月27日　第1刷発行

著　者　北岡 伸一

訳　者　ジェームス・M・バーダマン

発行所　一般財団法人出版文化産業振興財団

〒101-0051 東京都千代田区神田神保町3-12-3

電話　03-5211-7282（代）

ホームページ　http://www.jpic.or.jp/

印刷・製本所　大日本印刷株式会社

定価はカバーに表示してあります。

Printed in Japan.

ISBN978-4-916055-62-0